Advance appreciation for
Romance & Reality: a real life love story

"The story Greg and Joyce tell is a powerful and true report of God's reconciling power. God likes to bring broken things together—especially marriages. So, to all couples young and old who have wondered whether there is a future for a struggling relationship, this is a story for you. It's the testimony of how there is always hope when God is placed at the center of a marriage."

—Dr. Greg Waybright, Senior Pastor of Lake Avenue Church

"*Romance & Reality* is, indeed, a real life love story. The Millikans' marriage is a perfect example of how Jesus can transform something broken into something beautiful. This book gives real hope that it's possible to have a strong marriage no matter what has happened in the past. God does work all things together for good!"

—Jim & Debbie Hogan, Co-founders of Standing Stone Ministry and authors of *Shepherding Shepherds: The Standing Stone Story*

"The life course of a marriage can be like a river: there are stretches of both calm and turbulence. In *Romance & Reality*, the Millikans give us a great gift—a deeply honest and vulnerable memoir of the real-life flow of marriage, of waters that part and come together again. And through it all, we glimpse the presence of a gracious God who wants more for them than they sometimes want for themselves. Read their story, and receive a generously given word of hope for your own."

—Cameron Lee, PhD, CFLE, Professor of Family Studies & Director, Fuller Institute for Relationship Education, Fuller Theological Seminary, Pasadena, CA

"What an engaging story! *Romance & Reality* will be difficult to put down once you start reading. This true story of young love, lost love, and love that lasts will touch you and give hope to those who may be longing for a more fulfilling and intimate love life."

—Dr. Clifford & Joyce Penner, Sexual Therapists, Educators and pioneers in bringing healthy sexuality into the church and greater community.

"What a wonderful, inspiring, and informative story of love, broken hearts and restoration. *Romance & Reality* inspires couples to never give up on striving for a great marriage. Greg and Joyce share vulnerably their own story as well as give meaningful insights on how to grow, overcome and heal a broken marriage. Their story is a modern-day love story from sweet love to the edge of the cliff to falling back in love. It inspires young couples to grow and gives hope to stuck couples who feel restoring their marriage is impossible. As a marriage and family therapist and Founder/Director of Safe Haven Relationship Center, I spend most of my days in the counseling room with couples on the edge of the cliff. But most couples, even though despairing and afraid that all is lost, are longing for hope that their marriage can be restored. Greg and Joyce's story gives hope that no matter

how hopeless, you can grow, heal and restore your marriag
I am so glad Greg and Joyce finally put their story to pape
Now other couples can learn of the hope of a restored mai
riage."

ROMANCE & REALITY

a real life love story

To Sue ~
Warmly,
Joyce and Greg
2/23/24

GREG MILLIKAN
&
JOYCE MILLIKAN

Working Faith

Pasadena

Published by Working Faith
958 Mar Vista Avenue, Pasadena, California 91104 USA

First Printing, April 2014

Cover design by Chris Dalton, www.thestoryhaus.com

ISBN-13 978-0692026502

While all the stories in this book are true, some names have been
changed to protect the privacy of the individuals involved.

To our grandchildren and their parents.

"*I would have despaired unless I had believed that I would see the goodness of the LORD in the land of the living.*"

- Psalm 27:13 (NASB)

Contents

Introduction

Learning to Dance Together

The Millikans are Joyce and Greg. Therein lies the challenge. And therein lies potential.

In this book, we tell the facts of our story as objectively as we can. You will find our individual perspectives and our *opinions* about the facts—which are not always the same—in sections labeled:

- Joyce's Take
- Greg's Take

In these sections we give readers insight into our emotions, personal background, rationale; the dreams and desires that led us to do what we did, and sometimes our thoughts about what we might do today.

This book is not a "happily ever after story," but a *real story* of our actual lives as they developed over time . . . what each of us and our two children had to suffer on account of our choices.

We have faced trials and troubles—from within ourselves and in our marriage, as well as external crises—some of which have rocked other couples, in our nation and around the world. There are lessons to be learned. People can learn from successes, but more often we learn from failures. This book is written so that you might examine our marriage, and then determine what might work for you, and what is likely *not* to work.

Of one thing we are very certain: no two marriages are the same. There may be similarities, but since no two people are completely alike, no marriage can be like any other. Each marriage is unique.

We hope our real life love story will give you insight into your own marriage journey, and in your more significant journey of faith in God.

Joyce's Take

When I was a teenager, one of my favorite movies was *The Sound of Music*. I saw it again recently, and the part that spoke to me most was when the Captain and the young nanny, Maria, start dancing a familiar Austrian folk dance together on the garden veranda of his mansion. Both of them know the steps—but each of them is surprised by the intensity of their emotions as they dance together. When Maria notices other guests nearby approaching them, she suddenly stops dancing and says, "I don't remember . . ."

Had she truly forgotten the steps? Or was she unprepared to dance them in front of others? Was it proper for her to be dancing there in front of the Captain's guests, when he was their host? All viewers are allowed their own interpretations.

This is an appropriate metaphor for many moments in my marriage with Greg. At the beginning of our marriage, we both *thought* we knew the right dance steps. Our emotions were strong for each other. I imagined our feelings of love were strong enough to hold us together forever.

But then, in the harsh glare of life's Reality, we each discovered that we didn't know the dance . . . and often we were afraid to try dancing again. Eventually we both became distrusting of our dance partner. Loss of trust made dancing together nearly impossible.

Greg's Take

Nothing in this book is intended to glorify Joyce or Greg Millikan. We are not the main focus . . . we are merely the "case in point."

As a lawyer, I have reviewed thousands of case studies through the years. In law school we learned that a close examination of a case study could yield some important lessons about "what to do" and "what never to do."

This is the spirit in which we offer our crazy, mixed-up, real-life love story marriage. My prayer is that God will give you insight into yourself and your current marriage situation through our story.

God isn't simply involved in my life or in Joyce's life, but He is active in the world around us and in our lives *together* doing His work and accomplishing His purposes. Joyce and I welcome this relationship with Him each morning.

I hope that you, as readers, will enjoy the incredible journey of how we both came to know and find ourselves through God's love. Receiving *God's love is* how we each learned to extend *real love* to our spouse—the love God the Father gave us all in His Son Jesus Christ. May your joy be full!

For Contemplation or Conversation

We would also like to call your attention to the segments labeled "For Contemplation or Conversation" at the end of each chapter. There, we have placed several questions to help you reflect on the chapter and allow you an opportunity to discuss your thoughts with your spouse, a person who may *become* your spouse, or with a small group that is exploring ways to improve marriage or other relationships.

This real-life love story is not intended to be the *entire story* of Greg and Joyce Millikan. That would be too long to read. We have intentionally selected to write only what is relevant to the love story of our marriage.

Whether you are reading this book individually or studying it with a group, we suggest keeping the following questions in mind as you read:

1. Can You Relate? Can you relate to what is being told in the story? If so, in what way is the story touching your life? Is this situation one that is common to individuals and their relationships, or is this something that applies only to married couples? If so, in what ways?

2. What's Under the Surface? As you perceive the relational issues that develop beneath the surface of Greg and Joyce's relationship, how does this perception help you recognize what may be going on under the surface of your own life and relationships?

3. Knowing What You Don't Know. What do you see that Greg and Joyce didn't know or understand at specific times? How does this insight help you recognize what you don't know or understand in your own life and relationship? To whom might you turn to gain another perspective beyond your own?

4. The Importance of Wise Counsel. To whom might you turn for wise counsel when needed? What are your criteria for determining who is wise? What type of counsel is best suited for the situation you are facing (peer or friend counseling, pastoral counseling, marriage mentor counseling, a medical opinion, or psychological counseling)? In what ways does the Word of God serve as wise counsel for you?

Introduction

You may choose to turn to the end of a chapter and read through the questions before reading the chapter. Or, you may find it beneficial to read a chapter twice, once without an orientation toward the discussion or contemplation questions, and then a second reading with those questions in mind.

We are thankful for the opportunity to share our story with you. Happy reading!

— Greg and Joyce Millikan

1   The Meeting

Mr. Murray was definitely in charge of the classroom. He slapped a yardstick across his desk; but in spite of his raw exertion of force, the waves of his graying hair remained fixed. The chatter abruptly fell silent. He glared at his students, his imposing stature at full height. Today, his eighth grade biology class would be dissecting frogs and there wasn't a moment to be wasted.

Every lab desk in the room had a metal pan with a small green cadaver in it. The students eyed their specimens: the slender limbs; the sleek rubbery belly; the mouth stiff with rigor mortis.

The appalling smell was what first caught the attention of fourteen-year-old Joyce Jones. Although she was repulsed by its acrid odor, Joyce found herself curious about how she and her classmates would progress with their frogs. Normally, she found schoolwork uninteresting. For Joyce, school was all about the people. She had little desire to excel academically. This project, however, was definitely capturing her interest.

After calling the class to attention, Mr. Murray stiffly introduced a newcomer to the lab: "Greg Millikan will be joining our class today as my lab assistant. If you have questions, he can assist you."

Joyce looked up from her frog to see who this newcomer might be. She immediately blushed, hardly believing her eyes. *Who was this handsome young man with golden brown hair and an athletic build?* She thought *why haven't I ever seen him before?* Prior to that moment, Joyce was sure she had already seen all the good-looking guys at school.

Greg was a ninth-grader. Apparently as smart as he was handsome, Greg already had a certain amount of polish. He gave a cheerful smile as he surveyed the class and prepared to help. His smile gave him a confident air that he didn't truly feel. Actually, he was a little clueless as to why Mr. Murray had asked him to be excused from another class to assist with this particular lab assignment. Only moments before his introduction, Greg had been in the science department's supply room trying to find a lab coat that fit. He had no interest in a science-related career and had never heard of another student being conscripted into the role of lab assistant. But he shrugged off his questions, content to let the mystery be a mystery.

Mr. Murray barked out instructions as he drew on a chalkboard at the front of the room: "Make a slit here. Observe the body cavity. Identify the large intestines...the gall bladder...the liver...the reproductive organs...the heart."

Joyce wasn't paying much attention—her focus was on the lab assistant. She raised her hand, caught his eye, and smiled wider at him with each step he took toward her. "Can you help me with my frog?" she asked him, by now beaming.

For his part, Greg could not recall ever being greeted so warmly by a girl. Her inviting demeanor and smile made him conclude that she thought his presence in the room was the greatest thing since sliced bread. He blushed a little. At fifteen, he was still in the discovery phase of the social world and girls in general. He didn't have a clue when it came to the concept of flirting.

Greg and Joyce worked together for a few minutes probing the frog's anatomy with forceps and scalpel in hand. She asked questions. He answered. They shared a laugh over the horrid smell.

The frog, however odious, was made bearable for Joyce by the wonderful man-creature by her side. Another student from the far side of the room raised a hand for Greg's help. He smiled at Joyce and moved on. After a few minutes, he looked around to catch the sight of a girl's hand raised high above her head. It was Joyce, eager to ask another question. He walked to her lab station and spent most of the remainder of the lab session there.

Greg's Take

I had met some of Joyce's friends through other guys I knew in baseball and football. I had also noticed her before on school days when she wore her Candy Striper uniform. From a distance, I thought she seemed to mingle easily with a fairly social group. She seemed neither prudish nor bookish—and in all respects, admirable. I had never heard anything bad about Joyce. And up close, she was very appealing! On that day in lab class she was wearing a sleeveless striped dress with a thin belt and a white Peter Pan collar—nothing fancy, but quite feminine. Joyce was attractive and tall, with brown eyes and medium length light brown hair styled gently to the middle of her neck. But it was her smile that I found completely irresistible. There was a depth, and yet innocence that I loved about it, and about her. Joyce was altogether engaging and sincere. What a wonderful day that was for me.

At the end of the lab session, the students disposed of their frogs and cleaned their stations. Greg slipped out of the room and out of his white lab coat, then hurried to his next class. But the magic had begun.

Joyce clutched her books close to her chest as she walked out of the classroom. Before that class, she had not yet experienced such a rush of normal teenage hormones, and the feelings that accompanied them. Her mind was swirling with treasured thoughts of the handsome new boy she had just met. He had actually come over *twice* to help her. Greg seemed to respond to her and it seemed to her that they had connected. Joyce was hopeful, even confident, that she might have a conversation with him again—soon, she hoped.

When Joyce arrived at home after school, she could barely contain her excitement while telling her mom about meeting the lab assistant in class. "His name is Greg Millikan," she exclaimed.

Her mother answered pleasantly, "Oh, yes, we know his family. His Aunt Shirley was in my wedding."

"You do? You know the Millikans? Why haven't you introduced me to him before? I didn't know the Millikans that *you knew* had a son so good looking!"

Her mom laughed.

Prior to that day, most of the boys Joyce found interesting were friends of her older sister, Martha, and Martha's boyfriend, Scott. Both Martha and Scott were seventeen, and juniors at nearby John Muir High School in Pasadena. Joyce had been on several double dates with Martha and Scott and some of their friends.

Joyce's parents considered Martha and Scott to be safe escorts for Joyce and their friend to be with, but this was hardly the reality Joyce experienced. The four of them often went to drive-in movies—those were forbidden destinations by Joyce's parents. Not surprisingly, Joyce's date would observe Scott and Martha making out in the front seat, and naturally assume that Joyce would follow their lead. Joyce felt socially trapped and over her head, but all the same, she felt privileged to be included with her sister's older friends. Joyce was neither prepared nor able to say no, to set boundaries, or even to think wisely about the challenging situation. When her parents finally caught wind of what was happening, they unilaterally shut down Joyce's double dating with her older sister.

For his part, Greg was a happy kid in elementary school, but he was not pleased with his new life in junior high. It would not have bothered him in the least to have slept through the entire experience and awakened in high school. La Cañada Junior High had students from seventh to ninth grades, drawing students from several elementary schools in the area. Greg quickly perceived that his elementary school had been socially slow compared with some of the other schools. There were boys who seemed adept at boy-girl parties and relationships. Greg was not, but felt an anxious urge to try to learn. He was, after all, a healthy young teenager with his own set of raging hormones, and he wanted to avoid the subtle mocking and sense of rejection that seemed to go with being one of those who was *out of it* – whatever "it" was.

And then there was the cello. From the time he was in the fourth grade, Greg had developed a strong love for classical music from listening to his dad's record collection, and had jumped at the chance to take up the cello. By the time he arrived in junior high, Greg was an avid, if not accomplished cellist and gladly took a seat in the junior high orchestra.

Playing the cello was not, however, a badge of honor among most of his junior high acquaintances, especially his athletic friends. He resented the jab "Cello?" they gave him, but his compensatory athletic ability helped him ride out their teasing. He excelled in athletics, especially baseball, football, and track. In the end, Greg's desire to succeed in athletics overcame his future cello career. By the end of eighth grade, the conflict between music and athletics became too intense, and Greg abandoned the cello.

Academically, Greg was way above average. He could also come off as a know-it-all, even a bit arrogant when he was convinced he was right. His intellect, however, didn't keep him from acting like a foolish teenager. He frequently clowned around when the occasions presented themselves. He once received a quarterly grade of A-S-S from an English teacher for his class behavior and academic achievement. When Greg asked about it, the teacher said, "You deserve the A. The two SS's are because I don't want you to act like one anymore." With Greg's dad on the local school board, Greg felt a bit embarrassed at this reproof. However, he also had a secret sense of satisfaction that he had earned an A without having perfect behavior. And then there were girls—there was so much to discover.

Like Greg, Joyce struggled with her emotions and sexuality. Her parents gave her no guidance, only open or closed doors about dating, and the silent, unspoken rule: *Don't do it or you'll get pregnant!* There was no talk at home about sex—not that questions were ever asked directly by Joyce about it. Sex was the big, silent elephant in their home. With no words of wisdom or teaching, Joyce had no idea whether there was such a thing as normal or good teenage dating behavior. Joyce was just doing her best to navigate what she assumed was *good enough*.

What Joyce's mother was interested in was social status and acceptability, which was completely incomprehensible to Joyce. Neither of Joyce's parents encouraged her to excel academically or to lead anything. In school, Joyce enjoyed taking physical science classes, like physiology and biology, but other than those, she was mostly interested in cooking and sewing classes.

In seventh grade, Joyce joined the YMCA swim team with three of her girlfriends. This extra-curricular commitment presented an ongoing physical challenge for her—with workouts three times a week plus weekend swim meets. Joyce enjoyed the social aspects of being part of the swim team, learning to make her body work, and winning races alongside her friends and teammates. The swimming medals she earned added frosting to the social cake of being on the team.

After their first meeting in the biology lab, Joyce and Greg stopped to chat from time to time when they saw each other in the school hallways. Then one day Joyce spotted Greg leaving school in the afternoon after the final bell. Suspecting it was a long walk home for him, she asked if he would like a ride. Joyce's grandmother, Grandma Wells, lived next door to Joyce's family, so she regularly helped Joyce's mother by picking up Joyce and her younger sister from school. Joyce normally felt terribly embarrassed by the behemoth size of her grandmother's white '63 Cadillac, but on this day she was delighted at the prospect of sharing that space with Greg. Greg quickly accepted the ride offer, hopped into the car next to Joyce, and Grandma Wells greeted him warmly.

As Greg gathered his books and began sliding out of the car after they arrived at his house, Joyce spoke up boldly, "Do you think you might like to come to our house some evening for a visit?"

"Sure!" he replied, "That would be great."

It was a crisp California spring day, with summer on the horizon. Romantic feelings between them were beginning to bloom.

For Contemplation and Conversation

1. How did you and your spouse meet?

2. What first attracted you to your spouse? Was it love at first sight or did you appreciate something else?

3. Was your family any better than Joyce's at training you to save your body for your spouse alone? What advantages or disadvantages does this moral stand present to a young woman? A young man?

2   From Flirting to Engagement

Joyce and Greg soon shared their first kiss. It happened during his first visit to her home. After a family dinner, Greg and Joyce went into the den to watch television. There, finding himself alone with Joyce, Greg seized the opportunity. A little tentatively, he placed his arm around her, putting to work what he had learned at the boy-girl parties over the past two years. Sensing her warm response, he turned toward her and they kissed. Joyce rather enjoyed Greg's attention. Her parents were in the living room reading, totally oblivious to the need to check-in with their middle daughter and her friend.

From the perspective of Joyce's parents, Greg Millikan was a very acceptable choice as a boyfriend. Greg's family embodied much of the pioneering spirit of the West. They were a conservative, yet progressive family that attended a Methodist church. Greg's paternal grandmother was a strong-minded temperance advocate from the 1920s onward and well known locally. In the early 1960s, Greg's family helped start a new Methodist Church in La Cañada, and Greg's father served on the local school board. The Millikans apparently valued church attendance and education. Joyce's parents admired all of this.

Throughout Greg's childhood, his father, Brad, regularly arrived home in time for dinner with the family. Brad always accepted Greg's invitation to play catch after dinner and he often made time to attend Greg's Boy Scout meetings. But after these family times, he often spent long hours working on legal files he brought home for clients, or he went back to the office to work late. Apart from that, Greg's dad seemed to enjoy disassembling, fixing, and reassembling the family's home appliances and cars—perhaps to satisfy his engineering instincts. He approached such projects as elaborate puzzles to be solved by a mixture of concentration and logic. All of his father's propensities—from athletics, to scouting, to disciplined work, to fixing things, were passed on to Greg.

When Brad addressed any of Greg's shortcomings, he always did so in a logical manner. These talks often took the form of a Socratic interview in which Greg inevitably had to acknowledge that he was wrong, thoughtless, inconsistent, foolish, or lazy. Greg routinely found himself having to agree with his father that he, Greg, was his own worst enemy. His father's response to that admission was nearly always a sigh, leaving Greg with unvoiced feelings of foolishness and angry shame. There was little if any opportunity offered for Greg to express his genuine thoughts or feelings to either of his parents.

The Millikan family was polite by anybody's standards. Course talk or obscenities were neither tolerated nor practiced. Anger was not expressed at all. Like his own father, also a lawyer, Brad had a high regard for semantics, and he believed that words, carefully chosen and placed, were far more powerful than any form of profanity. Greg admired that approach and sought early on to become personally adept at wielding words like his dad. Greg's mother had worked as a teacher and was similarly well-spoken, but mostly she was the homemaker, arising early each morning to cook breakfast for her husband and four children, of which Greg was the eldest.

The Millikans were not active in political circles. Their names would not be found on any social club roster or mentioned in any society column. This did not mean they were unconcerned, uninvolved, or that they were social wallflowers. They simply preferred a low-key, no-fuss lifestyle. If any disagreements arose between Greg's parents, they were dealt with privately. As a couple, the Millikans were openly affectionate with each other. Neither of them traveled alone without the other, and there was no hint of infidelity.

With the end of the school year, Joyce had completed the eighth grade and Greg the ninth grade. They both were anticipating a move over to the newly built campus for grades 9-12 at La Cañada High School. There was a lot of excitement about this, and much for them to talk about. But their early summer conversations also included casual talk about Joyce's upcoming month-long trip to France with Grandma Wells, Grandma's friend Wilda Bernard and Joyce's sister Martha—an exciting travel adventure for the sisters.

Joyce had been overseas once before with her parents and siblings when she was nine. She was more grown up now—and very excited this time to be invited to go to France just with Martha, her grandmother and Wilda. Joyce and Martha were especially eager to see Paris and the French Riviera. The more Greg and Joyce talked about her upcoming trip, the more he began to realize how much he was going to miss Joyce's smile. To him, this was love, and it felt great.

Several weeks after she left, Greg received a photo postcard from Joyce somewhere in France. His heart leaped as he flipped the card over to read the neatly penned greeting.

It was brief. France was beautiful and Joyce was having a wonderful time. While on the beach in Nice, she and Martha had met two very nice American sailors from New Jersey, and the four of them had shared coffee and dessert. Then she closed and wished Greg a good summer. *What does that mean?* Greg wondered. He hoped that the message wasn't what he *feared* it might be.

It was.

After Joyce returned, Greg called her at home. He was aware she had already been back for a week—with no call to

Greg. When he finally reached her, she casually said, "Oh, didn't I write to you about Nicky?" Nicky was the sailor she met in Nice. She affirmed that she really liked Greg, but that their dating relationship was over. Greg replied, "That's it, huh? We're over, just like that?" Joyce said she was sorry but Nicky was the one who now had her attention. Greg said, "Okay, well good-bye, have a good summer."

Greg was miserable, feeling that his heart had been ripped from his body and thrown to the ground. *What was the meaning of all this? Hadn't his feelings been strong and deep? Weren't Joyce's feelings equally strong before Europe? How could she be so fickle? And who on earth was this Nicky guy?*

Then logic kicked in. Greg started to put a few pieces together. Nicky was a sailor stationed in Europe. Odds were, Joyce would never see him again. Greg accepted that his relationship with Joyce might be over—for now. But perhaps they could get back together in the future.

Joyce received a letter from Nicky and she wrote back. The dream of a romantic pen-pal relationship with a sailor seemed perfect to her. She waited for a second letter to come from him. But it never came.

When fall arrived, Joyce and Greg saw each other occasionally at the new high school. They talked and flirted a little. Neither of them held a grudge against the other. In an odd way their relationship seemed to have developed a new level of trust and friendship. They both had moved on and started dating other people.

Two years later, by Joyce's junior year, she had developed a steady relationship with Steve, a recent graduate of their high school who was now a freshman at Brigham Young University (BYU). Joyce considered her relationship with Steve to be one that might lead to marriage, so she began learning all she could about his Mormon religion. She took early morning classes before school with Steve's sister and attended church each week with his family. Joyce was drawn to Steve and his family on account of the commitment all of them made to pursue God.

Greg dated several different girls, but he didn't feel the same attachment to them that he felt for Joyce. By winter of his senior year in high school, Greg had made a decision that he was going to pursue Joyce. Greg knew about her relationship with Steve, but by now, Greg was an Eagle Scout and a strong achiever. He sized up the competition and believed he had both an opening and an edge—Steve was in Utah. Greg fully believed that a combination of tenacity and skillfully calculated moves might work to win Joyce's heart.

One day as he and Joyce talked casually, Greg revealed his interest in dating her. "I'm already committed," she said. "You're just going to get hurt if you try to pursue me."

"That's fine," replied Greg, surprisingly confident. "If I get hurt, I get hurt."

Joyce really didn't know how to respond to that. Feeling a little uncomfortable about Greg's comment, she also found it rather exciting that two high-quality men were interested in her. They each made plans and followed through on them. Joyce liked that. For her, that kind of behavior spelled security and maturity. Joyce and Greg continued to talk often during school lunch breaks, developing a stronger friendship but not yet dating.

That spring, Greg's baseball career as a left-handed pitcher began to take off. It was his senior year and he won thirteen games for the high school team, compiling an impressive number of strikeouts and giving up less than one earned run per game. Professional baseball scouts began to come around to see how Greg was performing. Although Joyce was happy for Greg's athletic successes, his athletic achievements did not overly impress her. To Joyce, Greg was merely applying the natural skills he had to give. In a way, Greg found Joyce's longing for something deeper and possibly more genuine than the fame associated with a possible baseball career to be very appealing.

For all that Greg and Steve had in common, neither of them had much in common with Joyce's father, Bob, who was both good-looking and fun loving, but not particularly well-organized or purposeful. Joyce loved and looked up to her father. He was charming and debonair. Bob was highly adept at tickling the ivories and smoothly dancing across a dance floor with Joyce, her mother, or sisters. But Bob was not one to be saddled with logic or pragmatism. This had nothing to do with his intellect—it had to do with his personality—as he was an engineering graduate of Stanford University.

Joyce's family relationships were complicated by the fact that Bob was very tough on Joyce's brother, Dean—often criticizing Dean harshly during family meals, even though Dean was the first-born child in the family. Their difficult father-son relationship created a tense relational dynamic that was a source of ongoing, unrelieved family tension. In contrast, Bob had an easy-going relationship with his three daughters, and he was especially fond of Joyce. Aware of his tendency to be too lenient with the girls, Bob often deferred his parental decisions to Joyce's mother, saying to Joyce and her sisters, "Go ask your mother."

Joyce's mother, Elizabeth, was something of an enigma to Joyce. Joyce often felt chosen by her mother as a favorite daughter, but later Joyce assumed this was probably on account of her physical similarity to Grandma Wells and not because of anything special in her mother's relationship with her. When it came to temperament or personality, Joyce thought she had little in common with her mother.

Elizabeth was a disciplinarian and social butterfly. She organized her daughters' lives around etiquette, community service, proper attire, social structures, and what she considered as appropriate friendships. Whether organizing the *perfect* dinner party for her friends or a holiday meal for the family, Elizabeth was fully versed in all aspects of entertaining and hospitality. She emphasized to all her children the importance of thank-you notes, well-kept appearances, and socially appropriate clothing. Her aspirations for Joyce seemed to be very simple: become a debutante, graduate from USC, marry well, and be at her house for every holiday gathering.

Growing-up years for Joyce were somewhat chaotic—juggling rule-making, rule-breaking, and family fines for the broken rules. As the third of four children, Joyce observed her older brother and sister getting into heaps of trouble with their parents. They were constantly under watch for the problems they caused. Joyce preferred to live without conflict with her parents, if at all possible. She often studied the behavior of her older siblings with an eye toward what *not* to do, rather than what *to do*. Joyce preferred to play quietly with her younger sister Robin than to be caught up in one of their older siblings' schemes.

If she had a choice, Joyce preferred being outdoors, playing games, rather than being indoors. It was when the four children went indoors, under the close scrutiny of one or both parents that life became more complicated and family tensions manifested themselves.

Joyce's mother ruled the indoors with a code of conduct that she strictly enforced. Each child paid a fine of ten cents into the fine jar for each infraction of the family rules. For example, if a child was caught leaving their bedroom without turning out the light, the fine was ten cents. Since Joyce's allowance was only ten cents a week for several years, she didn't dare risk losing a whole week's allowance for a left-on light. Her brother's fine for throwing rocks was substantially higher.

As the end of Greg's senior year in high school approached, he asked a classmate of Joyce's named Beverly to be his date to the Senior Prom. Joyce had not budged on going out with him. He and Joyce were both friends with

Beverly, and had been so for many years. In some ways, Beverly had become Greg's confidante regarding his relationship—or lack of relationship—with Joyce. Joyce and Beverly had been Brownies and Girl Scouts together, all of which made Beverly a good source for advice. On one occasion Beverly advised Greg, "The thing about Joyce is that if you let her know you're after her, she'll run away. You've got to keep yourself at a distance. Create some space and let her come toward you a little."

That sounded like very good strategic advice to Greg. He considered his options and drew up a plan of attack.

In mid-May, Joyce received a "Dear John" letter from Steve at BYU. He said that he had not planned it, but he had met someone new while at college and they were planning to be married. Joyce was disappointed and a little hurt by the news, but she felt worse after she learned that Greg was taking Beverly to the prom and another classmate, Charla, to his Senior Class Grad Night at Disneyland. These two additional bits of news left Joyce with terrible sorrow, thinking *if only Steve had written me sooner!*

Joyce owned up to the truth that she had never completely lost interest in Greg—and with his plans to celebrate his graduation with girls *other than her*, she felt sad and little jealous. She spent Greg's prom night and Grad Night at home sulking, wishing she were the one enjoying these graduation parties with Greg.

The Dodger Game

When Joyce finally told Greg that Steve had broken things off between them, Greg's heart nearly flipped. Even so, having gained a new stand-back strategy based on Beverly's advice, he tried to adopt an air of indifference. He had decided to take a casual approach and invite Joyce to two upcoming un-romantic events after his graduation. The first was the *Los Angeles Times* track meet at the Los Angeles Coliseum. The other was a Dodger baseball game the following week. Greg had decided that if things didn't work out with Joyce this time around, he would end his pursuit of her once and for all.

The track meet went well for both of them; in fact they really enjoyed it. When the Dodger game went into extra innings, Joyce felt delighted. She was entirely comfortable and pleased to be with Greg, and was glad that something seemed to be developing between them again. There was an easy rhythm between them. Perhaps the time spent apart during the previous several years had shaved off a few rough edges in their personalities.

Whatever the cause, they both had a new appreciation for each other. Joyce also concluded that Greg had grown even more handsome and more focused in the last couple of years—and more muscular.

After the Dodger game, they drove from the stadium back to Joyce's driveway, and there, they talked for more than a half hour in the car. Although there was a definite physical chemistry between the two of them, they didn't resort to kissing as they once had. Rather, they began to talk about serious issues of life, asking each other what they believed and knew about God. It was unlike any conversation either of them had ever had with a peer.

What do you think God is like?

What have you heard or learned about God?

Is God knowable?

Joyce spoke with thoughtful responses from her Presbyterian background and her more recent studies of Mormonism. Greg spoke from his Methodist background. Both of them realized that *neither of them* had a firm grasp on any substantial answers to many of their questions.

Joyce knew some Bible verses that her mother and grandmother had taught her, including Psalm 23, Psalm 100, and John 3:16. Beyond the few widely known Biblical texts and a few Bible stories they had picked up, attending church had seemed more of a family religious tradition or a social responsibility than something personally or spiritually meaningful or satisfying for either of them. Easter and Christmas, even at church, seemed somewhat opaque spiritually, more tied to culture than to God personally. In fact, neither of them knew what to say about the importance of Jesus.

What was most memorable to both of them about that night was that each of them had similar questions about God, and that they both wanted to seek and find God. Neither of them, however, knew where to begin.

Greg had been active in the local Methodist church growing up. His father sang in the choir and was apparently a believer, as was his mother. The family went to church together every week. Greg even participated in Methodist Youth Fellowship and preached a sermon on a Youth Sunday. But Greg readily admitted to Joyce that he knew more about Methodist traditions than he knew about God. Although Greg knew the story about Christ's resurrection, he did not understand its significance, or the importance of believing at all that it actually happened.

On this very issue, Greg had sought out the counsel of his pastor at a high school winter church retreat just that year. He had asked the pastor, "Can you tell me why it is important that I should *believe* that Jesus was raised from the dead? I know you are always pointing to Jesus as the model. But why is it important that I believe Jesus was raised from the dead? I don't see what that has to do with anything in my life."

His pastor paused and then hesitantly replied, "Well, I can't tell you *why* it is important . . . but it is."

This answer didn't set well at all in Greg's logical mind. At first, he was surprised by the answer, but then he became a little angry, saying, "Well, if you can't tell me why it's important for me to believe in Jesus' resurrection, then I'm not going to believe it!"

After that conversation, Greg refused to take church seriously. He wasn't about to be an atheist, but he was convinced that after all of his years in church—and all that he had learned during those years—that the message of the church wasn't really worth much. It seemed most of the theological information he had acquired in church was pretty useless. He had little interest now to consider thinking about God in terms of religion. There were other more interesting subjects to consider.

And yet there he was, parked in the Jones' family driveway, on a pleasant Southern California summer evening, talking with Joyce about God, about their mutual questions and beliefs regarding His existence. Greg found their mutual curiosity endearing.

To Joyce, Greg suddenly seemed to fit the model of her perfect guy. He was a balanced combination of athlete and thinker. Her boyfriend Steve had been smart, but he was not very athletic. Greg seemed to draw out of Joyce the more physically active lifestyle she had enjoyed in previous years. That summer, she and Greg spent much of their free time together playing Frisbee along the long driveway at her house, swimming, hiking, and sharing their dreams of future possibilities.

At the end of Greg's high school season, the Yankees baseball organization said they would be able to offer Greg an opportunity to play professional baseball if he were willing; but on his dad's advice to stay in school, Greg chose instead to study and play baseball at Occidental College. Although his dad hoped Greg would accept the baseball scholarship offered to him by the University of Southern California (USC), Brad's alma mater, Greg stuck with his first choice: Occidental College. Oxy was smaller and would be less intimidating for him socially.

Greg's decision was further cemented by an introduction to the Oxy baseball coach by a family friend. Coach

Dunlap was pleased to meet Greg and offered him a starting position on the varsity baseball team as a freshman under new rules just adopted. The coach told Greg that if all went well with his pitching, he would support Greg playing three varsity years at Oxy and then going into pro baseball after his junior year when he turned twenty-one. For Greg, this kind of thinking had the ring of an appealing life plan.

Greg's Take

On the outside, I felt pretty confident about where I stood at that point. I knew nothing was guaranteed, but I thought I had the smarts to get by in school and follow my dad into law if baseball didn't work out for me. After talking with Coach Dunlap at Oxy, I thought baseball might work out even better than I had ever imagined! And I had a girl friend I enjoyed, with real long term potential. But I was also like an onion, with inner layers of doubt and intimidation. I was a loner and a poet at heart, in love with words that could touch upon and convey genuine personal meaning to others. But I had no firm values or beliefs. I had no idea that God might love me, only the barest idea that God existed in some holy way that I didn't and probably wouldn't ever understand. I only knew that I didn't want to die, and I believed that life just had to be worth living. I was glad to have survived the social mysteries of adolescence, or so I thought.

In the fall of 1966, Greg arrived at Occidental College in Los Angeles—not at all prepared, as it turned out, to absorb the college social scene he encountered. Parties and drinking were far more prevalent than he had expected.

He also faced the intellectual challenge of competing with the other students. They may not have been as brilliant as *he thought* they were, but he soon felt intimidated. In a class small-group discussion early that fall, the young professor asked the half-dozen students present for their thoughts on how a personal philosophy might be developed. One of Greg's classmates answered, "I think Camus put it best when he said . . ." and then proceeded to quote from Camus *in French*! When she finished her quote, Greg glanced around, waiting to see what would happen. Everyone in the group, including the professor, seemed to be nodding knowingly.

Greg was thinking *Camoo? Who or what is Camoo, Kahmoo, or is it Kehmoo?* He had no idea, and he suddenly felt sick at the thought that he was the only one who didn't have a clue. Staring out across the campus he concluded *what have I done? Except for baseball, I've come to the wrong place!* It didn't matter one bit that Oxy was his mother's college or both of her parents' alma mater.

Although Greg was smart, and a capable student, he felt academically miserable—and he remained miserable for his first two years at Occidental. He couldn't seem to figure out *how* to get good grades, even when he put the work in. There always seemed to be far more work required than he could keep up with and still play baseball. During those first two years at Oxy, through the end of his sophomore year, he managed a 2.0 C average. Although he hadn't given up entirely on academic success, Greg still didn't know where to begin to acquire the skills he needed to compete on the academic stage.

Feeling frustrated and helpless, Greg found himself placing more and more time and energy into winning rambunctious rounds of ping-pong, shooting pool and playing bridge than into studying the courses in his major, which was political science. He also found himself agreeing to go to a movie with an Oxy girl who pursued him. As fate would have it, the two of them were seen at the theater by one of Joyce's friends. After hearing about it from her friend at high school, Joyce confronted Greg. Greg's failure to draw firm lines with an assertive female really surprised him, and wounded Joyce. This personal weakness frightened Greg a bit, but he didn't admit that to Joyce. Rather, he apologized to her and promised to take their relationship more seriously and *exclusively* from that time on.

Joyce's Take

I felt dumbfounded, not understanding Greg's explanation of how the date with the other girl came about. His inability to talk with me about this situation was disturbing. Perhaps if I had been in a church youth group, or if I had found a trusted adult mentor to talk with, I might have gained some wisdom from this experience. Officially Greg and I had made no promises. We weren't engaged. We both, especially I, had just assumed we were going steady—*but what did that mean?* The entire situation might have served as a red flag, at least for me, but I overlooked it and didn't recognize it as such. Sometimes such redflag behaviors left unaddressed, can return again.

Baseball became the silver lining for Greg at Oxy. That spring, Occidental finished fourth in the NAIA national small college championship. As a freshman, Greg won ten games for the college, including a 1–0 victory over UCLA. He finished the regular season allowing less than one earned run per game. And his relationship with Joyce seemed to be going equally well.

Joyce graduated from high school at the end of Greg's freshman year at Oxy, and she enrolled at USC as a pre-dental hygiene major. At the fall Sorority Rush, she had hoped to pledge Delta Gamma, her mother's sorority, but during rush week she noticed that most of the Delta Gammas were now short and blonde. Being tall and brunette, she was axed. Although she felt like dropping out of the sorority scene altogether, Joyce pledged Alpha Chi Omega and her exclusive relationship with Greg continued.

The following spring, Greg asked his fraternity friends to drive down to USC from Oxy to serenade the Alpha Chi girls, so he could pin Joyce with his Sigma Alpha Epsilon (SAE) fraternity pin. Socially at USC, this activity was seen as a pre-engagement announcement, which pleased Joyce very much.

The physical chemistry between Greg and Joyce had by now inclined them to sexual intimacy, which seemed both natural and unavoidable to each of them. Neither of them had continued attending church, nor were they seeking any guidance on such matters. Socially and culturally, at least in college circles, having sex in a committed relationship before marriage seemed entirely acceptable. It was 1968 and the era of free love was blooming. Greg and Joyce occasionally smoked marijuana with some of Greg's friends at Oxy, and alcohol drinking was an every-weekend party occurrence.

That summer, after Greg's sophomore year at Oxy and Joyce's freshman year at USC, Greg invited Joyce out one evening for a special dinner at a French restaurant in Hollywood, Joyce's favorite. After a lovely dinner, Greg drove up into Griffith Park in the Hollywood Hills and parked. "Let's get out of the car and look at the lights," Greg suggested. Joyce nodded, mystified about Greg's reason for wanting to get out of the car to view the lights that were fully in view from inside the car. She followed his lead, however.

Together they climbed a small hill, Greg assisting Joyce with his hand as she walked up the slippery gravel trail. From the top of the little hill, they could fully appreciate all of the flickering lights of Hollywood and the Los Angeles basin. It was a breathtaking sight.

Fumbling in his pocket, Greg pulled out a small box and opened it. The single diamond sparkled in the evening light.

Greg paused, looked at Joyce and hesitantly said, "Joyce, will you marry me? Will you become my wife next June?"

Joyce smiled back at him and she also paused. She had been hoping, and suspecting, that Greg might propose, but suspecting it didn't make this moment any less special. Then she answered brightly, "Yes, I will," beaming with the same smile that had first captured Greg's heart just over five years before.

Greg slipped the ring on her left hand, thankful that he had taken care to have it sized correctly. They embraced, feeling that something very special—a new depth of love they hadn't known before—was established between them that night.

Soon after that engagement evening, Greg called his father to ask for his advice on marriage, now that he had proposed to Joyce. Greg met with his dad in his Pasadena law office. After some initial small talk, Greg went ahead and asked for his dad's advice. His father thought a moment or two, and then said, "I want you to remember this, Greg. This is really my one and only piece of advice for you: Always remember that Joyce is the most important person in the world to you. Don't ever forget that." He closed with an air of finality that left Greg reluctant to ask any more questions.

Greg was a little surprised, and frankly, a little disappointed with his father's brief piece of advice. It seemed too short to explain all that Greg saw in his parents' marriage. He didn't really know precisely what his father *meant* by his words, but neither did he ask him any further questions. His father's advice was, in an odd way, engraved on his mind. Greg just simply replied, "Okay, thanks, Dad."

For Contemplation and Conversation

1. How long did you date your spouse before marriage? In what ways does Joyce and Greg's dating relationship correlate with your own dating years? What advice would you offer a young dating couple today?

2. Men: In what ways does Greg's early home life and college experience remind you of your own experience?

3. Women: What are some ways you can relate to Joyce's early home life and college experience?

4. How might you learn and share more about your own families of origin so that you and your spouse can better understand each other?

3 Beginning to Search for Happily Ever After

The date on Greg's desk calendar said simply, Saturday, June 7, 1969. Greg glanced at it as though it could hardly be true and then frantically resumed pecking away at his typewriter. He was cutting it close, but he firmly believed that if he stayed focused, he could finish. Not only was he determined to complete this last final exam, but he was also focused on his strong desire to earn an A for the course and possibly finish his whole junior year with straight As. When he reached the end of the page, he sharply tugged the paper free from the typewriter's carriage and spun in another blank sheet.

It was a conversation with his father the prior June that had frightened Greg into academic overdrive. By comparison to other student-athletes at Occidental, Greg's grades were not all that poor, but college life had come as a shock to him. He had repeatedly felt overwhelmed by the exams he faced, intimidated by the other students and equally so by the professors. At the time of that conversation just after the end of his sophomore year, Greg's 2.0 grade-point average was a tender subject. He had let his parents know how he was doing, but he also had avoided talking with them about it.

But that one evening, with little fanfare, Greg's father had gently asked him, "Are you still thinking about going to law school some day?"

"Yes," replied Greg, a little defensively, caught off-guard.

Greg's father said, "Well, the last I heard, you have to have a 3.0 to get into law school."

"Really?" Greg gulped, stunned and surprised, instantly aware that this would require a 4.0 average, all As, for his two remaining years. He had only received a single A thus far, in a course on Cervantes' *Don Quixote*, which offset a D in a required course in religious literature. His face fell.

"Yup," his father answered colloquially.

"Oh, wow," responded Greg, "That means a 4.0 from here on out . . . !"

The conversation hadn't gone any further. It didn't need to. Greg's father had made his point and walked out of the room, leaving Greg with a sobering feeling that the time had come to clean up his act and somehow throw himself more whole-heartedly into his studies. He moved into an extra room in an off-campus apartment with some senior SAEs who were excellent students.

In the fall, Greg began to spend long hours in the library and secured Joyce's help in typing his papers. Eventually he called his father to ask for help on one particular course, Constitutional Law. Professor Reath had told his Con Law students that their grade for the course would be based on one exam at the end of the quarter. He said the final exam would be designed to test the student's knowledge and understanding of forty legal cases that would be covered in the class. He recommended that all of the students *brief* the cases in advance of each class session to be ready for discussion, and to prepare themselves for the final exam.

Greg tried to follow his professor's instructions, but he knew he was falling behind the other students. The number of cases to study, write about, and put into memory was overwhelming. Plus, he had no idea what a brief was.

Greg's father responded positively to his plea for help and invited him to come over to his office, and to bring some of the cases he was supposed to brief. His father looked at one eight-page brief that Greg had written and said, "That's not a brief!" He added with a chuckle, "That's a long!" He then asked to see the case book for a few minutes and said, "I'll show you how to write a brief."

About ten minutes later, his father handed him a half page, handwritten. His father had scrawled a four-line list, "Facts-Issue-Holding-Reasoning" with a few sentences under each word.

Greg asked, "That's it?"

"Yes," his father explained. "That's why it's called a brief. It's brief!" Greg laughed, looking at the brief. He could see it was all there, in just a few sentences. He and his father looked at one another and smiled. "Okay, wow. Thanks, Dad!" Greg said, his hopes surging.

From that day on, Greg prepared his Briefs daily and asked Joyce to quiz him. He soon could recite the essence of the facts, issue, holding, and reasoning for every case that the class was assigned to study. His participation in class discussions suddenly came to life. When the multiple choice final exam came at the end of the quarter, Greg breezed through it and scored ninety-three percent, more than twenty percentage points higher than the next highest score in the class. Professor Reath personally called Greg into his office to congratulate him, remarking that he would have to figure out how to adjust the class curve to fill in the gap between Greg's score and the others in the class.

The success and confidence that Greg experienced in studying for that course spread to his other courses that fall quarter, in which he also received A grades. After the break for the holidays, the Dean of Men also called Greg to his office, just to congratulate him, saying, "I didn't know you had it in you!" Greg thanked him, feeling for the first time that he just may have an academic future, and that his law school ambitions might actually come to be a reality.

Greg's dedication to academics earned him new respect from many of the political science faculty members, and he was able to repeat with straight As in the winter term. Now

Greg had hopes of doing the same in the spring term—if he could just get this final paper finished and make it to his wedding! Several of his professors would be in attendance tonight. The typed exam was due by five o'clock, which would give him just enough time to make it to the church.

Greg finally pulled the last page out of the typewriter a little after four o'clock. Within minutes he changed his clothes, dashed out to his car, slipped behind the steering wheel and peeled out of the parking lot toward the professor's office. He jumped out, slid the typed final under the professor's door, then he took off immediately on the twenty-minute drive to the church. The wedding was to begin at eight o'clock.

By five o'clock, Greg was greeting his groomsmen at the door to the church. His best man, John, was just arriving. Nobody seemed to notice that Greg was a bit harried.

Joyce, meanwhile, was enjoying a delightful afternoon with her six bridesmaids and the photographer. It was a relaxed, happy day for her.

Her bridesmaids gushed at the beauty of her wedding dress and their lovely floral bouquets. They talked and giggled with excitement about how many friends they had seen arriving outside the church. Joyce was excited about exchanging their vows and kissing Greg after being pronounced husband and wife. After that, the reception festivities and her honeymoon with Greg! When her bridesmaids asked if she felt nervous about walking down the aisle, she replied no—after all, her dad would be walking down the aisle with her.

Joyce and Greg would have enjoyed planning their own wedding and reception. The entire affair, however, was mostly arranged and coordinated by Joyce's mother. And since her parents were paying for the wedding, Joyce acquiesced to nearly all of her mother's preferences—the wedding would be at eight o'clock in the evening, too late from Joyce's perspective, but her mother professed, "The best weddings are at eight o'clock."

Joyce stood firm on just three matters.

First, she insisted on a chocolate and vanilla marble cake rather than a plain, traditional white cake. Joyce's value of inclusiveness was to be expressed by the dark and white cakes mixed together. Although this would neither be appreciated nor understood by many at the wedding, for Joyce, a marble cake was essential.

Second, she wanted an airy lemon chiffon color for the bridesmaids' dresses, and the style of them was to be similar to her own gown choice. Third, she wanted to be free with Greg to move about and greet the guests informally at the reception. Therefore, she and Greg chose to dispense with a formal receiving line. Fortunately, Joyce's mother did not see these three preferences as major issues worth quibbling about, so everything from that point on went smoothly.

For Joyce, the wedding was not only a joyful new beginning in life. It meant freedom. She imagined many wonderful years ahead with Greg, far away from the strict social demands and preferences of her mother.

The church was packed with several hundred guests, including a respectable assortment of fraternity and sorority members, professors, extended family members, athletes, friends, and prominent figures in the community. Those in attendance hushed their quiet conversations as music signaled the start of the wedding march. As the door to the main sanctuary swung open, Joyce was awed at the sight of the dazzling white runner stretching before her from the back of the church down the center aisle to the altar. The flowers at each pew were beautiful. Every seat appeared full.

Joyce felt excited and yet ready for this moment. Unsure whether she would smile at the sea of guests on either side of the aisle, or look straight ahead to Greg, she finally opted for a mix of doing both. She recognized many faces of those in attendance and was pleased to see so many of their friends! She knew that those she did not recognize were probably friends of their parents.

Arriving at the altar, Joyce felt great relief. Greg reached out and took her hand. They had not seen each other all day, and it felt good to Joyce to feel Greg's hand and to see him return her smile.

Several months before the wedding, the minister had met with them in what he had called a premarital counseling session. However, when they met with him the only topic the minister wanted to talk about regarding their upcoming marriage was the ceremony. It seemed their meeting was mostly a matter of who would do what and when at the event.

Greg left the counseling session both perplexed and frustrated, as he had hoped for and anticipated a sober discussion about the meaning of marriage, and *how together they might live it out!* He had hoped and even expected that *some* adult in his life would address several of his concerns with less ambiguity than his father's brief advice that Joyce was to be "the most important person" in his life.

From Greg's perspective, this minister's premarital counseling was worse than ambiguity. It was *nothing important at all!* The pastor had apparently concluded that Greg and Joyce were a well-adjusted, well-educated young couple from upstanding stock. They appeared to have all the tools necessary for a healthy, thriving relationship. In retrospect, this pastor had made a very unfortunate miscalculation.

Outside the bubble of Greg and Joyce's immediate community, the entire world was in turmoil. The Reverend Martin Luther King, Jr. had been assassinated the year before, followed by Robert Kennedy's assassination a few months later. The Civil Rights Movement was in full swing, while divisions over the Vietnam War, social drug use, feminism, divorce, and the sexual revolution were changing society. Culture and political norms were shifting. The first no-fault divorce laws in America would soon be adopted in California, signed by Governor Ronald Reagan on September 4, 1969, and in just three years the book *Open Marriage* would hit the nation's bookstores and quickly become a best seller.

Despite the churning world outside, on the evening of their wedding, the ceremony was beautiful. It flowed smoothly just as planned. Greg and Joyce repeated their vows, exchanged rings, and finally, it was time for Greg to lift Joyce's white veil for the formal wedding kiss. Finally, they were married! The two of them turned joyfully to face their guests and everyone applauded. Smiling broadly, Greg and Joyce headed for the door at the back of the church. There they turned exultantly to one another and kissed again, celebrating that their shared dream of getting married had finally come true.

At the outdoor reception site in Joyce's parents' backyard, the dance floor was in place, flowers were floating in the swimming pool, and by four o'clock the sun began peeking through the thin fog around the hills. When the bride and groom arrived, the weather had cleared. Upon entering the garden setting, they were ceremoniously introduced as "Mr. and Mrs. Greg Millikan." Someone announced the bride and groom's first dance. While the photographer walked around them taking candid photos, Joyce and Greg moved to the music, looking at each other, not taking much notice of the song or the tune. The guests conversed casually, champagne glasses were filled and emptied, the music played, and the guests said the food was delicious. On cue from someone, Joyce tossed her bridal bouquet over her shoulder to the gathered single young women and Greg removed and tossed Joyce's garter to the single men.

Greg and Joyce agreed later that it would have been good for them to assign the best man or maid of honor to offer them some food from the buffet table. The only food Greg and Joyce had during the two and a half hour reception was a few ceremonial bites of wedding cake and a glass of champagne each. But other than this, their wedding and reception happened just the way they had hoped: the cake was delicious, the music was enjoyable for all, and their friends and guests celebrated happily together.

This important day also offered the two of them an unusually pleasant wedding gift, one they had both hoped for, but hadn't talked much about, because it was entirely outside their control. That very morning, June 7, was the day of the 1969 Professional Baseball Draft. Just before their wedding ceremony was to begin, Greg's father found Greg and told him the St. Louis Cardinals had selected him in the fourth round! Greg was thrilled with the news and thrilled to be marrying Joyce, all in the same day! He had a wonderful feeling that everything in his life was finally going his way, and according to his highest hopes. He felt more than ready to celebrate and relax on their honeymoon.

They departed for Hawaii by plane the next morning. It seemed like such an auspicious and luxurious destination to them. They had never imagined honeymooning in Hawaii, but the trip was a wedding gift from Greg's Great-Aunt

Nana and Joyce's parents. Now they were relishing the idea of two weeks alone together in paradise—what an incredible way to start their new life together. Immediately upon deplaning in Hawaii, they were engulfed by warm fragrant breezes and the beauty of clear smog-free skies and swaying palm trees. Almost heaven!

At their hotel in Waikiki, room service brought them fresh papaya with a dash of lime. Having never tasted papaya before, Greg thought *what sweet and satisfying fruit!* As they ventured out across Oahu, then Kauai and finally Maui during the next two weeks, they were overjoyed at the beauty and variety of the islands—stunning waterfalls and pools of crystal clear water surrounded by lush vegetation, sublime golden sand beaches, deep forests, winding rural roads, rocky coasts, and mountain views.

In the midst of their bliss, several doses of reality managed to creep in. It had been out of their control, of course, that one of Greg's fraternity brothers had thrown his handful of rice at the couple so hard that a grain of rice had become lodged in Greg's ear canal. Joyce was unable to remove it and by the third day of the honeymoon, the obstruction was becoming painful. Joyce encouraged Greg to call the hotel doctor, which he finally did. Happily, the problem was instantly resolved by the doctor with a long pair of tweezers.

Another learning opportunity arose a few days later when Greg saw a wide-open surfing break along the Lihue breakwater in front of their hotel. After lunch, he asked Joyce if it would be okay with her if he tried riding the waves using one of the hotel boards available to guests. "Sure," she said, "that's okay; I'll just stay here, enjoy the view and read my book on the hotel patio." She was glad for a few minutes of rest after their outing to Waialua Falls that morning.

Joyce looked out toward the breaking waves several times, hoping to catch a glimpse of her surfing husband, but the surfers were too far out to be seen clearly from anywhere on the patio. It was almost three hours later when Greg returned. Joyce was sullen, feeling hurt and a little angry. She told him that she had thought he would be gone about thirty minutes or so—no longer! It had not occurred to her to ask Greg how long he planned to stay out in the water. Greg was so enjoying the water and waves in his first chance to surf in Hawaii, he had lost all track of time. "Yes, I'm upset," she finally said. "What about our honeymoon, and being together?"

A little light bulb lit up in Greg's mind: *Yes, this is our honeymoon. Of course!* He understood her being upset and apologized.

The third dose of reality—and an opportunity to learn more about communicating with each other—took place on the island of Maui the next to last day of their honeymoon. Greg loved maps and the hotel had a pretty good one of the island. They were staying at Kaanapali on the west shore of Maui. Their destination was Hana and the Seven Sacred Pools on the east end of the island. To Greg, this looked like a perfect destination for a day trip. They planned together to share a picnic lunch in Hana—only forty miles from their hotel in their rental car—on the way to the Pools. It didn't occur to Greg to ask anyone at the hotel for input, and he didn't. After breakfast and a swim, they set off for Hana at about 10:30 in the morning, anticipating a nice lunch there and then visiting the Seven Sacred Pools just down the road.

The drive to Hana became a three-hour-plus adventure. True, they saw lovely jungle-like scenes as they bumped along a windy, narrow road at about ten miles an hour. In order to avoid a collision, they had to be especially aware of all oncoming traffic. Well before they finally arrived in Hana at two o'clock, they both had become hungry, irritated, and very cranky with each other. Finding no place to eat in Hana, they finally found the Hana General Store where the best available food was a can of Spam and a box of crackers which they devoured quickly in front of the store. Disappointed, but no longer hungry, they pushed on to see the Seven Sacred Pools. The beauty of the Pools mollified their slim lunch and they decided the treacherous driving experience would be something to remember. They were both surprised, however, that they had responded to this traveling surprise with such irritation toward each other.

On the last day of their honeymoon, rather than celebrating their final honeymoon lunch in a fancy restaurant with the extra cash they still had from their wedding gift, they decided to visit a nearby Dairy Queen for an authentic Hawaiian plate lunch. The two of them shared a good laugh together, imagining what Aunt Nana and Joyce's parents might say about that!

And then, it was time for them to fly back to reality. Soon after their return to the mainland, Greg signed a contract with the Modesto Reds, the St. Louis Cardinals' Single A farm team in the California League. Happily, Greg's father had worked out the details of the negotiation with the team representative while Greg was on his honeymoon. Brad had managed to get Greg a good signing bonus plus education expenses for his final year at Occidental College. Two weeks later, Greg and Joyce were packed and driving north to Modesto, California, where they began their married life together in professional baseball.

Greg's love for the game seemed to have been imprinted on his life since birth. His parents spotted Greg's potential as a pitcher after observing their five-year-old son engaging in rock fights. Greg could throw faster, harder, and more accurately than any of the other boys in the neighborhood, even *older* boys. To distract him from rock fighting, Greg was given his first baseball glove and a ball for his sixth birthday. He oiled and cherished that glove as a prized possession, and by the age of eight, Greg was relishing every hour of playing baseball on youth league teams.

Greg's affinity for baseball fit neatly into the Millikan family mythology. Greg's paternal grandfather, Pat, had played for and coached USC's baseball team before World War I. Greg's grandmother, "Baba," often entertained Greg with stories about Pat and his athletic career, pointing proudly to the large silver trophy on her sideboard. It was the Spalding Cup given to "Pappy," as he was affectionately called, for his Southern California batting championship in 1913. She also had a photograph of Babe Ruth that had been personally signed and addressed to Pappy. Someday, Baba promised, if Greg chose to follow in his grandfather's footsteps, she would give him the trophy and photograph. Part of following in Pappy's footsteps, Baba added, meant no drinking, no smoking, and no swearing. Proudly reminiscing, she told Greg, "One day at USC, Pappy told the other players on the team, 'If you don't stop cursing, I'm not going to play!' And he was such a good ball player, they all stopped because they didn't want to lose him!"

Baba also told Greg that his grandfather had been invited to play pro ball for the Chicago Cubs, but that Pappy's father, a Methodist minister, had not allowed him to accept the offer since baseball games were often played on Sundays and because the sport was known for a lot of drinking and smoking—things the Millikan family found disreputable.

Greg had a lot to live up to. The image he had of Pappy was always in the back of his mind, even though he never really knew his grandfather, who died of a heart attack at the age of fifty-nine, just after Greg's first birthday. For Greg, there was just the trophy and the personally addressed Babe Ruth autograph, plus a single picture of Pappy holding little Greg on his first birthday, looking at his grandson with serious interest.

As the days passed toward their departure for Modesto, Joyce was sorting through their wedding gifts with her mother. All of them were laid out in an orderly fashion on Elizabeth's dining room table, each one carefully numbered by her in a gift book, along with the name and address of its giver. The dining room glistened with a sea of treasures—sparkling crystal, silver serving pieces, beautiful china and lovely vases—as gift registries didn't include everyday items at that time.

As the new wife of a minor-league baseball player, Joyce had no idea how or whether she would ever be able to use such lovely and costly items. She was truly surprised by the elaborate gifts they had received from their parents' friends, gifts that went far beyond the items that Joyce and Greg had requested. From the many gifts displayed, Joyce selected a blender, some cookware, and a few other practical items to take with them to Modesto. She placed the remaining items in her former bedroom closet until they returned in the fall.

Frankly, Joyce was planning a fresh, simple start to her married life with Greg. As usual, she was bewildered by her mother's inability to see the disconnection between the beautiful, formal gifts on the table and her impending mobile life as a ballplayer's wife. At age twenty, Joyce had neither the desire, the confidence, nor the maturity to reason with her mother. The best she could do was to stall for time on the storage and dispensation of their many wedding gifts.

For months, Joyce sat down regularly to write thank-you notes—two or three at a time, one to each person or couple listed in the wedding gift book her mother had prepared. She felt burdened by the gifts, although thankful for those who had given them. She could not wrap her mind around the thought of ever putting many of the gifts to use.

Greg's first day with the Modesto Reds was July 3, 1969. He and Joyce met the team in Fresno, just as the Reds were finishing a road trip with a three-game series against the Fresno Giants. After the game that night, Greg and Joyce followed the team north on US Highway 99 to Modesto, with all their possessions packed tightly into their Ford Cortina GT. It was after midnight when they pulled into downtown and checked into Hotel Modesto. Their intention was to start apartment hunting the following day.

The next morning they were jarred awake by blaring trumpets, trombones and tubas, thudding drums, and clashing cymbals outside on the street. The local high school marching band was leading the Modesto July 4th Parade right past their hotel room!

They quickly dressed and went outside, only to find the hotel parking lot filled with parade-watchers and surrounded by flag-draped vehicles. They were trapped. Fortunately, the hotel had breakfast available. After breakfast, they made some calls to realtors but no one answered, even though it was Friday morning. Then it hit them—of course, it was the 4th of July! Apartment hunting would have to wait until the next day. Working to shrug off his disappointment, Greg studied a local map to find a park where they might at least get away from the noise until the parade festivities were over. In the park, the weather was very hot and humid, far from romantic. Overall, they both felt isolated, powerless, and a little depressed. Joyce was feeling so frustrated that she cried. In the mid-afternoon, Joyce drove Greg to Del Webb Field for his first day of work as a professional ballplayer.

That evening during the game, Greg asked his teammates for ideas on where to stay. Some of the players talked about month-to-month apartments available up on McHenry Avenue. This was welcome information! By Saturday afternoon, Joyce and Greg had signed a month-to-month lease and moved into their very first home together—a one-bedroom furnished apartment on North McHenry Avenue for $95 a month. It was a great find in their opinion, something well within Greg's monthly salary of $500.

Their daily routine was soon adapted to fit Greg's baseball schedule. This meant free time from waking up at nine or ten o'clock in the morning until three in the afternoon, when they would have a large dinner, as long as Greg wasn't scheduled to pitch. Joyce would take Greg to the ballpark by four o'clock, or he might carpool with one of the other players living in the same complex. Before the game began at 7:30, the team would have batting practice—"BP" as the players called it. The pitchers would work on their pitches, shag BP fly balls for the batters, and then run wind sprints. Infielders would take ground balls almost endlessly, working on their fielding and throwing. Games were usually over by 10:30 as long as extra innings weren't required. Joyce would usually wait for Greg, and when they arrived home, they'd watch Johnny Carson's *Tonight Show* on the new television they had purchased soon after receiving Greg's first paycheck. As several of the teams in the California League were in locations nearby, few overnight road trips were necessary. Both Greg and Joyce were glad that baseball life afforded them so many days to share together.

Being married and living together seemed to come naturally to them. Joyce did not miss her parents—she enjoyed the freedom of making decisions with Greg, having a small income and deciding how to spend their money. This was the very first time she was outside the confines of her parents' control and mother's expectations. Joyce relished her new independence. She was excited for the opportunity to learn how to plan meals and cook. Joyce's mother had not taught her daughters to cook, as Dorie, their family's housekeeper and cook, had done most of the cooking. Joyce's mother cooked occasionally, but mostly for social occasions. Prior to their wedding, Joyce had not done much cooking other than the fried eggs she loved, smothered in cheese, as her after-school snack.

Joyce had enjoyed watching Dorie and appreciated talking with her as she worked. Watching Dorie, she had acquired the sense as a young girl that cooking was *doable* and could be fun. She had really enjoyed helping Dorie roll ground beef into meatballs. In fact, on one occasion when Joyce and her sister, Martha, were helping Dorie, Martha said, "Let's make meat cookies!" so she and Joyce each grabbed a small handful of ground beef, placed a chunk of butter and some sugar into its center, rolled it into a ball—and popped it into their mouths. Dorie burst into laughter! Although it was a great novelty to Joyce, the instant she tasted the concoction, the idea quickly lost all appeal.

Joyce did bring to Modesto both cookbooks they had received as wedding presents—one with a red and white checkered cover from *Better Homes and Gardens*, and the longstanding blue-covered mainstay, *The Joy of Cooking*. The *Better Homes and Gardens* recipes seemed easier for Joyce to follow, so she began reading through it to try out various dishes. Breakfast and lunch were a cinch. She usually made her famous fried eggs with cheese or they had cereal for breakfast, and always sandwiches for lunch. Greg never complained and he seemed to have tastes that were easy to satisfy. Greg always wanted ice cream for dessert.

Joyce made sure to follow every detail provided with each recipe. In cooking her very first spaghetti dinner, Joyce sautéed the ground beef and onion just as directed, feeling excited about the dinner she had planned. This was her first try at spaghetti—something Greg said he really enjoyed. Then, following the recipe closely, she added oregano and garlic to the beef and onions in the large frying pan, and finally a can of tomato sauce. The pasta was just about ready, simmering in a pot on the back burner.

But when she spooned a serving of the savory meat sauce over the noodles on Greg's plate, she was surprised. There was an odd-looking orange film oozing to the side of the plate. This didn't look like any spaghetti she had eaten before. It certainly didn't look like the picture in the book next to the recipe!

Greg had watched his mother cook often with ground beef so he was able to identify where things had gone awry when Joyce set the plate on the table before him. He asked, "Did you drain the fat after cooking the ground beef?"

"No," she answered, "Do I need to?"

"Yes, you have to drain the fat from the ground beef before mixing it with the tomato sauce," Greg said softly, trying to ease Joyce's disappointment.

"Well, the recipe didn't tell me to do *that*," she said with a pout.

Greg bravely loaded a fork with a large helping of noodles and sauce, took a bite, and nodded his approval. It was a meager attempt to placate his wife's distress. It was also something to laugh about later.

In following weeks, a corn and chicken casserole recipe taught Joyce another valuable lesson. It only took one bite for Greg to know that something was definitely amiss with this recipe. After asking Joyce about the ingredients, he learned she had *not* been taught that meat left in a refrigerator did not have an indefinite shelf life! The chicken had gone bad before she cooked it. They both were glad they hadn't actually swallowed more of the rancid casserole.

To her credit, Joyce was not dismayed by these mistakes. She was a fast learner and very soon became a good cook.

What Joyce truly *enjoyed* was managing the household finances. Greg's minor league salary was enough to live on if they were careful, and she liked the challenge of making ends meet. They had a brief hiccup, both writing checks against their joint checking account, and quickly learned that communication was essential when one of them wrote a check. Since their income and expenses were fairly stable, it was easy for Joyce to find ways of balancing their account, and that kept them on track.

Joyce's Take

While I was in high school, my dad talked with me about investing in the stock market. Together we would watch stocks and how their prices fluctuated. For my Economics class I was to select a stock and pretend to purchase it at a certain price, recording the cost of my investment. After two weeks, we checked to see where the stock had moved to learn if we had made money or lost money. Although I really didn't invest anything, if I had, I would have made money investing in Channel 7, ABC. Dad and I enjoyed doing this together, anticipating how various stocks might rise and fall. These few conversations were some of the best adult talks I had with my father. I found that I enjoyed learning how to invest in good companies, and that my money could work to support a company's future. My dad's influence carried over into my later life, so today I remain very selective about investments. Greg and I consider carefully how our investments might impact the lives of others around the world.

One challenging newlywed adjustment to married life in baseball was living in very small towns and accepting that their baseball team was a kind of artificial family for the two of them. There were certain rules in the Cardinals' organization, such as not wearing shorts to the field or in the hotel on road trips. However, professional baseball players were not what Joyce had anticipated. Instead of being the clean-cut heroes as she had imagined, many of them seemed to take advantage of their status, and regularly behaved poorly. She was surprised to see some players smoking after the game, and to hear some coarse language. Greg's mental appraisal of their new social order quickly divided the players into three categories: singles; newlywed players; and older, married players with small children. The team had a diverse mix of personalities, ages, and ethnicities. Some of the players were recent high school graduates, others were long timers—veterans that would soon be on their way out of baseball. Players came from across the nation and Western hemisphere—from virtually every place baseball was played—and from every socio-economic background. Some had little education, and yet others were Ivy League grads.

Greg tried to be friendly with all his teammates, but he was cautious about becoming too close with some of them. He knew that a poor choice of friendships could influence his career. It was already mid-season when he joined the club. Relationships on the team were already in place, and no one on the team had any knowledge of who Greg was, or vice versa. On road trips, Greg commonly sought to room with a married player, trying to steer clear of teammates who exhibited wild or unstable behavior. He purposefully tried to connect with players who had the background, talent, and drive that might carry them into prosperous futures, with or without baseball.

Overall, however, Greg soon saw that it would be difficult to establish the same degree of camaraderie that he had enjoyed previously with his college teammates. He found it somewhat disconcerting that a player might be traded to another team, or released, on a moment's notice without warning. A player with the team the night before might simply be *gone* the next day, his locker empty. Furthermore, since everyone on the team was trying to stay in the game and make it to the next level—ideally to the major league level—teammates were not just teammates, but *competitors*, which naturally added relational tension. Each player had to focus to some degree on his own performance and statistics with concern for his individual future. Greg had not anticipated this—neither had he experienced this kind of stress or pressure in college baseball.

Making friends and developing a social circle among the players' wives was a far less stressful endeavor for Joyce. She enjoyed the other women and shared good times in their company. The wives commonly sat together in the stands during home games, cheering on their husbands whether the team lost or won. When their husbands were traveling to away games, the wives would gather at one of their apartments and socialize while listening closely to the radio broadcast of the game.

The players and their wives, however, rarely socialized with one another when a game was *not* involved. Throughout the season, which ran through Labor Day, the team played nearly every day with occasional doubleheaders, so there was little extra time to develop meaningful friendships that were not focused exclusively on baseball.

Beginning Professional Performance

Soon after Greg's arrival in Modesto he was placed into the pitching rotation. His first start was to take place in Bakersfield against the Bakersfield Dodgers on July 20, 1969. Joyce drove south from Modesto and his parents and siblings drove north from Los Angeles to attend the game. Today few would remember whether the Reds won or lost that day—for the record, they lost 3-2. Greg pitched well, but it was neither the game nor his pitching that was most memorable. Everyone was excited about the moon landing by the Apollo 11 crew. Astronaut Neil Armstrong was expected to step out onto the moon from the lunar lander at any moment! In the stands, transistor radios were tuned to the live broadcast.

Sure enough, just as Greg finished the bottom of the first inning with a groundout, Armstrong descended the ladder of Apollo 11 and onto the surface of the moon. At 7:56, his words audibly echoed throughout the Bakersfield stadium, "That's one small step for a man, one giant leap for mankind." For Greg the moon landing was a distracting coincidence, but he was glad to have pitched through the first inning without trouble.

After five creditable innings in which Greg gave up two runs and several hits, the manager lifted him, explaining that five innings was the max for his first start. Greg was disappointed with his outing. He had hoped to dominate, to pitch very well, but he had been only average. It was a smaller step for him than he had wished. Nonetheless, he accepted his family's congratulations without complaint after the game.

Overall, it seemed perfectly acceptable to both Greg's family and Joyce's family that after their wedding, the young couple would live completely independently of their parents and families of origin. There were no lengthy or frequent phone calls or visits requested or expected. It never occurred to either Greg or Joyce to question whether this distancing from their original families was normal or healthy.

Joyce and Greg felt it natural to see their families only on holidays. They did not think it strange that their brothers or sisters or their parents never asked how they were getting along or if there was anything they might do to help them. Being entirely apart and on their own after marriage was evidently expected. The basic cultural and family understanding on both sides was that everything would be all right, and that Greg and Joyce would find their own way, autonomously, independently, and without ongoing family support. For each of them, launching out into the next generation of family life was a pioneering venture across a new frontier.

At the end of Modesto's baseball season in early September, Greg and Joyce returned to Los Angeles to complete their college studies. They rented a studio apartment midway between USC and Occidental College and adapted themselves to a new, very different routine. For her evening work, Joyce brought home small blocks of wax she had been assigned to carve precisely into life-size teeth for her dental hygiene program. Greg read volumes of political science books and journals and devoted himself to a yearlong senior honors project funded by a foundation grant—a different universe from his experience with the Modesto Reds.

Based on his birth date, Greg had drawn a vulnerably low military draft lottery number of sixty-five. With St. Louis' blessing and the Vietnam War continuing, he planned to stay in school and graduate the next June so that he could keep his student deferral another year. Greg had a back-up plan as well, based on his bad knees and a previous surgery on his right knee in high school. Armed with a clear set of X-rays and advice from a lawyer recommended by his dad, Greg hoped, if and when the call for a physical exam came, he would fail the exam and get classified 1-Y—which meant "unfit for active duty service."

With school by day and homework by night, nearly six months into their marriage things were going well enough, but Joyce found herself increasingly frustrated with her husband's silence and with his mental and emotional stoicism. It seemed to her that almost nothing would draw Greg out of himself to share his feelings or his own opinions openly and directly. Joyce had assumed that Greg was identical to her, and that if he wanted, he would be able to speak freely and openly about himself and what he cared about. Not hearing much at all from him, she began to wonder, *what really matters to Greg? What does he really care about? Does he really care about me?* Joyce, however, didn't think to ask him meaningful questions. In her family, asking one another questions had not been the norm.

One Saturday morning the two of them began to have a disagreement. Rather than back down, Joyce purposefully allowed the argument to escalate. She wanted to elicit *some kind* of emotional response from Greg, but he refused to go in that direction. Analyzing their argument, he strategized a way through it, and worked to explain his point of view so the two of them might come to a clear understanding. The more Greg tried to plow through the situation, the more

Joyce pushed back. It seemed that nothing he could do or say would satisfy her.

Finding this situation completely absurd and exasperating, Greg finally exploded. Sucking in a big breath, he suddenly turned and punched his fist through the particleboard cabinet door next to him in their bedroom. But even in this impulsive act, born of sheer frustration, he showed some restraint. Greg had punched through the cabinet with his right hand, not with his pitching arm.

Shocked and surprised by his outburst, Joyce silently exulted in the moment. She had successfully evoked an emotional response from Greg—not one she had hoped for or expected, but to her it seemed like a start. "Oh honey, now I know that you care!" she exclaimed. "Now I know that you actually have *feelings*!"

"*What*?" Greg was taken aback. "You *wanted* me to do this?"

"Well, I didn't want you to punch the cabinet," Joyce replied. "I had no idea you would do that. I just wanted you to share with me how you were feeling."

Greg was dumbfounded, feeling bamboozled by Joyce's statement. He had never had anyone intensely desire a genuine, unromantic emotion from him. His parents had modeled a very placid way of relating, at least in regard to emotionally difficult things. His father was hyper-mental in his communication, and his mother always asserted that things were *fine* whether they might have been or not. Neither of his parents expressed or welcomed any words that openly stated non-positive personal emotions, even in a disagreement!

Greg was completely unprepared for Joyce's desire for him to express such emotions to her. He simply could not understand her asking him to openly recognize his own emotions. Greg's self-focused, logical way of analyzing life led him to conclude that strong emotions or their expression signaled something negative, not positive. And furthermore, he believed it would be *his fault* if a negative situation ever did erupt between them. Greg's solution for any emotional conflict, especially with Joyce, was to shut down communication and to disconnect until, like a volcanic eruption, the conflict was far enough away not to be dangerous.

The more Greg did this, however, the more frustrated Joyce would become—and the more she felt her desire for closeness and security was threatened. She knew that things were not being said that should be said, and that ultimately, their relationship was not growing and developing as it would if they were able to work their way through disagreements. For her, leaving things unresolved seemed only to drive the two of them further apart.

Joyce's Take

When problems came up early in our marriage, I commonly responded with a head in the sand approach. Greg admitted to me later that his approach was to "ignore the smoking car and hope the problem would disappear." In essence, Greg and I both chose to duck down and look the other way. We kept moving forward from circumstance to circumstance without ever really taking stock of what was going on, what we valued, what was truly important, or how we each were feeling. With my head in the sand, I had no way of knowing or learning if there was something either of us could do to improve our communication and our overall relationship. It seemed I was living an external life only, not really having an internal life experience—at least, not a positive one.

Greg's Take

Joyce and I seemed to set each other off into a negative spiral. Down we would go—reacting against whatever was perceived negatively by the other. We had neither the skills nor patience to look carefully and deeply into what the other said, what was meant, or what the most helpful response to the other person might be at that moment.

Greg's inability to deal with his own emotions and with the emotional aspects of their communication led Greg to feel like a failure, and to conclude that *he* was solely responsible for the relational difficulties they were experiencing. He didn't know where to turn for help, and frankly, he wasn't sure that help was possible. Although he wouldn't have admitted it to anyone, deep inside Greg began to feel discouraged and helpless. He began to assume that if he wasn't satisfying Joyce emotionally, he probably wasn't going to succeed in satisfying her sexually either. He did not see that this erroneous assumption on his part would lead to all kinds of problems for him and Joyce in the coming years—problems that did not need to happen.

Greg graduated from Oxy on schedule in 1970, and was assigned to Lewiston, Idaho, with the Lewiston Broncs of the Northwest League. Greg pitched well and made the Northwest League All-Star team. And due to his bad knees, he failed his draft exam in Spokane, just as he had hoped.

Joyce and Greg were surprised and delighted that summer to learn how much they enjoyed the slow pace and quiet life of Lewiston. In future years, they would look back on that season, even with the team's long bus rides to Coos Bay and Bend, Oregon, as something special and difficult to recapture.

The Cardinals invited Greg to their fall instructional league in St. Petersburg, a good sign, so he went to Florida and Joyce moved in with her parents to complete her fall semester at USC. On Greg's return in December, they rented a flat over the garage at a family friend's beach house, and found that they loved living at the beach, even though they could stay only a few months.

The following spring, Greg was assigned again to Modesto as one of the starting pitchers, with solid hopes of moving up to AA or beyond as the season progressed. Joyce arranged to finish her last semester classes early so that she could join Greg in Modesto.

A month into that season, their high hopes were derailed by a failure of Greg's left knee. One afternoon in late May, while leaping to catch a fly ball during batting practice, his left knee buckled, and he collapsed with what turned out to be multiple cartilage tears. He was flown to St. Louis the next morning, where the Cardinals' team doctor examined the knee. Two days later reparative surgery was performed to remove torn meniscus on both sides of his left knee. For her twenty-second birthday, Joyce flew to St. Louis to meet Greg in post-op. She did her best to comfort and encourage him, but to little avail. He was miserable and in great pain. Greg was placed on the disabled list for the rest of the season.

A few days later, they returned to Los Angeles with Greg on crutches. He began working hard immediately on what he hoped would be a full rehabilitation, but they also had to find a place to live. Having become mutually enchanted with beach life, they decided to take the remaining portion of Greg's signing bonus to make a down payment on a small duplex in Hermosa Beach in Los Angeles' South Bay area. They planned to live in one unit and rent out the other.

While waiting for escrow to close, they stayed with Joyce's parents. One Saturday afternoon while Joyce's parents were away for the day, a call came in on the home phone. Greg picked it up. It was Joyce's mother, in a panic. She announced that Joyce's dad had just drowned during an after-lunch scuba dive with their instructor.

Greg knew that Liz and Bob had gone to Catalina Island that day for a scuba-diving certification exam. It was a new activity for them, suggested by their marriage counselor to help them get back on track together after a marital crisis. Greg asked her where she was and if she was okay. She was still on Catalina Island with the Sheriff and the Coast Guard. She was not doing well.

Greg put Joyce on the phone, and she walked her mother through it all again to be sure to get the facts right. This stunning news and turn of events would change many things for Joyce and Greg and the rest of her family, but they were nevertheless glad, for her mother's sake, that they had been there to answer the phone.

Greg was fully recovered when he reported to spring training the following March. He was pushing hard for a promotion to AA. But the Cardinals seemed committed to keep him on their single-A team in St. Petersburg for further rehabilitation. This left Greg feeling frustrated and angry. He would be twenty-four years old in May, and he feared that time was running short for him to make it to the major leagues.

On the last day of spring training, Greg's former Modesto manager, now managing the Cardinals' AAA club in Tulsa, gave him a chance to pitch against the Oilers. He told Greg that if he did well, he might get a reassignment to Arkansas, the Cards' AA club in the Texas League. Greg shut out Tulsa for six innings, and then was pulled from the game and summoned to the box by the farm director. "You'd better pack up," he said. "I want you to report to Arkansas the day after tomorrow. The team will be playing in Memphis by then." That was the breakthrough Greg had been hoping for. He thanked the farm director and almost sprinted back to the locker room.

Still elated, Greg called Joyce, who was unpacking their stuff in their new St. Petersburg apartment. He told her what had just happened, and asked her to start packing the car again for Little Rock—they would need to leave early the next morning!

It turned out the Little Rock manager didn't realize Greg was coming until hours before the game in Memphis, and he had no spot in mind for Greg to pitch. Greg would be the twelfth pitcher on an eleven-man pitching roster. However, the manager did need a left-handed closing reliever. He asked Greg if he had ever relieved. Greg said no, but said he was sure he could learn. The manager showed him how to get warmed up in five throws and told him to be ready to pitch that very night! Sure enough, in the bottom of the ninth, with his team ahead by a run and two outs, Greg was called in to pitch to Memphis' left-handed clean-up hitter. Happily, Greg got him to pop-up and end the game. Thus, Greg moved into a new job description: left-handed short relief; and he flourished in the assignment.

A few months later, on the team's road trip to El Paso, Greg and some of his teammates went across the border to Juarez, Mexico, after an evening ball game and slipped into a bar to order drinks. While they were there, Greg and his friends were approached by a woman in the bar. She was there to earn her living by having sex with whomever she might persuade to join her. Greg was the one she succeeded with. He was not immediately certain why he followed her to the back room. After he and his teammates returned to El Paso that night, he was not only remorseful; he felt repulsed by his behavior!

He called Joyce to say hello the next day. His guilt was so intense that he later believed that he had *surely told* her over the phone what he had done.

When Greg arrived back home after the road trip everything seemed normal between Joyce and himself, as if nothing had happened. This puzzled Greg, because by now he had experienced his wife's strong emotions about many things. Surely she would have a strong emotional reaction to his lapse with a Mexican prostitute.

Greg was surprised when Joyce greeted him with a kiss. They shared dinner, caught up on the team's games, watched some TV, went to bed, and made love. Early the next morning, Greg decided he had better say something about what he had done in Juarez, wondering why Joyce had not said anything about that earlier.

Joyce listened, not quite comprehending what Greg was saying even as he spoke. It had never entered her mind that Greg would cheat in their marriage—she thought something like that simply wasn't in his character. Joyce felt betrayed and devastated... almost speechless. In the midst of many tears she said, "How could you come home like you did, share dinner, the evening, and sleep with me without talking with me about this first?"

Terribly hurt, Joyce couldn't imagine how life could go on normally between them again. With a sullen and downcast countenance, Greg slumped down into their couch and sat quietly for a long time, not knowing what to do.

Greg's team was not scheduled to go on the road again for two weeks. The tension in their tiny apartment was palpable. Finally Joyce said sternly, "I'm willing to forgive you only if you promise that this kind of thing will never happen again!"

Greg promised. They agreed not to discuss the unhappy incident any further. And they didn't. The silence between them didn't heal anything or resolve any deeper issues. Ignoring their pain and uncertainty, the incident was buried. Neither of them knew anything better to do.

Greg's Take

By the time my friends and I returned from across the border, I was filled with remorse about what I had done. This woman had not been attractive to me, but she had been persistent—she was earnestly determined to find at least one of us at the table that would go with her to the back room. After all, this was her livelihood. From her perspective, *why else would these men be here?* For reasons I could not understand until years later, I was the one who went.

Nothing was said about this afterward among us ball-players, but once we were back, I went to the team trainer and asked him if there was medicine I might take in case I had picked up anything south of the border. He gave me medicine that I gladly took.

What I came to realize later was how my parents, and especially my father, taught me that a man *never says no* to the sincerely expressed desires of a woman, if she is not at fault in expressing them and he is in a position to satisfy them. If a woman made an earnest request—and she was firm about it—then I was taught it was *my duty* to fulfill her request. I have resented that kind of power that determined women have exerted over me from time to time, whether it was my mother, grandmother, or some other woman in an authoritative role. I resented it because it seems I almost always yielded to their power, which made me resent it all the more.

After my behavior in Juarez I also had a tremendous feeling of guilt. I couldn't believe I acted in this way, yet I couldn't deny that I had. Denying it wouldn't change the historical fact. It would only change me, and for the worse.

I feared and believed that if I didn't confess the act to Joyce, then I was somehow embracing my behavior as acceptable—something that I might be willing to do again. I did *not* want that to be the case!

I was grateful when Joyce finally said she would forgive me if I promised never to do such a thing again. I was quick to make that promise, and I meant it.

For Contemplation and Conversation

1. Did you and your spouse think you were *prepared* for marriage? What expectations did you have for the role of husband, and for the role of wife? If you received premarital counseling, what was the *best piece* of advice you received?

2. What are one or two of the happiest memories of your wedding? Your honeymoon? Do you have any difficult memories of those events that you have not discussed with your spouse?

3. What were some common *do's* and *don'ts* required of you in your family of origin? Do you think those were good ones? Has your perspective changed? If so, how?

4 A New Life in the Midst of Difficulty

As a pitcher, Greg had a very good season in Arkansas, finishing with nine wins, four losses, and a 1.6 earned run average. To his surprise, before the season was over, the Cardinals offered him a Winter Ball contract running through December with a team in the Mexican Pacific League, the Guasave Algodoneros ("cotton workers"). Greg quickly learned that such offers were generally made only to players who were considered bona fide prospects for the big-leagues. It was another potential breakthrough, one he felt lucky to have. He didn't want to miss it, and he wanted Joyce to go with him. That was possible because they had just bought a 1972 VW Bus—with air conditioning—in Little Rock to handle all the moves they were making.

As they felt ready for travel, Greg quickly told the Cardinals he would accept the offer and join the Guasave club for the 1972 winter season. The winter season for the Algodoneros was scheduled to begin October first. He was to arrive in Guasave the third week of September.

Joyce's feelings were mixed as the season came to a close in Arkansas. She was excited about Greg's season and how his pitching had improved, yet she wondered *will we be glad to spend three months in Mexico? Is there any chance that this Winter Ball will truly make a significant impact in Greg's baseball career?* On and off, she found herself thinking about a childhood incident she observed between her mother and her grandmother—Grandma Wells was crying—and the word "divorce" was spoken. That was how Joyce learned that her grandfather had left Grandma Wells. He had gone off with his secretary.

Joyce was only five years old at that time. Grandpa Wells was the man in her grandmother's life—the one who carved the turkey at Thanksgiving, bounced Joyce on his knee, and made funny noises with his mouth. He was still her grandpa, but Joyce never saw him again and there was no more talk about him. She had missed him.

Now, as she prepared to move to Mexico for a few months, Joyce found it odd having these memories of loss and betrayal that had happened twenty years before. She wondered if Greg's south of the border infidelity was some-how bringing this to the surface. *What would happen now that both of them would be in Mexico?* Joyce didn't say any-thing about this to Greg. She wanted to keep her muddled thoughts and worries tightly corked inside. Her main desire was for both of them to move beyond the terrible one-night stand in Juarez. Just the same, Joyce couldn't ignore the fact that nearly all of the men in her life had fallen to marital infidelity.

Only eighteen months earlier her father had announced his intention to divorce Elizabeth and marry another woman with whom he had been having an affair. Joyce knew the woman and her husband, as they and her parents had social-ized together as friends for years.

The discovery of her father's deceit had sickened Joyce, but it was never discussed within the family. The other wom-an backed out of the arrangement and Joyce's parents had decided to try marriage counseling. The scuba diving was part of their therapy. When Joyce's father died in the acci-dent just a few months later he was only forty-nine years old. Any possibility for mutual discussion and closure with Joyce was completely cut off. Six months after Bob's death, Joyce's mother sold her home and remarried a local widower—also named Bob. Now, only a year after her father's death and just six months after her mother's remarriage to a man Joyce barely knew, Joyce would be going to a remote city in Mexico with Greg to advance his baseball career.

For Joyce, the ground under her own marriage wasn't feeling all that solid. Since her marriage to Greg two years before, Joyce's heart had been unexpectedly broken, and she felt triply betrayed by her father: first, by his extramarital affair, then by his expressed intention to divorce her mother, and finally by his death. Perhaps Greg's infidelity had reopened, maybe even deepened these wounds.

With only two September weeks open between Little Rock and their departure, Greg and Joyce quickly loaded their things and Greg's baseball gear into the VW Bus to begin the Mexican adventure. Off they went to Nogales, Arizona, then over into Mexico, aiming to drive down the coast through Guaymas, Ciudad Obregon, Navajoa and Los Mochis to Guasave, about five hundred miles south of the border.

After several days of driving, Greg and Joyce finally arrived in Guasave. The agricultural town of 40,000 was located well off the main highway and about forty miles from the coast. The streets in the center of town, about eight square blocks, were paved. The rest were simply hard-packed dirt. Almost no one understood or spoke any English.

They found their way to the team's office and inquired about housing. After looking at the two choices offered by the team, Joyce and Greg opted for a two-story house on a paved street downtown which they would share with another American player—a African American outfielder with the Tulsa Oilers, his wife, and their three-year-old daughter. They quickly learned that they were now instant celebrities. Whenever they went out, wherever they went, they were stared at and often followed by groups of giggling young children.

So this is fame? Joyce mused, feeling embarrassed and somewhat uncomfortable. *The experience of fame is far more difficult than people commonly talk about!* At the same time, she enjoyed the cultural differences she encountered, including trying to speak Spanish with locals. Securing local food and figuring out its preparation was another cultural surprise since there were no supermarkets. The couples did find eggs, peanut butter, jelly, and white bread in a small neighborhood market. A nearby deli offered imported ham, cheese, and bread—but at very high prices. The only local place they found to purchase meat was an open-air market where animal carcasses were hanging from hooks, unrefrigerated, unpackaged, and unbutchered into familiar cuts. Just one visit to this market was enough for Joyce, when she encountered a fresh cow's head, placed right there on the counter—for sale! Joyce decided that from then on, purchasing and cooking fresh beef in Mexico would not be an option.

Within a few weeks of their arrival, a local widow named Lupita was introduced to them. Lupita was willing to cook and serve them dinner in her home. Each person paid Lupita six dollars a day for dinner and a sack lunch. Under the circumstances, this seemed quite reasonable.

On one occasion, Joyce helped Lupita prepare sandwiches for the sack lunches. As Joyce spread a normal amount of mayonnaise on the bread, she noticed Lupita wince. In response to Joyce's questioning look, Lupita reluctantly explained that mayonnaise was a luxury—she had to travel by train 500 miles north to Nogales every few weeks to purchase supplies, including mayonnaise, to cook for the ball players. Mayonnaise was expensive and packaged in heavy glass bottles. Naturally, it had to be used very sparingly. This was eye opening for Joyce. Lupita's life seemed so very difficult, not at all like Joyce's *normal life* in the USA.

The baseball stadium in Guasave was fairly new. Placed in the midst of cotton fields about a half-mile from town, it seated 10,000. Like many of the stadiums in the Mexican Pacific League, the stadium had no water piped into the locker room for showers, so the ballplayers had to arrive at the field dressed in their uniforms and return home to shower after the game. Their soiled uniforms were picked up, laundered and returned to them daily at home by someone from the team.

The crowds at the games were often quite large and boisterous, ranging anywhere from 3,000 to a packed stadium of 10,000 fans—or more. Even though the quality of play in the Mexican Pacific League was quite high, Greg wasn't sure if Guasave's fans cared all that much about the individual players or the quality of play. They mostly seemed concerned that the Algodoneros win the Mexican Pacific League championship, as they had the previous January.

Although the team was having its ups and downs this season, Greg continued to pitch well, seeming to pick up where he had left off in Little Rock. He was determined to make a good showing that might advance him past the AAA level and possibly onto the St. Louis big club the following spring.

By mid October Joyce was starting to feel a bit nauseated each time she faced food, even Lupita's good home cooking. Eventually a doctor was called, and he asked as he examined her, "Con niño?" ("With child?")

Joyce wasn't sure how to answer. She and Greg were trying to get pregnant, but she couldn't really know whether her nausea was caused by tainted food or morning sickness. The doctor gave her some pills that she hesitated to take, but finally did, hoping they would be all right for their baby, if indeed she were actually pregnant.

By Thanksgiving, Joyce felt certain she actually was pregnant. While that was potentially good news, she and Greg agreed it would be best for her to return to California. Their housemates agreed that this was a sensible choice. In fact both couples decided it was time for the wives to return to the United States, and the husbands would move into the Hotel Guasave with the other American ballplayers. Greg and Joyce packed everything except Greg's clothing and baseball gear into the VW bus. The day after his next pitching start, Greg drove to Nogales with Joyce. From there she drove home by herself and Greg returned to Guasave by train. The season would end the first week in January, unless the team made it into the playoffs.

A few days after Greg's return, one of his American teammates—a AA infielder with the Dodgers—stepped into Greg's open door in the Hotel. "IIcy!" he enthusiastically announced, "Greg, have you heard the news? You're a Dodger!"

"What? What are you talking about?" Greg shot back confusedly.

"Haven't you heard anything? You got traded to L.A., man! One of the scouts told me. You and Rudy Arroyo were traded for Larry Hisle." Rudy Arroyo was another left-handed pitcher in the Cardinal organization.

Greg was dumbfounded. He hadn't heard anything from anybody about the possibility of being traded, and he had no inkling that the Dodgers were interested in him. The trade had actually happened almost a month earlier, but no one had contacted Greg about it, perhaps a sign of just how far removed Guasave was from the rest of the world.

On reflection, Greg was pleased with the prospect of being a Dodger, but very puzzled about the trade. The Dodgers had a good organization. Having grown up in the L.A. area, Greg was certainly a Dodger fan. On the other hand, from what he knew, the Dodgers already had a number of left-handed pitchers on their major league roster. Greg wondered what his chances would be with the Dodgers. He also felt disappointed at losing the opportunity he'd been working toward—a spot with the Cardinals. Alone in Guasave, he felt a little displaced.

Without Joyce, Christmas in Guasave was also a lonely experience. There was no ball game scheduled on Christmas Eve or Christmas day and the team did nothing to observe the holiday. For whatever reason, the American players didn't do anything to brighten one another's day either. Greg thought *professional baseball may be exciting and full of adventure, but hanging out alone here in Mexico is sure no fun!*

The Algodoneros were eliminated from making the playoffs the day after Christmas. Greg made his last start a few days later and was then allowed to leave for home. He managed to make it back to Hermosa Beach just in time to share New Year's Eve with Joyce, now three months pregnant. This was a real high compared to his Christmas low.

After a few days off with Joyce, Greg made contact with the Dodgers. He signed a AAA Albuquerque contract and was invited to January workouts at Dodger Stadium with the other Dodger pitchers and also to Spring Training in Vero Beach with the big club. He was glad for the invitation, but he was also sobered because he would be there as a non-roster player. Despite his success in Mexico, he was not one of the eleven left-handed pitchers on the Dodgers' major league roster. Even so, Joyce was thrilled to see Greg on television with the big team as they boarded the Dodger jet for Vero Beach. She was able to keep tabs on how he was doing and was glad to see he was having a pretty good Spring Training, even if he didn't make the big club.

By the end of March, Joyce was in her sixth month and feeling far less nauseous. She and Greg were looking forward to the 1973 season and to the birth of their first child. Becoming parents was something the two of them had discussed while dating. Both Greg and Joyce were from fairly large families and felt confident about taking on the tasks of parenthood. Joyce did not feel compelled to take advice from parenting books or to follow the current child-rearing experts, not even Dr. Benjamin Spock who was still highly regarded by her parents' generation. Joyce's mother had breastfed all four of her children, so even this seemed a natural part of motherhood to Joyce.

Greg's performance in Vero Beach gained him a starting position in the five-man pitching rotation for the Albuquerque Dukes. With the trade and move up to AAA, Greg's salary would almost double to $1,250 a month during the season. Joyce was looking forward to a larger paycheck for their family. With the AAA team flying direct to Albuquerque from Vero Beach, Joyce packed up and drove their VW bus from Los Angeles to meet Greg there when he arrived. They found a very nice apartment in a new complex—a large one-bedroom unit on the ground floor—with a lawn, swimming pool, a flowing artificial mountain creek, and lovely pine trees throughout the property. Two other married ballplayers with small children were also renting there. It felt good to find and be able to afford this upgrade from their previous apartments.

As Joyce settled in to the apartment, Greg and the Dukes were completing their exhibition games before the official start of the 1973 Pacific Coast League season. The last evening before opening night, the Dukes played a final exhibition game against the University of New Mexico (UNM). It was Greg's turn to pitch that night. As the game got underway, he felt healthy and strong and glad to get a feel for the Stadium and Albuquerque's famed light air that the hitters liked so much. Even so, Greg also felt a little impatient at what was essentially a meaningless game, though it was supposed to be fun for the fans and UNM.

In the third inning, a batter topped a slow roller about twenty feet to Greg's right in front of the mound. Greg sprinted to scoop up the ball to make the play to first base. As a left-hander, he had to set his left foot and pivot around back to his right to make the throw. In the two years since his surgery in St. Louis, Greg's left knee had given him no problems at all—he had almost put it out of his mind. At that moment his left heel cleat stuck firm in the grass, and as he began the pivot, his left knee buckled and gave way. He felt an awful grinding as the joint twisted and his knee gave way.

Greg collapsed in silent pain. There on the grass, before the trainer reached him, Greg's mind raced, *what happened? The surgeon said there was no more cartilage left to tear in that knee! I can't miss another season—at twenty-five, I'm too old to start over again.* He gritted his teeth, waved off the trainer, got up off the ground and hobbled off the field, grateful not to be carried off.

It was a deep setback. Greg was placed immediately on the disabled list for six weeks, but he told the team the knee was really fine and that he just needed to recuperate. Privately, all he could do was to hope for the best and do everything possible to speed the knee's healing process. Greg wasn't saying much to Joyce or to anyone else about how afraid he was that this might permanently derail his chance of success in pro baseball—not because he couldn't recover, but because he would be viewed as damaged goods when the Dodgers or any other team made their plans for the future—unless, that is, he could come back strong after his recovery. Greg silently set himself to come back hard as soon as his knee settled down. The six week healing period would end just a few days before their baby's due date, a coincidence that gave Greg a bit of hope that everything might turn out okay after all.

Joyce enjoyed baseball life with Greg and she was excited that soon their family would have three members. As her girth increased, Joyce and Greg took a series of Lamaze classes, as she wanted to deliver their baby by natural childbirth, with Greg in the delivery room as her coach. Although Greg adjusted well to this idea, the prospect horrified Joyce's mother, but Joyce was not dissuaded by that disapproval.

As the baby's due date approached, Joyce looked down at her sizeable mid-section with increasing dread. She would occasionally wonder *how is this baby going to make it out of me safely? Will I be able to survive this child's birth?*

Happily, the baby arrived just fine in mid-June. Joyce went into labor at four o'clock in the morning while the club

67

was on a road trip in Salt Lake City. Knowing Greg would have to catch a quick flight back to Albuquerque to make the delivery, Joyce immediately called him to tell him their baby was on the way.

The Dukes' manager had been forewarned to expect Greg's sudden departure when that call came, so it was no surprise when Greg grabbed his things, called a cab, and hopped on the first flight to Albuquerque, which included short stops in Denver and Pueblo, Colorado. He finally arrived at the hospital early in the afternoon to find Joyce panting in the studied, rhythmic breathing they had learned in their Lamaze class. Their Lamaze coach had helped out by driving Joyce to the hospital and standing in for Greg until he arrived in the labor room.

Greg was just in time for the climax of Joyce's labor. With sweaty palms, Greg jumped into place, guided briefly by their coach. Breathing in rhythm with Joyce, Greg encouraged her, mopping her brow with a damp cloth. Within a short time he followed along as she was wheeled down the hall and into the delivery room. Joyce was relieved that Greg had actually arrived in time for the big moment and she was proud of him for coming home to be with her.

After a few big pushes, their baby, a boy, was safely delivered. Geoffrey had arrived.

Greg was able to stay and watch over Joyce and newborn Geoff for a few hours before he took a taxi home to catch some sleep. He had an early flight the next morning to join the team in Tucson. Greg was scheduled to pitch against the Toros—and this would be his first start after coming off the disabled list.

Although Greg's knee still felt a little stiff, he fantasized a storybook outcome for the game, imagining a solid outing and a win for his first decision of the season. Unfortunately, in the actual game he was nervous and couldn't get his fastball or his curve down where he wanted them. He walked a number of batters, got hit pretty well by the Toros, and took the loss. After his travels, *lost* sleep and birthing adventures, and long layoff, everyone congratulated him for a pretty good outing, but Greg was secretly very disappointed. Pulling his pitching back together in time to make a difference was going to be harder than he imagined.

Joyce's mother immediately flew out from California to help Joyce with baby Geoff until Greg returned back home and settled in from the road trip. When the team returned from Tucson, Joyce and her mother attended Greg's first home pitching start, parking the VW Bus in the leftfield drive-in section. Five-day-old Geoffrey slept soundly bundled in a cardboard box between the two front seats. That night the team lost again. Greg was still having difficulty keeping his fastball down, and his breaking balls weren't breaking well in Albuquerque's light, dry air. Although Joyce didn't say anything to Greg, she also noticed that he was falling behind in each batter's count.

As he dressed after the game, Greg was sorely discouraged. It was another missed storybook ending, another loss instead of a win. Although he was still recuperating from his knee injury, he knew he couldn't afford to lose many more games.

Despite his pitching difficulties, Greg and Joyce adapted quite well to having a newborn at home. As they had commonly done before, they dove into this new parenting challenge and figured they would learn as they went.

At the start, they were able to keep nearly the same lifestyle after Geoff was born as they had before his birth. If friends visited or there was a party to attend, Geoff just went along with them. Greg was glad he could spend long hours with Joyce and baby Geoff on days when the team had home games. However, after Geoff's birth, Greg became quietly and unexpectedly anxious about providing well enough financially for his family.

Looking Further Down the Road

Greg was discouraged by his largely mediocre pitching statistics following the knee injury. With the season slipping away, Greg didn't see much chance of improving his stats significantly unless something miraculous happened in the last month before the season ended. The roster of left-handed pitchers ahead of him in the Dodger organization was deep. He would need at least four full years at the major league level to qualify for the player's pension. He could see that it might take him eight more years, performing well with various minor and major league teams to get to that point. That meant he would be at least thirty-three years old before he had any assurance of a worthwhile reward for his efforts in baseball. Though he didn't say anything to Joyce about it, Greg was beginning to doubt his future in baseball.

He thought about other ball players he knew who had families, reflecting on how they had struggled with fear of failure and uncertainty about their futures. He further factored in the several injuries he had experienced, two of which had put him on the disabled list. It never occurred to him that he might be harder on himself about his chances than he needed to be, nor did it occur to him to talk with anyone in the Dodgers' organization, or anyone else, about these concerns to see if he was on track or not.

Without mentioning it to Joyce, Greg was also concerned and feeling guilty about leaving her alone with Geoff while he was on road trips. Greg wanted to be home, and he also wanted to make sure his marriage with Joyce was stable and sound. How could he do that if he was in Cleveland? Finally, Greg felt sure that the AAA baseball salary offered would not be enough to support his growing family—at least not in the fashion he wanted to provide.

Greg decided to keep his hopes alive by aiming for a winning season. There was a glimmer of a miracle when he threw a complete game shutout against the Hawaii Islanders in Honolulu to bring his record to 5-7. He needed to win his last three starts and he would finish 8-7. Instead, he lost all three games.

In his final start, Greg gave up a go-ahead, three-run home run in the sixth inning. His manager, a kind man, apologetically removed Greg from the game at that point. Greg, however, felt furious. Something inside Greg snapped. He railed back with an angry outburst and thrust the ball at the manager as he stomped off the mound in a dejected fury. He was angry at his own failure, and a tremendous feeling of isolation swept over him—a feeling he couldn't understand. It was a grief he could not talk about.

A few days later, near the end of the season, Greg disclosed to Joyce that he had decided he would retire from baseball after this season—his fifth season after all—and that he thought it was time for him to pursue that career in law as he had always planned. To Greg, this announcement had a nice, comforting "lick your wounds and get on with it" feel to it. He figured that Joyce would think his decision was a good one, and that she would be excited to settle down in Hermosa Beach.

Instead, his announcement was a complete surprise to Joyce, as they had not discussed the topic at all before that moment. She knew Greg's career had hit a few snags but it still seemed to Joyce that his baseball career had real promise. She also knew Greg well enough to know that he would not make such a decision and announce it without being very certain that this was what he would do. Although Greg's stress about the decision was evident, Joyce wasn't sure exactly why he felt such stress. There certainly was no pressure from her.

Joyce wondered if Greg's stress had to do with his fears of financial insecurity. His parents had weathered the Great Depression as children. Their prevailing attitude, especially as expressed by his mother, was generally to pinch pennies—always with an eye to obtaining financial security. Greg's father was competitive by nature and didn't seem to think much at all about the *possibility* of not earning enough money. His philosophy was that hard work inevitably led to success, if you were good at it. While Greg enjoyed hard work and excellence, his innate drive was for inner satisfaction, not *beating others*.

A conflict had developed inside Greg that he didn't see coming: The threat of financial insecurity seemed to have taken away Greg's *intrinsic enjoyment* of baseball. He wasn't *good enough* to make an assured living playing baseball professionally, and that took away his joy. He had to find something better.

After the end of the baseball season, Greg and Joyce left Albuquerque in their VW Bus and returned with Geoff to their Hermosa Beach duplex. It was in an attractive location, within easy walking distance to the beach. It seemed perfect for their family while Greg began to pursue his new career in law.

With a lead from his dad, Greg soon found a law firm in West Los Angeles that had an opening for a law clerk. Greg thought this would be a good step for him on the path to a legal career. His dad's law partner gave Greg a good recommendation based on work Greg did for him during Greg's recuperation from the knee surgery two years before, and Greg was immediately hired. Less than a month after leaving Albuquerque, he was at work daily in the firm's library, writing briefs, researching laws and organizing documents for use in the firm's litigation cases.

Unlike baseball, Greg didn't feel threatened by law studies or the risks of a career in law. He had grown up watching his father navigate legal matters, and think and speak as a lawyer. Greg was comfortable in that world.

Within months of being hired, a surprising new life goal emerged out of his participation in a highly contested litigation case involving a large-stakes construction project. It showed him that he might work in the future to help business people create and preserve value and avoid squandering it in needless disputes. He was so strongly inspired by this case that going forward it shaped his studies and directed his future law practice, but his focus remained on himself and his work, not on his marriage or his family.

Greg's Take

Business litigation was like baseball. A lawyer could play great and get paid well, but the results for the client were unpredictable and often decided by others. In a lawsuit even a win was not necessarily a win for the client after the legal bills were paid.

In that important construction case, our client was a local builder who played a very small part in the construction of a huge power plant. His company was being dragged along in a big lawsuit over the plant's delayed completion. He had to fight because a contract clause put his company on the hook with others for more than three hundred million dollars ($300,000,000) in damages if his company were found at fault—probably forcing him into bankruptcy. Our firm was able to get the client's company off, but only after a year of work at great expense. In the end, our client had to pay much more in legal fees than all the money his company was paid for the project. If a lawyer had just properly reviewed his contract before he signed it, he would have either deleted that clause or skipped the project and his company never would have faced such a lawsuit.

I decided that as a lawyer, I wanted to help clients put deals together, not take them apart or pick up broken pieces in court. I might have seen my marriage in the same constructive light, but I didn't. I didn't yet have any light there.

New Opportunities—Big Challenges

As Greg filled out his applications for UCLA and the other local law schools, he and Joyce laughed with relief when they learned that new admission policies meant Greg's GPA from his first two years at Oxy would be ignored. So far as the law schools were concerned, he had graduated from college with a 4.0 grade point average. By Christmas, Greg received the news that he had been accepted at each law school. As UCLA Law School was highly regarded and less costly, he made plans to begin his studies there the following fall.

Greg and Joyce knew nothing about how Greg's law school education would impact their relationship. No longer were there automatic times when the two of them could be together. Law school created more distance between them—emotionally, mentally and physically. Perhaps following his father's example, Greg didn't think there was anything about his law studies that would be interesting or important for him to discuss with Joyce. She in turn felt Greg was too busy to be interested in hearing about her day-to-day life as a young mother.

When he entered UCLA Law School at age twenty-six, Greg was older and in a different stage of life than many students. Most of them had come straight out of college and were single. The environment was intimidating. Many law students felt the need to compare themselves to one another, sizing up one another, guessing who among them would be smart enough to excel in law. Greg's background and experience inclined him to be one of those students who was both admired and successful. As a result, and on the heels of his self-defined failure in baseball, he was easily pulled into the social competition to excel and prove his intelligence in the study of law.

For her part, Joyce was lonely during the day, solely taking care of toddler Geoff. She knew nothing about how to connect with others in Hermosa Beach. She had no thought of visiting a church or finding social outlets for young moms. Joyce felt dead in the water, craving stimulating conversation beyond the toddler level! In this quandary, Joyce decided to take on a part-time dental hygiene job, not only for the adult conversation but also to fill her need to feel appreciated by others.

Parenting two-year-old Geoff was presenting Greg and Joyce with some new challenges. For example, neither of them knew how to handle Geoff's bedtime behavior. Soon after they put him to bed, he would hurtle himself over the railing of his crib and scurry out to reconnect with his parents and their activities. Taking him back and closing his door securely, with firm instructions, didn't work. Geoff would still jump out of bed, place his little face as close as possible to the crack of light at the bottom of his door and scream loudly for his parents to rescue him from the darkness. Joyce felt for Geoff, and his tantrums played on her emotions. She was at a loss about how to deal with the situation. Greg also had no clue, but he could escape to law school or his work and avoid the problem. Perhaps there was no choice but to suffer through it, however, the additional stress of Geoff's struggle added weight to Greg and Joyce's relationship in the midst of their inability to communicate with each other.

Joyce easily found a job as a dental hygienist three days a week with two dentists who were partners in practice, and she found a nearby neighbor who was available and happy to sit with Geoff on those days. One of the dentists was a recent dental school graduate who was easy-going, amiable and conversational. The other was the senior partner. The work environment was very professional and pleasant. Joyce was glad at last to feel involved and productive, using her talents in tandem with other adults at work.

Staff members often shared the lunch hour together outside the office. Joyce initially shared lunch with other staff members, but one day the younger dentist asked her to join him and share their sack lunches together by themselves. Having attended the same dental school, the two found talking at the professional level easy, but then after several lunches together, their conversations drifted into many other topics. Before long Joyce became concerned about their relationship, wondering whether it was right for her to continue sharing lunch alone with him.

One evening after dinner, she brought it up with Greg, "I think I'm becoming attracted to Dr. B. at work. We've been sharing our sack lunches together. What do you think about this?" Her tone was serious, direct, and dispassionate. She felt she had nothing to hide. Recalling Greg's indiscretion in Juarez and its impact, Joyce was sensitive to the risk of undermining her marriage. She knew her attraction to someone else might challenge her own vow of fidelity.

"Well, sharing lunch together with him sounds okay to me," Greg said, outwardly calm as though he were indifferent, "so long as you're enjoying yourself."

This was not at all what Joyce hoped to hear. She had wanted him to say, "What? Don't become involved with someone else. I care about you and I want you for myself!" It had not occurred to her that Greg might not care, or that he might have some other agenda, conscious or unconscious! She saw Greg's response as another example of his oblique communication style. It seemed impossible for her to know or *even* to dig down and find out what Greg was *really* thinking about or feeling. Often Greg's statements didn't make much sense to her, and this time she was sure there was nothing to be gained by trying to dig further into him.

Greg's laissez-faire attitude toward their marriage seemed to echo the views presented in the widely publicized, newly-released book, *Open Marriage*. It had become popular (and notorious in some circles) for its overt encouragement to share one's sexual intimacy with others outside one's marriage.

In reality, Greg was not sharing himself at any level with anyone besides Joyce. He was too overwhelmed by his work and law school assignments. Ironically, Greg was terribly frustrated at what he perceived was his own sexual inadequacy to satisfy Joyce. Without talking with her, Greg reasoned that Joyce's involvement with Dr. B might help her learn how to interact with Greg himself at an intimate level, perhaps in a more satisfying way. Perhaps she could get some experience that Greg wasn't able to give her. Greg had no ability to convey these thoughts and fears to Joyce, plus he felt too ashamed to try. Joyce, however, had no knowledge about Greg's frustrated thoughts or his fears.

Joyce's Take

From the time we began dating, Greg and I genuinely enjoyed spending time together. We thought we loved each other, but we *knew* we *liked* each other. Neither of us understood God's love or the power *His love* can bring to another person.

The lonely, unimportant feelings that arose in me from Greg's attitude toward our marriage and his keen attention to others in law school made me crave recognition from *someone*—and certainly the attention of a handsome male appealed to my pride and vanity. Despite Greg's odd encouragement for me to continue sharing lunch with Dr. B, I decided not to continue those lunches because I respected the man, his marriage, and his family. I knew I was getting close to being in trouble with him, going in the wrong direction.

Looking back on this, I was glad to have behaved somewhat morally. However, what I *really needed* was God's truth. I needed specific guidance and caring friends who knew Christ—friends who could help me become truly wise. Going forward without that kind of support, I was powerless and unable to continue honoring my moral code. I eventually drifted even further away from an honorable, true, and right path.

Most days when Greg arrived home from work or law school, he found sanctuary in the waves of the Pacific Ocean just a few hundred feet from their door. He would quickly slip into his wetsuit and head for the waves to body surf. He had learned this as a young boy when his family visited Aunt Nana on Sunday afternoons. She lived near the surf, along the Strand in Hermosa Beach. There was something wild, joyful, and strangely brave about diving out under the waves into the surf and beyond the break, then swimming furiously with the kick of fins to catch the rising, rushing wall of water and career toward the shore, an arm out to the left or the right depending on the shape of the wave, then ducking under and out just before it crashed over in the shore break, and swimming back out with a kick of fins to do it again.

Nearly every day, either in the early morning or late afternoon, Greg looked forward to catching the curling flow of Hermosa's waves, if they were rideable. Out in the water, he could let go of land things and relax, scanning the horizon for the moving lines that signaled waves on their way toward him. He could unwind and think about nothing except those waves and where he would need to be to catch them when they arrived. This was an entirely self-satisfying experience that he shared with no one. His life revolved around three points: law school, work as a law clerk, and body surfing. Joyce and Geoff were there, but they were more or less taken for granted in Greg's mind, not factored into his immediate priorities.

Greg was a closed book—he wasn't revealing his inner feelings with *anybody*. He kept his fears and insecurities deeply hidden. He assumed that negative emotions were his personal, private burden. Any desires he had to make changes, find solutions, learn something, or perform better—all were tethered tightly to his need to maintain some degree of control. And, the most he could control were his law studies, his law clerking, and his body surfing.

Greg and Joyce were married, living together in the same house, but in many ways they were living life separately, except for Geoff. Geoff served as a kind of glue that held his parents together.

For Contemplation and Conversation

1. What do you think young or newlywed couples need in their marriage? What does a wife need from her husband? What does a husband need from his wife?

2. Has a career change ever affected your marriage relationship? If so, how did you and your spouse adjust to the changes required?

3. How might a person's professional/career aspirations become connected or unified with his or her marriage or home life?

4. What kinds of adjustments does a new baby bring to a couple? What insights might you offer to couples contemplating the addition of children to their family?

5. What common signs of communication breakdown do you see in the story? What are some ways a married couple might recognize that their communication is breaking down?

5   Groping in the Dark for Paradise

From time to time, Joyce and Greg had discussed the possibility of establishing themselves beyond Los Angeles. Since childhood Joyce had hated breathing smog, and recently the growing population and traffic congestion of the Los Angeles area had become daunting. In his second year of law school, Greg was starting his search for a stable and challenging long-term position.

He had made Law Review and was in the top five percent of his class the first year, so he hoped to have a shot at a summer clerkship with a top-tier firm. Unfortunately, there was no South Bay firm in that category with a summer position to offer. However, Greg learned that a prestigious Santa Barbara law firm was scheduled to interview for clerks that fall at UCLA. He mentioned Santa Barbara to Joyce and she liked the idea, so he set his sights on a summer clerkship with that firm. He put his best foot forward at the interview and landed one of the two clerking positions there for the summer of 1976. Greg would be twenty-eight by then.

Joyce and Greg were thrilled with this new opportunity, hoping it would be a ticket to heaven—a perfect way to get out of Los Angeles. Santa Barbara seemed ideal to each of them—a wonderful location for family and career. Life ahead looked promising and wonderful again—at least on the surface.

Joyce became pregnant again that same fall, which meant their second child would be born in mid-August, when they would be living in Santa Barbara. Privately, each of them assumed that the change of scenery, the new job, and the additional child would certainly bring renewed excitement and satisfaction into their marriage—along with a permanent home in Santa Barbara.

Looking forward with confidence, yet with sorrow at leaving their familiar beach home, they decided to sell their duplex in Hermosa Beach in the spring. They were amazed to discover the property had doubled in value during their five years of ownership. It sold quickly, and the Santa Barbara firm helped them locate a rental house in the Goleta neighborhood of Santa Barbara for the summer. The rental was just right, with a large yard and twenty young avocado trees in the back that Geoff could climb. It seemed fortuitous that avocados were one of Joyce's favorite foods. Their move to the rental in early June went very smoothly.

The Goleta area and Santa Barbara in general were daily delights for Joyce. Assuming the best about Greg's work at the new firm, she and Greg started searching for a home to buy where they could raise their children long term. The sale of the Hermosa Beach house would provide enough for a good down payment, so they hoped to find something just right. When Greg wasn't at work, the three of them were out house-hunting together. Their aim was to find and buy the right house, rent it out during Greg's final year at UCLA, and then move back to Santa Barbara after his graduation. Greg would take the Bar exam, join the prestigious law firm, and they would live happily ever after. That was their plan.

It was a relaxed, memorable summer in the Goleta house. The avocado trees bore plenty of good fruit, and Geoff had lots of space to play and trees to climb. Upon arrival they had found Geoff's bedroom appropriately decorated with brightly colored airplane mobiles hanging from the ceiling, and a side yard with two rows of strawberries, bearing sweet, ripe fruit. For a three-year old, Geoff took a surprisingly keen interest in the strawberry patch. After harvesting some, he firmly decided he wanted to plant more. Although there was no summer surf in Santa Barbara, Greg enjoyed running on the beach and playing volleyball with some of the lawyers in the firm. Greg also learned to cook avocado omelets, which the family all greatly enjoyed. During the days, Joyce and Geoff explored the parks and beaches in Santa Barbara and Joyce prepared for their new baby's arrival. All in all, summer in Santa Barbara felt very good.

Greg and Joyce's hopes remained high, but socially and spiritually their little family was completely isolated, except for Greg's few relationships at work. At the one social gathering the firm sponsored that summer, Joyce felt distinctly unwelcomed by the lawyers and their spouses who attended. Greg and Joyce hadn't discussed God or spiritual issues for years. They didn't think to seek out or build friendships with people in the local community, or to find a spiritual home.

Plans Thwarted

Then their plan ran into a roadblock. Greg and Joyce had finally found what they believed would be a perfect house—located on a cul-de-sac, which made it more secure for children's play. They had seen no other house that would work so well for them. Boldly, they decided to make a full-price offer. To their shock and amazement, their offer was not only rejected, but the house was suddenly pulled from the market. Licking their wounds, they felt stumped and a bit dejected. They didn't know what to do.

By mid-August, Joyce's mid-section had expanded with child number two—and she was eager to deliver. When the baby's due date came and went, Joyce became frustrated. Little Geoff contributed his opinion to the dilemma, announcing to his parents, "Mommy is not really pregnant after all—there is no baby coming, Mommy is just fat!" Joyce laughed, but not convincingly. She was impatient, wanting desperately to deliver!

Deliver she did a full week after her August due date. Todd, their second son, was born healthy at Cottage Hospital in Santa Barbara. Greg was there during Joyce's labor and delivery, more confident this time. The joy of Todd's arrival somewhat tempered their housing disappointment.

Over the summer, Greg noticed that the Santa Barbara firm's work seemed largely focused on personal estate planning and investment matters for very wealthy clients who lived in the Santa Barbara area. The clients had lawyers in Los Angeles or New York who handled their most challenging business and professional matters. This discovery began to gnaw at Greg. He loved challenges. He was one of the top law students at UCLA, and what he found *most interesting* and challenging about legal work were the truly difficult business matters—they were like the large winter waves he enjoyed tackling in his body surfing!

On the positive side, the firm was quite pleased with Greg's legal work. In September, when it came time for him to return to UCLA for his final year of law school, the firm offered Greg a permanent position as an associate following his graduation. This was exactly the result Greg and Joyce had hoped for the previous spring, but now Greg and Joyce's perspective had changed. The job offer was also contingent on Greg's prompt response with a committed yes or no required before the end of the month—by September 30.

From Greg's viewpoint, the requested response time was too short. He had serious doubts about long-term work in estate planning—day in and day out—for the rest of his life. Greg talked about this with Joyce, an unusual step for him at the time. Joyce voiced her concern about feeling unwelcomed by the wives at the firm's social gathering. Also, they had not located a family home as they had hoped, so their housing situation was still up in the air. Deciding to let Santa

Barbara go, they both agreed that Greg would turn down the offer. On September 30, he told the firm, "Thank you for the offer, but I'm sorry, I just can't accept." Although the decision was necessary, it was very depressing and disappointing to Joyce and Greg.

As a result, Greg's last year of law school began without a vision or an acceptable job offer. He found himself with a wife, a three-year-old son and a newborn for whom he felt responsible—with neither a home nor a secure job.

Hawaiian Dreams Dawn

Joyce and Greg found a rental home in Westwood near the UCLA campus. It was in a lovely neighborhood—very clean, and it had a little backyard for the boys. Greg built them a two-story playhouse with a steering wheel and a ladder, which they adored. The UCLA campus was uphill from the house, but it was close enough for Greg to commute by bicycle.

Among Greg's classmates returning from summer clerkships was an acquaintance named Mike, who had a shared interest with him in bodysurfing. Mike had clerked for a large firm in Honolulu and excitedly told Greg and a few others about his summer adventures and the many benefits of life in Hawaii. Mike was nearly giddy explaining how glad he was to have secured a permanent position as an associate attorney with the Honolulu firm after graduation. It was a highly respected firm and Mike said it was growing rapidly. In fact, he understood that the firm was intending to interview students at their UCLA Law School in December. Seeing that Greg's interest was piqued, Mike added, "And you are just the kind of person the firm is looking for!"

Greg perked up at the strange thought of living and working in Hawaii. He would definitely find surf there. When he shared this most unthinkable possibility with Joyce, she was thrilled with the idea. They had lived in Hermosa Beach for five years, so being near the ocean had become natural to her. A life for their family in Honolulu truly seemed like *Paradise* to Joyce.

As it turned out, Greg did interview with the Honolulu firm, but not at the UCLA campus. Instead, he was able to interview at the firm's office in Honolulu before the firm came to interview students at UCLA. Joyce's mother and stepfather had coincidentally decided to celebrate Thanksgiving that year with their extended family at a resort in Maui. With Mike's encouragement and direction, Greg called and arranged with the firm to fly over to Honolulu from Maui for an interview during the holiday break—and Joyce was invited too. For the short time they would be away, Joyce's parents agreed to take care of Geoff and baby Todd, who was just 3 months old.

Greg did not know in advance that the Honolulu firm was searching specifically for a new tax associate—Greg's strongest area. They were interested to find a young attorney who could get along with their tax partner, Grant, who was in his late forties. Grant was brilliant, but mercurial and extremely difficult to work with. Mike had told Greg about Grant and about Grant's consuming passion, paipo-boarding, a type of bodysurfing with a small board designed especially for Hawaiian waves. Greg had a paipo-board and used it often.

When Greg arrived at the firm's expansive offices—two floors of the Pacific Trade Center downtown—for his interview, he was surprised to be escorted directly to Grant's office. Upon entering, Greg greeted Grant warmly, but he could hardly take his eyes off the panorama through the windows before him. Grant's office on the twenty-second floor had a 180-degree view of the Honolulu coastline from the harbor eastward all the way to Diamond Head.

Greg managed to stay cool, even as he noticed a telescope mounted on a tripod near the window. It pointed directly at Ala Moana, a notable surfing area. After chatting a bit, Greg gestured at the telescope and asked, "For the surf?" Grant replied, "It is." And then he added, "It's focused on the break at Magic Island. When the surf comes up there, it comes up really fast, so I have to get right down there. That's the best summer break in the area for paipo-boarding." He looked at Greg, "Do you surf?"

"Body surf and recently paipo-board, pretty much every day," Greg answered with a smile.

"Really?" Grant asked, brightening. Greg nodded.

Grant smiled too, narrowing his eyes a little thoughtfully, and then said, "Would you like to continue this interview tomorrow morning up at Waimea? There's supposed to be a nice swell coming in there early tomorrow. Body-surfing in the shore-break could be really fun."

"Sure, that sounds great. I don't think we have any plans tomorrow morning," said Greg. Then he added, concerned, "But I didn't bring my fins."

Grant grinned. "Large? I'll bring you a pair. My wife can make us a picnic lunch. Check with your wife and see if she can join us. Call me back and let me know. We'll pick you up here at 7:30 in the morning, and we'll be back by around 2:30 in the afternoon or so." They shook hands and Greg, smiling and feeling amazed, nearly floated out of the office.

Greg and Joyce shared most of the next day with Grant and his wife, Amy, a day they would remember for years to come. For Greg the body surfing at Waimea was delightful and thrilling, and Amy's picnic lunch was enjoyable to share together as couples. Incredibly, Greg's interview with Grant took place informally in the water, between sets. As the two of them awaited the best waves to ride, Grant checked to make sure Greg knew tax law. Fortunately, he did.

Greg's final interview was to be with a senior partner in the firm later that afternoon. To Greg's surprise, the partner offered him a position with the firm, to begin after Greg's graduation. Knowing Joyce's feelings, Greg jumped at the offer and accepted on the spot. The deal was done. That evening Greg and Joyce joined three of the firm's attorneys and their wives for dinner at one of the nicest restaurants in Waikiki to celebrate his joining the firm.

Reeling from all the excitement, Greg and Joyce returned on an early flight the next morning to the family Thanksgiving celebration on Maui. They poured out the exciting news: Greg had accepted an offer from the firm; they would be moving to Honolulu next June after Greg completed law school. The family was stunned, but excited and congratulatory. No one asked whether this was a sensible move—after all, this was Hawaii they were talking about! The fog of Santa Barbara's disappointment had disappeared in the warm Hawaiian sunlight.

Back in Los Angeles after the holidays, Greg's elation continued on the surface, but it did not penetrate his depths. Down deep, underneath, shapeless concerns lay huge and silent. Greg could feel them, but he could not name them. It wasn't anything he could mention to Joyce.

Personal Boundaries Tested

After this remarkable turn of events, Mike quickly became Greg's new best friend. Mike was an intelligent, sincere, and gregarious young man from the San Francisco Bay area. He had graduated from Stanford University and was quite up-to-date with the technological breakthroughs emerging in what would soon be known as Silicon Valley. Mike was a very interesting guy, unlike anyone Greg or Joyce had known before. Greg and Mike did some paipo-boarding and cycling together when they could find the time. Joyce joined them on occasional bike rides.

Mike was also into Sufi mysticism, Werner Erhard's "est," and other New Age philosophies. Amazed and fascinated by Mike's many interests and abilities, Greg soon persuaded himself that Mike's surprising spirituality must be the key to his successful and pleasant outlook. Although Greg had learned about some of these spiritual pursuits in college, Mike's was the first enjoyable and possibly livable spiritual perspective that Greg had ever encountered.

In contrast to Greg's church background, Mike's views had an easy sense to them that made the mystical elements seem palatable, even if they seemed odd in the context of Greg's past experience. Mike's perspective poured into the spiritual void in Greg's mind and soul. He began adopting Mike's approach to life as a pleasant mystery, hoping to leave the depths in his soul alone.

In committing to move to Hawaii, Greg hadn't given any thought to local schools for his children, to the kinds of homes available in their price range, to the right kind of neighborhood for his family, and certainly not to the kind of church their family might visit in Honolulu. Instead, he thought mostly about surfing and preparing to surf in Hawaii. Although he studied hard at law school to be ready for his work with Grant, Greg grew a beard and wore his hair in a shaggier style, gearing up for his soon-to-come beach life as a lawyer in Hawaii.

For Joyce, thinking about their move to Hawaii and deciding what to take with them from their California home felt exciting. The Honolulu law firm had agreed to pay all the shipping charges for their move. This was a real plus. Both she and Greg felt sure that Hawaii would finally pan-out as the utopia they had been seeking all along—it would be their "happily ever after" place.

In addition to his new beard and hairstyle, Greg made other changes. He bought a state-of-the-art sound system. He and Joyce started smoking marijuana socially with Mike and Mike's girlfriend Kelsey (who was raised in Hawaii and planned to move back to Hawaii with Mike). Greg rode his bicycle to UCLA in shorts, sandals, and an un-tucked aloha shirt. He was counting the months until he would live and work in Hawaii.

Joyce was increasingly astonished as she listened to Greg talk endlessly with Mike about the merits of their newly shared spiritual pursuits. She was far more skeptical about Mike's beliefs than Greg appeared to be, but she did enjoy hearing Mike talk about Sufism. Joyce's younger sister Robin and her husband had recently become Hindus, but Joyce had no idea what that meant. Joyce didn't know anything about Sufis or Hindus, or even much about her own spiritual beliefs—certainly not enough to talk out loud about them!

One evening Mike announced that a Buddhist retreat had been scheduled in March in a small town near Palm Springs, and a well-known Tibetan Buddhist Lama would be teaching there on meditation. Neither Greg nor Mike would be able to attend because of their law classes, but Mike suggested and expressed hope that Joyce might go and then come back and share with them what she learned. The first teaching session would be for two entire weeks as an intensive course. With hardly a moment's thought, Greg also encouraged her to go.

Joyce was surprised and flattered at their request and she agreed to go as long as her mother and Greg's mother would agree to help care for their boys—Geoff was now three and a half, and Todd was nine months old. Incredibly, both of their mothers agreed to the plan. Furthermore, Joyce invited Robin to attend the retreat with her. Joyce was very glad that her sister accepted so they could talk about the retreat together.

Joyce's Take

Going to Palm Springs for an intensive Buddhist retreat with my sister was truly an *outside the box* experience! I was thrilled for the opportunity to learn something that was meaningful to Greg—something he didn't already know about. Naturally, I was hoping that my learning there would allow me to become more important to him, but also I was excited to get away from my everyday life, which felt so limited and boring.

Self-Centered Longings

The retreat mornings in the town of Yucca Valley were quite cold and the meals were vegetarian. Joyce was delighted with the menu, although she found that just having one piece of fruit for dinner was way too meager. She ate everything she could at breakfast and lunch, but she always seemed to go to bed hungry. She was perplexed. *Does having no meal for dinner equate to some kind of important spiritual exercise?* During the many hours of the event, Joyce was exposed to ideas she had never considered before, and the guided meditations were surprising. She enjoyed considering new ways of thinking about life. But by the end of the two weeks she missed her boys and the routine she regularly shared with them at home.

As it turned out, however, the teaching Lama decided to offer an additional ten-day Intensive. Intrigued with the potential, Joyce decided she actually was interested to stay on. Missing her boys, she asked Greg if he would consider arranging his schedule to bring them out to the desert for a short visit and he agreed.

When Greg arrived he did not find the desert setting to be the peaceful place that Joyce had described, and that he had imagined. It felt foreign and forlorn to him, even desolate and uninviting. Geoff entertained himself playing around the campus and nine-month old Todd snacked at a highchair while Joyce and Greg discussed the opportunity for her to stay for ten more days in Yucca Valley. Robin had decided to return home, but Greg agreed it was okay for Joyce to stay on longer.

An additional, unspoken reason Joyce wanted to stay in the desert was to further a friendship—not with the Buddhist teacher, but with a younger man she had met at the session. She had enjoyed regular conversations with him and a friend who had come with him to the conference. Their conversations were friendly; mostly about the intensive they were experiencing. Joyce later admitted to herself, however, that she was enjoying his company more than she had told Greg. Her relationship with the younger man was slowly building toward an extramarital romance. *No harm done*, Joyce foolishly reasoned, *he knows I'm married!*

Joyce's Take

Looking back on this, I can hardly believe how selfish and ignorant I was! I didn't have one serious thought for the young man, for Greg, our kids, or myself. I just wanted to *satisfy myself* in the moment, to feel good, and to enjoy some good times. Back at home I felt unimportant to Greg and I feared that life was passing me by. Greg and I had never discussed the importance of raising two sons, nor did we consider what we, as parents, would teach our sons for their own lives and future families. From my perspective now, Greg and I both were like dead wood floating *aimlessly* down life's broad and mighty river. Neither of us knew anything about what could constitute a truly satisfying life.

When Joyce returned home after the retreat, Greg was shocked by her gaunt appearance. She had not only lost fifteen pounds, but now she also had a round tummy from no exercise and a steady diet of rice and vegetables. He feared she might be on the verge of an eating disorder, but he said nothing to Joyce about that. He was very relieved when she resumed her normal diet and activities and her lovely figure returned.

As it turned out, Greg and Joyce didn't talk much about the retreat, and Mike never asked about the benefits Joyce had gleaned on their behalf from her time away in Yucca Valley. Although Joyce had appreciated the teaching at the retreat, she didn't see much of a future in the practices she had learned as a potential way of life. Within a month, the retreat faded into the background along with the sparkling initial attraction to Tibetan Buddhism.

Looking forward now more intensely to their impending move to Hawaii, Greg, Joyce, and Mike all began in April to swim regularly in the Olympic-sized swimming pool at UCLA. This activity was for each of them to become prepared to swim and body surf in the large Hawaiian waves. Joyce's neighbor who also had two children was glad to assist Joyce in caring for Geoff and Todd so she could participate in these workout times. What Greg and Joyce weren't doing was spending the time necessary to find housing in Honolulu. No one suggested it, and the thought somehow didn't occur to either of them. This was Hawaii, after all, not Santa Barbara.

When the study schedule came out for the Hawaii Bar exam, Greg and Mike decided to forgo their UCLA graduation ceremony in order to arrive in Hawaii as soon as they could. Each of them believed they would be able to study better for the Bar exam in Hawaii than in California.

Arriving in Paradise

The firm sent two attorneys who had met Greg and Joyce during his Honolulu interview to meet them at the airport. Mike, his girlfriend Kelsey, and Joyce were greeted as soon as they stepped off the plane and into the warm Honolulu air, however, the two attorneys barely recognized Greg through all his shaggy hair and beard. Mike and Kelsey had previously made their own living arrangements. The firm was kindly providing the Millikan family with a Waikiki condo for a week until they could find rental housing. Knowing they needed to buy a home to offset taxes from their Hermosa Beach sale, Greg and Joyce aimed to purchase a house as soon as possible. Most of their stuff would wait in storage until a place was found. Within the week, a realtor found a short-term rental for them, a furnished two-bedroom condo in a Hawaii Kai high rise.

Greg immediately began attending the daily taped lectures at the Bar review course and studying outlines for the upcoming Hawaii Bar exam. While he did that, Joyce enjoyed some casual house hunting with the real estate broker and the boys. It wasn't long before Joyce found a three-bedroom house in a lovely Kahala neighborhood not far from downtown. The house was within walking distance to a good preschool and a convenient shopping mall. Joyce was delighted with the garden, which included six healthy mango trees and a banana tree.

Greg's younger sister, Laurie, was already living on Oahu, having moved there the prior year with two girl friends from college to enjoy the surfing life after they graduated. Laurie was clearly enjoying having Greg and Joyce and the boys nearby. She soon introduced them to her Monday evening volleyball league as a way for them to meet some local friends. Laurie also enjoyed being with the boys, gladly offering to help care for them when needed, if she was available.

One unsettling discovery that surfaced during their first few weeks was the use of the Hawaiian term, "haole" to refer to Joyce, Greg and the boys because of their European ancestry. Originally this was the word used for a foreigner (outsider or stranger) by native Hawaiians, but now *haole*—in Hawaii's multi-ethnic culture—was a label placed on all white people. Even whites born in Hawaii were called *local haoles*. Non-whites were not called haoles, no matter where they came from. By this measure, about 30 percent of the population in Hawaii was haole. Joyce was particularly sensitive about their family's new minority status, and she went out of her way to keep from offending native Hawaiians.

Joyce's Take

I could barely believe our little family was living in Hawaii—this really was a dream come true! Little did I know how fearful I would be, finding myself in a minority position culturally. I had never experienced this situation before, so despite the personal challenges, I look back on this as an incredibly valuable experience. I was now living in a position where so many others in the world live every day. However, even with the challenge of our ethnic minority status, overall our family remained privileged due to our education and Greg's job. Along with this important ethnic adjustment, I also discovered that mango trees are in the same botanical family as poison oak! Naturally in our new garden, I raked and gathered up loads of mango leaves that fell onto the lawn, placing them into the trash, in bundles, with my arms. Within a very short time, the inner part of my arms became covered with thousands of little itchy blisters—and I needed a doctor!

In August, soon after Greg completed the Hawaii Bar exam, he received his own haole education while board-surfing one afternoon at an outer reef off Queen's Beach. The surf was good-sized, and there were six to eight others surfing. Greg didn't know any of them and he was the only haole. When waves came in, he was careful only to take off on those that no one else was trying to catch. At last, Greg was the only surfer remaining outside to catch the sixth wave of a big set.

Just as he was catching the wave, one of the surfers paddling out veered and collided into him. The sharply pointed nose of the surfer's board rammed into Greg's right shoulder, impaling him just below the collarbone and dragging both of them to a stop in the water. Greg sat up in disbelief. As the man's board slid out of the wound, blood gushed out. Greg had tried hard to avoid him, and thought the man must have just misjudged Greg's speed and cut it too close.

Greg immediately stanched the blood flow by pulling his right arm across his chest, and looked at the surfer for some explanation or apology. He was about Greg's age, pony-tailed and part-Hawaiian. The man was briefly shaken when he saw Greg's bloody wound, but the shadow of alarm quickly passed from his face. He lifted his eyes to meet Greg's, glared at him, and said belligerently, "That's what you get, brah, for bein' out here!"

Completely stunned at this response, Greg replied with incredulity, "Take care, eh brah . . ." and turned away, knowing he had to get to shore. There was nothing more to be said to this guy today. Somehow, Greg managed to catch a wave, paddle himself to shore with his left arm, drive to the hospital, and then call Joyce to tell her what had happened. More than thirty stitches later, the wound was closed, but the memory would speak to Greg for a lifetime.

Greg's Take

The words of this man were what echoed in my mind—along with the look on his face. I saw him fight back his awareness of what he had done to me to focus instead on what he had to say to me. His words and facial expression were what I remembered—far more than the humiliation, violence, or insult—or even the fact that I missed riding that beautiful wave.

As I sat in the hospital ER waiting for the surgeon, I thought it wasn't because I wrecked his spot or stole his waves today—I didn't. But others before me probably did! When he was a kid, there were no crowds out there in the water, and especially no haoles cutting in and squeezing him and his friends out of waves. Now it's different because of people—haoles, like me. Of course! For him I was simply one of them. That's just normal prejudice, a handy tool in risky situations. His prejudice erupted in anger toward me today.

Suddenly I understood prejudice better than before. If I didn't remain open to the truth about myself in relation to others, my prejudice would harden into mistrust and resistance. I would later learn that about myself in relation to Joyce.

Greg never learned the surfer's name, though he might have. The news of the assault spread quickly but quietly in the surfing community. Greg learned that the other surfer was a longshoreman, perhaps a pretty tough guy. Even so, locals were apparently a little shocked at what had happened. As a result of Mike's recent influence on his life, Greg was now thinking in more spiritual terms, but he still knew nothing about a Christian perspective on forgiveness or reconciliation.

One of the firm's lawyers later asked Greg if he wanted to press charges against the guy. Greg couldn't see any future in that, so he said no. He already had plenty on his plate, feeling torn between his desires for external fun and the deep internal discontentment he felt, which seemed even worse after the challenges of the move, buying the new home, taking the Bar exam, and the continuing communication gap with Joyce.

Night Falls

To celebrate their completion of the Bar exam, Mike and another new lawyer in the firm planned a weekend camping trip to the renowned Kalalau Valley on the island of Kauai. Mike invited Greg and Joyce to join them. Though Joyce was already quite tired of Mike's influence on Greg, the trip did sound like a nice opportunity. Greg's sister volunteered to take care of the boys, so Joyce and Greg decided to jump on board. Unknown to either of them, Kalalau had become notorious for people hanging out in the nude and using drugs. The whole experience dragged them down individually and as a couple.

When they returned from Kalalau, Greg and Joyce quietly distanced Mike from themselves as a couple. They did their best to ignore and forget the whole experience, but its corrosive effect seemed to taint their outlook in the following months as they tried to settle into everyday life in their new location.

Greg was admitted to the Hawaii Bar in mid-September and officially became the firm's forty-sixth lawyer. He had been assigned his own office and had already embarked on his full time job. Greg was working with Grant on tax matters, and also with a half-dozen other partners in their real estate development projects, corporate finance matters, and international trade questions. There were consistent pressures and challenges in that kind of work that Greg would simply have to meet, regardless of what might be going on at home.

Joyce was rapidly learning more than she ever wanted to know about lawyers and big law firms. Based on what she was hearing and experiencing, she wondered if her marriage with Greg would be able to endure the additional strain.

Joyce also had desires of her own. She was educated and wanted a professional life. She was considering part-time work outside their home, so she aimed to secure her dental hygiene license in Hawaii, just as she had in California. She felt powerless in her relationship with Greg, and she didn't know what positive contribution she could make, or what she might offer of herself to help their marriage and family succeed. So she thought about her own welfare and wondered *will Greg ever be able and willing to make time in his busy life for me and our family?*

Their home in Kahala was in good condition. Formerly owned by an older Japanese couple, it was a 1950s suburban Hawaiian-style house with two baths, three bedrooms, a large patio opposite the bedrooms, and a well-maintained garden all around the property. Much about the house was very good, but within a few months after moving in, Joyce concluded that the enclosed patio was unhelpful. It didn't fit into the family's daily life and its central location made the functioning of their home feel awkward. She thought the unused space would serve them better if it were reorganized to connect with the kitchen and dining room.

The house was like their marriage at that point. From the outside it appeared normal and well maintained, but on the inside the house was dysfunctional, with the most important living areas separated from one another. As a result their life together often felt disordered and confusing. Greg and Joyce's lack of communication skills left them unable to solve these problems. Greg supported the idea of remodeling the house if it would make Joyce happy. They talked about the project with an architect, but when it came to details they kept running into roadblocks. Their plan was placed on hold for the holidays. Even so, their first Christmas in Hawaii was far more depressing than festive.

Greg was called out of town to San Francisco the entire week before Christmas and most of the week afterwards for a big year-end deal. He was part of a legal team working nearly around the clock to wrap up a hotel sale for one of the firm's corporate clients. Greg was able to return home Christmas Eve and Christmas morning, but had to fly back to San Francisco Christmas night. He brought transaction documents with him to work on during both flights. Joyce could see that Greg's mind wasn't much on Christmas or the family. He returned the morning of December 31—on a red-eye flight from San Francisco, with a briefcase full of signed legal documents. Business-wise his trip had been a great success.

After the holidays, Joyce simply did not want to talk anymore about the idea of remodeling their house. It was too tiring for her. Keeping up with Greg, caring for their two boys and keeping up their house and garden consumed all the emotional energy she could muster. Despite the *need* she saw to remodel their home, she was too discouraged to invest the time, energy, and money required. Although she didn't say it, Joyce considered her relationship with Greg too weak to take on the additional weight and stress of a major remodeling project. She knew they weren't connecting well at any level. Joyce had no knowledge how to begin a meaningful conversation with Greg about what was truly important to her.

Geoff, at four-and-a-half years old, was the first to notice how Joyce was feeling. One day he said, "Mommy, there's something wrong with your face."

Curious, Joyce asked, "What's wrong with my face, Geoff?"

Geoff placed his hands on her cheeks and said, "It doesn't go up anymore."

Surprised that Geoff had observed so clearly what she was unable to see in herself, Joyce realized she was miserable—and things weren't getting better. No one had come to visit them for the holidays, so Joyce was feeling even more down and blue than she might have if Christmas had been more enjoyable. As she looked at her life, she was baffled. She couldn't help but wonder, *Hmmm...I live in a very nice*

house in Hawaii, there are two cars in the garage, and I'm rais-
ing two beautiful sons. Why am I so miserable? What's wrong?

From everything Greg and Joyce had learned thus far, a
happy life was all about their position in society: the security,
the money, the vacations, *all the stuff* they could buy, and
the fun they could have—if only *their spouse* would do a better job of making them happy! It didn't occur at all to Greg
or Joyce that God was trying to get their attention. But for
both of them, God didn't attend church. Church was just a
place where people gathered to sing songs *about God* and to
socialize with one another. The religion they each had experienced seemed a powerless waste of time, and the Eastern
alternatives they had recently encountered were no better.

On a lazy Saturday afternoon in mid-February Joyce approached Greg. He was reading, sitting comfortably in the
living room. The boys were playing together outside. Ap-
prehensively, Joyce drew near and stooped down by Greg's
feet. Having pondered their situation carefully, she was very
concerned. Looking up into his eyes, she said, "Greg, I think
we've been going in the wrong direction in our marriage.
Let's stop all this nonsense we've been up to recently and get
our relationship going in the right direction."

Without much hesitation or thought, Greg responded,
dropping the proverbial bomb. Bluntly he responded to
Joyce, "Well, I've been thinking about things between us,
and I've decided to make up for lost time. I think I want to
go out with Kelsey." Greg had learned at work that Mike
and Kelsey had broken up. Greg thought she was attractive
enough for him to pursue.

"Please don't do that," Joyce said firmly, completely
baffled how he could say such words following such a trans-
parent plea on her part.

"Yes," Greg replied defiantly. "It's my turn. You've gone
out with other men."

Joyce admitted, "Yes, I have," but she quickly added,
"and now I think I was wrong to do that. I had many con-

cerns about it, but when I asked you about it, you *encouraged* me to go out with other guys. But now it is not okay with me *for you* to do this!" Greg had finally crossed Joyce's boundary. She was ready to stand her ground, and she hoped Greg would comply.

"Well," he said, "I'm going to go out with Kelsey anyway."

"No, you're not!" asserted Joyce, and she took her glass of water and threw its contents in his face.

Greg's Take

This conversation with Joyce didn't occur in a vacuum. It was precipitated by the very bad advice that I had given Joyce—advice she had taken. I had told myself it might improve our sex life if she went out with others. I believed (without confirming it with Joyce) our sex life was unsatisfying for both of us. This short conversation with Joyce not only exposed how my advice had failed, but it revealed that my real intention all along was only to get pleasure for myself, not to provide anything good for Joyce.

Our behavior exhibited such foolishness and self-deceit. The negative impact was magnified by three factors:

• There were people in the early 1970s, reputed experts, speaking and writing books advocating open marriage and multiple partners as a way of improving one's marriage and sexual experience. Neither Joyce nor I were Christians or had anything to do with a church. My traditional beliefs lacked depth. When "Jesus people" accosted us on the Strand in Hermosa Beach with warnings about hell, they seemed laughably naïve and misguided. I thought we were *just fine spiritually*, and that we were sure to find a better way by having an open marriage.

• We had no way to assess the wisdom or foolishness of what we were doing. We had no compass points to follow and no agreed coordinates for our marital destination. All we had to go on was a vague fantasy of happiness ever after, plus our impulses, our desires for self-satisfaction, and whatever external constraints we were willing to accept.

• We were socially isolated. There was not one person in our lives that we could mutually point to and say, "That person is wise. He or she has wisdom." Smart, yes. Wise, no. In many areas of our lives, including sex, Joyce and I tried all sorts of things that were *wrong*. In fact, now when we mentor engaged or married couples we often say, "You can't shock us— we know everything that *doesn't* work!"

J oyce's Take

I had no desire for a relationship with anyone but Greg— until he suggested that I go out with other men. I didn't really want that, neither did I understand his suggestion that I should do so. The idea itself was confusing, and yet the thought of it was somehow intriguing to my ego and pride. At that time, much was being written about women's sexuality. There were high expectations being spelled out for *women* as to what was normal, enjoyable, and what might be possible.

As I discovered later, Greg thought I had told him there was something wrong with the way he related to me sexually. That was not at all what I remember saying! What I was *trying* to tell him was that I felt there was probably something wrong with *me,* not him! But, because he voiced the going out idea with such persistence, I began to believe it, thinking *maybe that is what I need.* All of this was a huge misunderstanding—and one that escalated our situation ever closer to divorce.

Dripping with water, Greg didn't reply. Instead, he got up from his chair, walked out of the house and drove off in their yellow VW Rabbit. Joyce knew he would probably follow through on his words. So after he left, she began packing his belongings into boxes and bags. She was not willing to discuss that topic again with Greg. If dating others was the kind of fun he wanted in marriage, she didn't want any part of it!

As the boys played outside, Joyce kept going over their brief conversation again and again in her mind. She felt shocked, betrayed, abandoned, and alone. She realized that many things had taken priority over marriage and family in Greg's life—work, sports, friends, and now, apparently, sexual pleasure. She had resigned herself to accept Greg's remoteness and do her best to raise the kids—but now, suddenly, she felt afraid and shaky. Her marriage with Greg seemed to be crumbling apart.

When Greg returned home later that afternoon, he found all of his personal belongings on the front porch in boxes and bags. Atop them was a note that said simply, "Goodbye." As far as Joyce was concerned, her relationship with Greg was all but over. Greg was twenty-nine and Joyce was twenty-eight. They had been married eight and a half years. Geoff was four and a half. Todd was eighteen months old.

Greg crammed all his items into the Rabbit and drove away, wondering where he might go. He stopped and called Mike. Without sharing the details of his spat with Joyce, he asked Mike if he could hang out at his place for a while. Mike agreed, offering Greg an extra room downstairs in the split-level house Mike rented with two other bachelor lawyers. The house was nestled among ironwood trees just off the Pali Highway high on a hillside in Nuuanu Valley. As he headed there, Greg had no clue how he might deal with Joyce, but he was glad for some time out. He hoped that maybe Joyce would cool down and the atmosphere between them would clear up in a day or so.

No one was home when Greg arrived. Mike had told him where the key was, so he let himself in. One of the guys who lived there had evidently left the sound system on. As Greg entered, a hauntingly beautiful orchestral piece, Vivaldi's *Four Seasons*, flowed resonantly throughout the whole house. He had never heard it before and at the time didn't know what it was. It evoked such poignant emotions in him that he stopped and stood in the entry, frozen and almost breathless. For the moment, he didn't care who had composed the song or what it was titled—he was wrapped up in the beauty of the music. Standing there alone, against the backdrop of wind-rustled ironwoods and the spacious valley below, Greg felt he had found a calm port in a big storm.

Instead of clearing up, the situation with Joyce became even more confused. Greg made some calls to Joyce, ostensibly to discuss things other than their conflict. Given the threat Greg had made, Joyce remained firm and closed to his indirect approaches. Greg's single friends commiserated with him and happily allowed him to stay a while longer if need be. So Greg waited—hoping Joyce would make the next move. Even though the animosity between them was palpable, he could not fathom that they would not make *some* mutual effort to repair this break in their relationship. At the moment, Greg didn't have the stomach to pursue Kelsey, as he had told Joyce he would do.

For her part, Joyce decided to reach out to her Yucca Valley friend Ron, whom she had met at the Buddhist retreat the year before. She wasn't seeking a romantic relationship with him, only some attentive adult with whom she could converse and commiserate meaningfully. She left him a phone message.

A couple of days later, Ron returned Joyce's call, announcing that he wanted to fly over from California to visit her. She felt complimented by his interest, and although she had mixed feelings about this impromptu visit, she agreed. During Ron's visit, he and Joyce took the boys to a local beach one Saturday morning. By coincidence, Mike happened to be there with other friends and gave Joyce a warm hello. She introduced Ron and Mike to one another. After a few pleasantries, Mike said he had to be on his way and departed. As Joyce had no plans for an ongoing relationship with Ron, she had little concern about any fallout from their chance encounter with Mike.

Back at the Nuuanu house later that day, Mike mentioned to Greg that he had seen Joyce and the boys at the beach that morning, and that he had met Joyce's friend Ron, from California. When Greg heard about Ron, he was stunned. Joyce had never said anything to him about Ron.

Greg hadn't yet reached out to Joyce to rectify or apologize for his behavior, but he still imagined that Joyce would eventually *settle down* and things would get better between them. Hearing about Ron's arrival and visit with Joyce was an unexpected shock. Greg flipped.

Similar to the moment on the mound four and half years earlier when his manager took the ball from him in his last game with the Albuquerque Dukes, something snapped and blew apart inside Greg. He said reactively to himself *well, if that's the way it is for Joyce, then I'll just divorce her. We're finished!*

Propelled by frustration and pain, Greg called Kelsey that afternoon to see if she would be available to go out with him. Kelsey was the only single woman he knew in Hawaii besides his sister. This too bore no fruit. She turned him down. Greg sank into an angry, self-pitying funk.

The following Monday, Greg sought out one of the lawyers in his firm to fill out divorce papers. When Joyce was served, it was her turn to be dumbfounded and stunned. She thought, *Wow! Why is Greg doing this?* But rather than ask Greg any direct questions, she decided to take a hardened, impassive approach to his divorce proceedings. She began actively arranging with Greg by phone how to split their belongings and sell their house. If she was now to be on her own, she decided she would do better moving with the boys to California, where her earning potential as a dental hygienist was far better than it was in Hawaii. Santa Cruz was a place where Joyce could see herself living. She thought *I might as well move to Santa Cruz where I know at least one person—Ron. Maybe the two of us can work something out together after all. And if not, fine.*

To placate Joyce's mother, Joyce and Greg agreed to fly to the mainland to meet with the marriage counselor who had previously counseled with Joyce's parents. Neither Greg's nor Joyce's heart was in the counseling effort. At the end of the session, the counselor agreed that they might as well get divorced.

Greg asked Joyce to consider the idea of continuing to co-own their house together and to it rent out. After all, he noted, they had lived in the house for less than a year and it seemed a waste of money to sell it. Subconsciously, he later realized he was probably trying to keep some contact alive with Joyce. But Joyce remained firm, still hurt and offended by his unrepentant attitude and lack of apology. She wouldn't even consider his idea. The house was placed on the market and it sold almost as quickly as their marriage had spiraled into dissolution.

In less than five months, they had gone from discussing a remodel of their home, to Joyce moving Greg out, a friend of Joyce's strolling in, divorce papers being filed, and Joyce and the kids departing for a life in California. Their uncontested divorce was promptly concluded. Greg agreed to give Joyce custody of their boys. Their marriage was over.

Greg was not there to say goodbye when they left for the airport. Though he knew the day and time they were leaving, Greg hadn't called or said anything to Joyce or the boys. Strangely though, he *felt* them leave. He sat alone in the lower bedroom of the Nuuanu bachelor house, listening to the trade winds blowing down the valley through the ironwood trees and into the city below. To him, the sound was forlorn. He felt alone, utterly alone.

Joyce's Take

What Greg didn't know about me, is how I *really needed* him to *apologize to me* for his threat against our marriage relationship—for expressing his interest and determination to go out with someone else. After he said those things to me, I felt an apology was required! Until then I was not open to discuss anything else with him.

Without telling Greg what I needed and wanted from him, I just shut completely down. I assumed that Greg should already know that an apology was the right and necessary thing to do! I was living in an irresponsible dream world. I did not yet know that people I care about need to hear what I'm thinking, what I'm feeling, and what I want from them.

For Contemplation and Conversation

1. Have you ever had to deal with an inappropriate or unhealthy friendship? How did you detect this problem? Whether you are married or single, how were you able to gather the strength you needed to move beyond the unhealthy situation?

2. Have you ever found yourself in an emotional situation with your spouse that seemed to spin out of control? What is needed to guide the situation toward the positive side?

3. What have you learned about yourself that might help you begin a conversation with your spouse about a sensitive topic?

4. Does your spouse know what communicates love to you? If not, let your spouse know which of the following actions you enjoy receiving the most: Physical Touch? Acts of Service? Words of Affirmation? Receiving Gifts? Quality Time? (see Gary Chapman, *Five Love Languages: The Secret to Love that Lasts*).

6 Alone and Lost in Paradise

Greg's sanctuary in the Nuuanu Valley became a very bleak place. He was alone in Honolulu and his children were thousands of miles away. His attempts at connecting with his sons over the phone were very disappointing. Geoff was turning five, and there was only so much Greg could convey over the phone to him. Greg realized he had taken his fathering role for granted. Now that he was separated from the boys by thousands of miles, he felt he might as well be on the far side of the universe! The distance between them was incomprehensible to Geoff, not to mention Todd, who was not yet two.

Things might have turned out differently if Greg and Joyce had been sincere about seeking help from a capable counselor. Separately each of them had imagined the possibility of reconciliation if the other one was willing. The two of them actually had more in common than they were willing to admit. Joyce thought if Greg had been willing to apologize, she probably would have softened enough to take Greg back and start over. She was not committed to Ron—he was only a friend with whom she could talk. That was all. Joyce had no idea that Greg was so angry about her friendship with Ron. She saw *Greg* as the problem, with him always looking outward and away from their relationship, rather than inward to care for her and their family.

In the weeks after Joyce's departure to California with the boys, Greg decided that his personal dreams needed retooling and his goals needed to be reset. At the office, he was frequently recognized and praised for being a bright, up-and-coming lawyer. He also had an office on the twenty-second floor, with a west-facing window. Through it he could see the Honolulu International Airport and Pearl Harbor, and beyond them, the Waianae Mountains. To Greg, this was the kind of office that conveyed tremendous success—high as it was in the Pacific Trade Center in downtown *paradise*. Greg thought he must have been doing *at least* as well, or better than his peers. He just needed to recalibrate his life and form it into reality a bit better.

He was sure about one thing—the New Age religions, and especially the Buddhist and Sufi paths, were dead ends as far as any relevance for his future. He had studied them enough to find only futility and emptiness. Greg was still intrigued by the importance of the spiritual realm—at least in theory—but everything he found there seemed like distractions from real life.

In the evenings at the Nuuanu house after work, Greg talked about his predicament with Harry, a housemate who was a first year lawyer in their firm's litigation department. An alumnus of the Harvard Lampoon, Harry was good-humored, bright, and well read. A Midwesterner who had moved to Hawaii to attend law school after graduating from Harvard, Harry commiserated with Greg. He suggested, "You need a new philosophy on life, Greg, something more lively and enjoyable than that mystical stuff." Then Harry announced, "Hemingway! Read some Hemingway. He'll help you learn to enjoy life!"

Greg had heard of Ernest Hemingway, but he was unfamiliar with Hemingway's writing and had not read any of his books. After hearing the suggestion, Greg recalled how affected he was as a boy when he watched the movie version of *For Whom the Bell Tolls*, with Ingrid Bergman and Gary Cooper, on late night TV. He welcomed Harry's idea. It seemed worth a shot.

Greg purchased a copy of *The Old Man and the Sea* and began to read it each evening in bed. He enjoyed the dramatic flair and the visceral feelings of Hemingway's words and his descriptions. Without a doubt, Hemingway clearly saw and spoke with a masculine voice, capturing so well the gritty, heroic, and frustrating reality of life. His type of lone-wolf hero was someone to whom Greg could readily relate. Greg could feel his hopes rising as he neared the end of the book. Then in one of their evening talks, Harry offhandedly mentioned that Hemingway had committed suicide.

"What?" Greg fired back. "What kind of successful life philosophy is *that*?"

"That's just it," Harry replied. "Hemingway said the point is to drink as deeply as you can from the cup of life, and when you realize that you have fulfilled your desire to the fullest extent possible, you demonstrate that you are still in control by killing yourself."

Greg was aghast. After a brief pause, Greg replied, "Well, no thank you to that!"

Harry laughed and shifted gears. "Okay, then I think you ought to try reading Camus—Albert Camus. Try *The Plague*. He deals seriously with the meaning and purpose of life. I think you'll really like this one."

Albert Camus? Greg brightened. Could this be *that Camus*—the very writer—the one that Greg had never heard of in his first year at Oxy? Greg laughed to himself, thinking it funny that some things in life seem to come around full circle.

Harry was obviously sincere in recommending Camus, and Greg enjoyed Harry's company, so Greg went ahead and bought an English translation of *The Plague*. He began reading it bit by bit, more cautiously and carefully than he had with Hemingway. In the coming months, the message of this book would be instrumental in ways Greg could never have imagined.

On the social side of things, Greg found being single quite awkward. To him it felt like learning how to drive a stick shift for the first time. He didn't hesitate to party and date anybody he could find. Though the party scene sometimes bewildered Greg, overall he found it to be pleasurable but tiring. Ultimately Greg didn't find partying a very satisfying use of his time, although it seemed more real to him than other activities that had been suggested by the Eastern religious philosophies he had previously explored.

Greg picked his way through *The Plague* in between work, partying, surfing, and bouts of lonely journaling late at night. Greg was beginning to journal his inner thoughts for the first time. Sitting alone in his room, he scribbled mangled thoughts onto a yellow legal pad. Most of his thoughts were self-pitying. A few of them were self-loathing and filled with sorrow, written with the conviction of a man searching for a new life perspective, yet with no emotional security. Greg wondered how a self-centered hedonistic way of life could possibly turn out better for him in the end. He wondered where he was going. He had no clue.

It wasn't long before Greg grew tired of the bachelor pad and its forlorn winds. He wanted to live closer to the beach, where there would be less rain and fewer shadows. Harry said he felt the same way and suggested they might find a house to rent in Kaimuki, near to Waikiki. Glad for a change, Greg agreed. They found a suitable place and made the move fairly quickly. Despite the good location, Greg still found himself frequently casting his imagination toward California, over the northeastern horizon, wondering *what's going on with my boys? What kind of future will they have? What part will I play in that future?*

Finally, Greg gathered his courage and arranged with Joyce to visit the boys. One evening in early June, he took a red-eye flight from Honolulu to San Francisco. There, he rented a car and drove south to Ben Lomond, where Joyce

114

and Ron had rented a little house in the redwood-forested hills near Santa Cruz.

Joyce enjoyed the fact that Ron was an elementary school teacher who was caring and kind with Geoff and Todd. Although he was a few years younger than Joyce, their age difference didn't seem to matter to Ron, so she decided it wouldn't matter to her.

Ben Lomond was a rural, quiet place with an agricultural bent. Joyce had searched out a private, family-owned school for both of the boys. And it was just a short drive up the road from Ben Lomond. Having secured a good job in downtown Santa Cruz—four days a week as a dental hygienist—Joyce's work schedule still allowed her a good amount of time with the boys.

On Greg's arrival, Joyce introduced him to Ron. The two men shook hands stiffly and Ron left for his Saturday morning fencing practice.

The atmosphere between Greg and Joyce was odd, uncomfortable, strange—and yet familiar. There was little outward hint of acrimony. Although the 1970s myth of an amicable divorce had now become well known, Joyce and Greg were both struggling to live that out. A popular saying at the time advocated, "As long as nobody gets hurt, you can do whatever you want in life." Somewhat uneasy, Joyce flirted a little with Greg, which he soundly rejected. Greg wasn't in any mood to have fun or be playful.

The boys seemed glad to see their dad, but neither of them was particularly overwhelmed by his arrival. They were happy enough to leave the house with Greg for a day of adventures. The three of them started off at the Roaring Camp Railroad and took a train ride through the redwoods. After hot dogs for lunch, Greg drove them up the peninsula to the San Francisco Zoo where they spent the remaining hours of the day. After pizza for dinner it was already dark by the time Greg had them back home. Greg kissed each boy and said good-bye as they went down the hall to get ready for bed.

Finally Greg said farewell to Joyce, and then he drove off to San Francisco to catch the last flight back to Honolulu. The visit had been a major financial investment for Greg—flying over from Hawaii to spend just one day with his sons, but he felt surprisingly glad he had done so.

Back in Hawaii, Greg continued his dating, surfing, and non-stop legal work. The regular, warm sunlight of Kaimuki had driven away his journaling urge, but he continued picking his way through *The Plague*, looking for insight into his life predicament. Greg's recent visit with his sons had intensified his newly kindled desire to be with them. He suddenly wanted to find a way to have an active, ongoing role in their future, but he had no idea how that role might be forged. Within weeks, Greg decided to call Joyce again to schedule a second visit—this time in early July.

On his second visit, Greg accompanied Joyce and the boys to their school. He wanted to see where the boys were spending their days and what they were learning. Joyce was pleased that Greg was now caring about the boys' schooling. The school was called Circle School and was family friendly—it even had a toddler program for Todd. Joyce had worked hard to find a school that offered a curriculum that *she* would have enjoyed at their age.

At the school, the children took care of farm animals in age-appropriate chores. There was also a pond with a rope swing for the children to use for jumping into the water. Many caring families were involved with the school and there was a spiritual emphasis, which Greg saw as a positive factor. He decided the spiritual focus was probably Christian, which seemed like a good idea to him.

During this second visit, Greg began talking with Joyce about the possibility of his taking the boys to Honolulu for a couple of weeks in August during his vacation and before the start of school. Greg said he knew this would take a lot of time and extra work on his part, but he wanted to spend some extended time with the boys. He volunteered to fly both ways with them—picking them up and then returning them to California. Joyce agreed, feeling pleased and yet irritated by Greg's increasing interest in the boys. Incredulous, she asked herself why *has Greg waited so long to care proactively about his sons?*

In early August, when Greg arrived at the house, he found that Joyce had already packed the boys' bags and that they were all ready to go. As he gathered up the children's belongings, Greg noticed Todd sitting on the floor, working carefully to tie the laces on his shoes. Although Todd was just turning two, Geoff had managed to teach him how to hold the laces and make the bows all by himself. For some reason, this was a poignant moment for Greg.

Greg's Take

I couldn't take my eyes off Todd, intently focused on tying his own shoes, which he actually completed quite well. He was so little, and yet so much about him had changed from the infant he had been when I had last lived with him seven months previously! I saw how Geoff had been able to influence Todd constructively by being there with him and caring for him. It struck me that time was flying and there was none to be lost. And it struck me that good results could come from time well spent, if I cared enough to try.

In the Kaimuki house Greg and Harry shared, there was a third bedroom available for the boys. Harry warmly welcomed them and cheerfully encouraged Greg in his single-fathering role. Within a week, however, Greg realized that keeping the two boys full time wasn't just fun and games. It was a completely absorbing and demanding experience—and there were no *off hours!*

At night, after the boys were asleep, Greg spent some time imagining a future life for his sons. If they moved to Hawaii with him, he would have responsibility for their full-time care. If he allowed them to be raised in the Santa Cruz Mountains, he imagined they would probably learn to do fencing and Buddhist meditation with Ron and Joyce, and he would likely see them only for a few hours every few months. While Greg couldn't fathom just how he could be a full-time single dad, he found it impossible to warm up to the alternative of them living with Joyce full-time in California. Greg wanted to be more involved in their lives than to visit them every few months. He also saw right away that a revolving door between full-time fatherhood and the partying bachelor life wouldn't work.

One evening Greg finally came to the point of considering whether, if he searched for it, he might find suitable daycare for Todd and a good school for Geoff. If that were possible and if he were able to find a three-bedroom house for all of them, he just might be able to make the role of full-time dad work. Harry supported the idea and thought Greg ought to check it out. What did he have to lose? Greg decided to look into it, but he had no plans to communicate anything about this yet to Joyce.

The very next day, Greg called the realtor who had recently sold their home in Kahala. The realtor told Greg he knew about a three-bedroom townhouse out on the east end, in Hawaii Kai, that Greg could probably afford with seller financing—assuming the money from his share of the Kahala house sale could be available for the down payment. If so, Greg and the boys could possibly move in by Labor Day.

Greg drove with the boys to the townhouse and looked it over. Amazingly, it looked just right. It was in a nice neighborhood, a short distance to school for Geoff, with a pre-school for Todd just around the corner. Greg felt great about the idea of becoming a full-time dad—making his life work with the boys under his roof. To Greg, it seemed clear-cut—either buy the townhouse and make the switch, or forget about parenting altogether. He wrote out a check for the deposit and gave it to the realtor. Then he called Joyce.

When Joyce answered, she heard Greg fumble for a moment, and then announce, "I'm not bringing the boys back to California."

Unable to grasp what he was saying, Joyce answered, "What?"

"I'm not bringing them back. I'm keeping them here in Hawaii with me," he answered.

Dumbfounded and in disbelief, Joyce shot back at him, "What do you mean you won't be returning the boys? We had an agreement—four weeks—you *promised!*"

"Look," Greg pleaded after a moment's silence, "it was just too hard for me to set up house here with the boys temporarily. I want to be a dad more than once or twice a year. Once they were here with me, I realized that being a dad is something I really want to do . . . and I'm ready to do it full-time! So I've bought a condo in Hawaii Kai. We're moving in at the end of this month. What I'm saying is that I've decided to keep the boys here—and I've enrolled them both in school." For his part, Greg could hardly believe how calm he sounded.

"Well, that's a fine how do you do!" Joyce exclaimed. "You asked me to honor you by allowing you to take the boys on a four-week vacation and then you unilaterally buy a home and enroll the kids in school without even talking with me? What a creep you are!"

Greg knew his announcement was risky. His decision to take the boys away from Joyce wasn't malicious, at least not consciously. Yes, Joyce did have physical custody of the children according to their divorce documents. He knew that if Joyce insisted on his returning the boys to California, he would probably have to go along with that decision—or end up in a bitter legal battle that she would probably win in court. But he did not tell Joyce any of this because Greg also wanted what *he wanted*.

Joyce justifiably felt hurt and thoroughly stunned. She protested, but she wasn't trained to think like a lawyer, and not fully understanding her legal rights, she yielded to Greg's surprise tactic. For years, Joyce had hoped that Greg would wake up and carry his fair share of the parenting load. She had always wanted him *to join her* in the family enterprise— to become a responsible husband to her and a good father to the boys.

"That rat," she said under her breath after hanging up the phone. "I can't believe the gall of that man! The boys were with him all along before the divorce proceedings, and now he wants to turn over a new leaf and become a loving father? Well, I guess for the sake of the boys, having their father participate late in parenting is better than not at all!" Not one to enjoy court battles or to fight openly with others, it never occurred to Joyce that she could have fought Greg in court and won.

Once Greg took responsibility for the boys and began making their home with him in Hawaii, Joyce's thoughts naturally began to drift west across the Pacific. She had loved living in Hawaii, not just for its weather and beauty, but also for its ethnic and social diversity. She thought *if Greg has the financial capacity to care for the boys in Hawaii Kai, maybe I could return to Oahu and make ends meet for myself as a dental hygienist. I could visit the boys regularly and take them to the beach on my days off.*

Since Joyce had never really considered a long-term future with Ron, she mused *why shouldn't I go back to Hawaii? If Greg wants to be a good dad, I'd like to see that for myself! At least I'd be there for the boys if Greg needs help.* She wondered if perhaps Greg might be open to some kind of cooperative childcare arrangement. *It would be terrific for the boys,* she thought, *if Greg and I could find a way to cooperate about their care. I think I will move back.*

A few weeks later, Joyce called Greg from the Santa Cruz dental office to discuss her plans to return to Hawaii. Greg was not thrilled with the news, but he responded warmly enough for Joyce to ask if she could stay for a short time at his condo when she first arrived. Greg replied to her non-committally, saying, "Let's talk about that when you get here and see how it goes."

Moving forward, Joyce gave her four-week notice at the dental office, held a garage sale of things she didn't want to take back, and loaded everything else into her VW Bus for its re-shipment back to Hawaii. It wasn't long before she was waving good-bye to Ron, who was bewildered by her enthusiasm for this move. After delivering the VW Bus to the shipping dock in Oakland, she headed directly for the airport, a one-way ticket to Honolulu in hand.

On arriving in Hawaii, Joyce rented a car and easily found her way to Hawaii Kai and Greg's townhouse. She hesitated briefly as she sat in her rental car looking up at his condo—486-B. She took in a deep breath, exhaled, and then strolled very slowly up the eight steps to the front door. When Greg answered, Joyce greeted him in her brightest voice, "Hi, Greg, I'm finally here! May I come in?" His eyes widened in a stunned look of horror.

Stepping aside to let her into the living room, Greg asked, "What do you mean, 'I'm finally here?' What are you doing here—I mean at my house?"

"Well, we talked about my coming here on the phone. Remember, I asked if I could stay with you for a while when I got to Hawaii? You said we could talk about that when I arrived, right?"

On the phone at the time, of course, Greg thought he had been making a non-committal "talking about it" statement to discuss her presence in Hawaii. Joyce, however, had taken his response as an invitation to stay there while the discussion took place.

121

In no uncertain terms, Greg replied that Joyce definitely could not move into his home or stay with them.

"Really?" Joyce said. "Then where am I supposed to go?"

"I don't know," answered Greg. "That's your problem."

"My problem?" she retorted. "Look, Greg, you agreed to allow me to stay here, even temporarily. You knew I was flying in today. It's crazy for you to turn me out and tell me I have to stay somewhere else!"

Greg felt a little panic begin to rise somewhere in his gut. He couldn't run away, nor could he punch a cabinet. He was happy for the boys' sake that Joyce was back in Hawaii. She was a good mom, and this kind of arrangement would be much more stable for them in the long run. But concerning his relationship with her—well, her arrival was not only shocking, it scared him! He thought Joyce was acting a little crazy, and her approach seemed like a bulldozer headed his way. Just the thought of renewing a relationship with Joyce threatened to tie him into an emotional Gordian knot.

"Look, Joyce," he said firmly, "I think *you* are way off base, even crazy for coming here like you have. Before I agree even to discuss the possibility of your moving in, I want to have you talk with a counselor and hear what he says."

That's incredible, thought Joyce. *Crazy? Now Greg is truly losing it!*

"Fine," Joyce retorted defiantly. "I'm glad to talk with a counselor. I assume you'll be there. Maybe this way we can clear up some things." Joyce was confident a counselor would understand the situation and help Greg gain a better perspective. Greg agreed he would locate a counselor and set an appointment for the two of them. In the meantime, Joyce would find a room to rent elsewhere.

"This is so typical of Greg," Joyce groused to herself as she went back to her rental car. "He always says one thing and then does something else!" She was tired from her travels and ready to rest. She picked up a local paper at a nearby convenience store and promptly found an ad for a room in a shared house for singles in Kapahulu. *Awesome*, she thought, *this place is just two blocks from the beach and Kapiolani Park. What a terrific location!*

Tired as she was, she made the call, set up an appointment, and went to see the house. Having never lived alone as a single adult, away from her family, Joyce was surprised to find it was a shared, co-ed situation with three others. But the rent for her bedroom would only be $99 a month. It had a lock on the door, so she thought the arrangement might work okay, and it might even be enjoyable! The house was just seven miles from Greg and the boys, so although her arrival had involved an unexpected glitch, Joyce felt quite happy to be back in Hawaii.

When the time came for their hour with the counselor, at Greg's expense, Greg was very surprised to hear that the counselor thought Joyce was quite normal, not at all crazy. The counselor completely understood her behavior, adding that for Joyce, trust between them had been broken. It appeared to the counselor that Greg often broke his agreements with Joyce in crucial matters. Greg was disturbed that he had misread Joyce so completely. After leaving the counselor's office and parting from Joyce, who now had no interest to move in with him, Greg wondered *how was it that Joyce seemed so crazy to me and not at all crazy to the counselor? Maybe I'm the one who's crazy!?*

Taking on the single father role with two young sons, along with his full-time job at the firm had been a major adjustment to be sure. Even so, despite the counselor's opinion, Greg was determined to prove his ability to be a good father for his boys, and to provide a stable home—and *never* to ask Joyce for help unless it was absolutely necessary. Greg had concluded that *she* was the problem in his life, and therefore, in his family's life.

Although Geoff's kindergarten was just three blocks away and Todd's pre-school just a little further around the next corner, Greg had not accurately factored in how much time was needed to drive the boys to their schools and still get to his downtown office on time. His commute required driving the Kalanianaole Highway in both directions—a dependable daily traffic jam during commuting hours. His schedule was very tight. After dropping the boys off at their schools, Greg faced a nine-hour workday. He was to return to pick up the boys at precisely 5:45 in the afternoon or pay a hefty fee, minute by minute.

Greg was glad to be fulfilling his plan to provide a stable home for his sons, but the arrangement wasn't always satisfying. Children at five and two years old couldn't take care of themselves. They certainly were not able to cook, do the marketing or the laundry. Greg missed surfing, partying with his friends, and even the opportunity to work late. None of that was possible. Beyond his nine-hour day at the office, he arose at five in the morning and stayed up until nearly midnight each evening just to keep up with the necessary parenting and housekeeping chores. Exhausted, he soon began taking the Express Bus into downtown Honolulu to avoid the hassle of daily traffic.

Some evenings, Greg pressed in to read and learn from Camus, bit by bit, with more urgency now. Camus did help him recognize some questions about life's purpose; but instead of fading away, those questions seemed to burn all the more intensely, yet Greg was gaining few answers.

In mid-October Greg finished reading *The Plague*. He understood Camus' basic premises—first, that hypocrisy and foolish pretense often masquerade as faith or wisdom but are neither faith nor wisdom; second, there is no truth in religious faith but choosing good is better than tolerating evil; and third, it takes courage to do good instead of succumb to evil.

Camus' philosophy was encouraging to Greg in his present course, but he saw that Camus wasn't able to answer the big question: If there is no truth, then how can I know what is ultimately good or evil? Greg wanted something reliable. He wanted something reliable to give his sons to live by. Camus was his last hope. Greg wondered almost out loud *where do I look for truth now? The boys will probably grow up okay, but what can I give them that they can teach their children? Humanity has made it through all these generations, and I don't want to drop the baton now!* It did not enter his mind to ask God or to visit a church for the answer.

One thing was certain—the boys could not search for life's answers at their age. It was up to Greg to find a worthy baton to pass on to them. Greg put *The Plague* on the top shelf of his living room bookcase. As Camus suggested, he was trying to choose to do good as a father, but other than that, the book gave him only one overall precept: Never succumb to what you know to be evil!

In the practical realm, Greg sorely needed to find someone to pick up the boys from school and take care of them until he arrived home. Through a note on a bulletin board at Todd's school, he located an older woman who might fill the bill. Somewhat hurriedly, he set up an interview. She had flaming red hair and talked a good talk, so he hired her on a weekly basis. As it turned out, the woman routinely brought in candy for the boys—saying nothing about it to Greg, which made them hyperactive. He arrived home once to discover she had invited some friends to visit with her while she was at his condo. Greg wondered whether he should fire her, but he wasn't sure what he would do without her help.

As perceptive as ever, Geoff finally confided to his dad after a few weeks of her care-giving, "Dad, she's really not very good." Geoff's perspective gave Greg the certainty he needed to dismiss her and begin another search, this time for someone who was experienced and verifiably trustworthy. With the holidays fast approaching, he was worried he might have to carry the full load by himself again until after the New Year.

About that time Greg noticed something unusual go-ing on. When faced with a dilemma about the boys' care, if he resisted the temptation to compromise and accept the lesser of two (or more) evils, even though it appeared he had no choice—so long as he *refused* to accept what was not good for the boys—somehow the universe opened up and miraculously rewarded him with a good option, right when he needed it! Looking back over the past few months, Greg saw many little coincidences like this that had enabled and encouraged him to persevere and stick with the very best choices he could make as a single father. He began to won-der *what or who was causing this good fortune?*

Greg's Take

Once the boys were living in my home, I could no longer escape any of the responsibilities of parenting, many of which I had too easily overlooked when Joyce and I were together. I no longer wanted to escape those responsibilities, but I had to face all that it meant to be a single father. I truly *did* want to be a dad, and a good one. But that desire alone did not make good things happen for my family.

My previous life seemed like an absurd game. For years, I had bounced pointlessly from misery to ecstasy, from pleasure to pain, going with the flow— and yet trying to get on top of what was handed to me. At the same time, I had an unquenchable desire to connect with something more reliable, more stable, and more secure. I *really want-ed* a different way to live. I just didn't know what that might look like; let alone how to find it!

I found the multiple responsibilities of being a new lawyer and a single dad almost impossible to juggle! There just weren't enough hours in a day to be a good lawyer and a good single dad. In the past, while living with Joyce, I had always felt free to compromise, and still feel satisfied that I was doing my best. Now I couldn't compromise. I couldn't play the kids off against work or vice versa. Having read Camus, I was sure I wouldn't have felt satisfied with that trade-off even if I had tried.

I was often tempted to think I could be in two places at once, doing two things at the same time, but that was not a solution. In the end, I just had to bite the bullet and accept all of my responsibilities, right where I was at the moment. Doing this seemed to open an invisible door for good to come to me from somewhere outside of myself, beyond any resources I had. I was grateful, but also completely mystified.

This is the way God first stepped in and showed me His hand. Even though I didn't yet know the Lord, or understand anything about God's ways, He gave me courage. He must have known I needed courage to seek and find a way of being both a lawyer (and provider for my family), and a good father. All of this took more courage than I had. When I received inflows of courage, I didn't recognize those as God's gift until years later. In retrospect, there could be no other explanation.

For example, one day at work, I was stuck on a very important conference call. Within minutes, I had to leave the office to pick up the boys or I would miss the school deadline. This was before cell phones, and my secretary had already gone home. In the past I would either have abandoned the call or I would have stayed and left late, hoping to deal with the day-care people the best I could. Both options were wrong, so I waited a few more moments. Just then, one of my legal colleagues stuck her head in the door of my office and asked if I needed help picking up the boys. She was leaving the office to run an errand that took her right by the day-care center, and she could easily swing by my house to drop them off. We were not close friends, I'd never asked her to do such a thing before, and she hadn't known about the conference call! Gratefully, I accepted her offer. As it turned out, I was able to complete the call and get home a few minutes before she pulled up to my house with my sons. Later that evening I thought *that wasn't just a coincidence.*

Late one evening just before Thanksgiving, Greg was alone in his living room. The boys were asleep and the only sound in the house was the tumble of the clothes dryer running on the back porch. While he waited for the dryer to finish, Greg noticed the bookshelf was a mess and he decided to straighten it up. He started sorting through the books, putting them into piles he mentally labeled "keep" and "discard." One was a little King James Bible from his childhood that had somehow made it there with him in the move to 486-B. He didn't recall ever opening it.

Greg picked up the Bible, wondering *was this given to me by Uncle Don or by my Sunday school class for memorizing verses when I was a boy?* He couldn't remember. He aimed to put it on the discard pile, but he couldn't quite bring himself to junk it so quickly. Looking at the blue leather cover, he remembered his mother's parents had a large, nicely bound Bible on their coffee table, with pictures and maps of Bible lands. *Maybe this one has pictures in it too*, he said to himself, flipping it open to check out that possibility.

The Bible fell open to the first page of *Ecclesiastes*. There he read, "'Vanity, all is vanity,' says the Preacher in Jerusalem." He read on, "'Vanity of vanities,' says the Preacher, 'Vanity of vanities, all is vanity.'"

The words struck Greg as odd, yet somehow familiar. He looked at the footnote in the Bible and read "vanity: void, emptiness, meaningless, futility."

Hmmm, Greg said softly to himself, *sounds like Camus.* Then he wondered *what is something like this doing in the Bible?* Greg sat down on the floor and continued reading the text, verse by verse, amazed by the stunning poetic vision and philosophical breadth of what he was reading—even in the language of King James. When he came to Chapter 3, he found more familiar words:

> To everything there is a season, and a time to
> every purpose under the heavens. A time to be born,

and a time to die; a time to plant, and a time to pluck up that which is planted; a time to kill, and a time to heal; a time to break down, and a time to build up. A time to weep, and a time to laugh; a time to mourn, and a time to dance. (Ecclesiastes 3:1-4, KJV)

Wow, thought Greg again, *now that's incredible! That's the exact wording of the song, "Turn, Turn, Turn" by the Byrds! What are these lyrics doing here in the Bible?*

Greg stayed right where he was on the floor, completely losing track of the laundry as he read through the rest of *Ecclesiastes,* devouring its poetry and timeless insights. When he read the final verses, Greg felt he had the answer for which he had searched for years:

Let us hear the conclusion of the whole matter: Fear God, and keep his commandments: for this is the whole duty of man.

For God shall bring every work into judgment, with every secret thing, whether it be good, or whether it be evil. (Ecclesiastes 12:13–14, KJV)

There really is Truth, Greg thought, stunned by the concept. *And not only that, whoever wrote this knew the Truth. And it hasn't changed for thousands of years! Camus knew the questions of life—no one ever put it more clearly than he did. But, whoever wrote this not only knew the questions, they knew the answers! So, who is God, so I can fear him? And what are His commandments, so I can follow them?*

Greg suddenly thought that perhaps the force or entity helping him with life might actually be God. It was just too late in the evening to think about that possibility. For the time being, God would have to remain an enigma, a powerful authority in an unopened black box.

In the days that followed, Greg didn't say anything to anyone about his reading of *Ecclesiastes,* or about the numerous circumstantial wonders that he had experienced in recent months. He just carried on, working at being a good father, and searching for the right kind of afternoon house-keeper and caregiver to assist him with his sons.

All the while, despite her aloneness, Joyce was striving to enjoy her single life in Hawaii. She easily landed a dental hygiene job four days a week in downtown Honolulu to pay her rent and other living costs. Ron continued to call her from California, but she was now dating Larry, a single man she met shortly after moving into the Kapahulu house. Joyce was neither inclined nor content to remain single. Larry was an easy-going man, unconcerned about status or success, yet he was athletic, a good worker and employed full time.

With the Christmas holidays fast approaching, both Joyce and Greg made plans to fly to California to visit their families. They agreed to shuttle the boys back and forth between the homes of the two sets of grandparents, who lived only two miles apart. The day after Christmas Joyce invited Greg over to her parents' home for a short visit. She wanted to talk.

"I just want you to know," she told Greg, "I never planned to have a long term relationship with Ron. He is a nice man, but he's out of the picture now. However, I'm dating a man named Larry who wants to get together with me. I don't want to become tangled up with him if there is any interest on your part to work toward a renewed relationship with me. Are we completely finished, or are you open to try working something new in our relationship?"

Greg was surprised by Joyce's candor and openness toward him. He could sense that she was earnestly seeking his response and that this was an important moment in their lives. He also felt somewhat intimidated by Joyce's transparency. He wondered *might there really be something to hope for, or would trying again be another lap around the track of craziness? Should I agree and try to reconcile with her somehow, or should I let this opportunity pass?*

Greg was still for a moment, surveying the question like a large wave rolling toward him, one that might be rideable or might smash him despite his best efforts. His emotional reservoir was still full with unresolved anger, pain, and fear. He couldn't see anything good coming to himself by choosing to make room for Joyce in his life. Without further reflection or deep consideration, he answered, "Nope, right now I have no interest in pursuing any kind of new relationship with you."

"Okay," Joyce replied. She was disappointed but not very surprised. She had thought it might be best for them to reconnect at least some of their separate lives, but she had no interest to argue with Greg or explore the reasoning behind his decision. That would be too risky and painful.

A few days later on his flight back to Hawaii after the holidays, Greg met an attractive stewardess on the plane. He told her about his younger brother's upcoming wedding in California in late January. On a whim, Greg invited her to go skiing with him at Lake Tahoe after the wedding. She replied with a perky, "That sounds fun!" Greg assumed the deal was sealed.

Arranging care for the boys for the January week he would be out of town turned out to be very difficult. Greg's search for a new nanny had not yet panned out. With little time left, he finally broke down and asked Joyce if she might take the kids for the week.

To Greg's surprise and chagrin, Joyce said she would be glad to keep the boys. She used the opportunity to tell Greg how concerned she was about the lack of childcare he currently had in place for the boys. Joyce said she was planning to move to Hilo (on the Island of Hawaii) in March, and that unless Greg was able to find a nanny acceptable to her *before he left for the wedding*, both boys would be coming to live with her permanently. Inwardly, Greg shuddered. He was scheduled to fly out the next Friday morning, just four days away.

Greg had by now faced this kind of dilemma numerous times. He knew staying home from his brother's wedding was not an option. He also knew he wouldn't give up the boys. There was no way for him to know what would happen if he failed to find a nanny. On his way to work that Monday morning, he wondered what he could do.

Later that morning, a co-worker poked her head into his office and asked Greg if he was still looking for a nanny. Greg nodded yes. She continued, "My sister and her husband have had a temporary *au pair* helping them with their children. The permanent *au pair* they have been waiting for has arrived early. Their temporary girl needs a new position right away. Would you be interested in talking with her?"

Incredible! Greg thought *maybe this is God's doing.* He said, "Sure, thank you for thinking of me!" and breathed a silent, weighty, yet hopeful sigh as he received the slip of paper from his co-worker with the phone number. He immediately called the au pair, whose name was Jennie, and arranged a time to meet with her after lunch that same day.

Jennie asked Greg during their afternoon meeting, "Do you believe in God?"

Uh oh, maybe she's crazy, thought Greg. "I think so," he replied.

"Well, I've been praying that I could become a nanny to a man with two boys," continued Jennie, "and God gave me assurance about that. In fact, I even had the distinct impression that the man would have a beard." Greg was still sporting a beard and his hair long at the time.

Upon hearing her words, he didn't know what to think, but couldn't help but wonder i*s this the same helpful hand working on my behalf, or is this my imagination, or both?*

If Greg hadn't been in such a desperate situation, he may not have acted as quickly as he did, but he found himself wanting to offer the job to Jennie. Although she was young, in her early twenties, she was enthusiastic, came with a good reference, and was said to have great rapport with children.

She was young enough to be a little sister to Greg, not one who would become romantically interested in him or vice versa. He explained to Jennie that she needed to meet Joyce, but that if the two of them got along well, she would have the job. Jennie assured Greg that she *would* get along with Joyce because she liked people and got along well with almost everyone.

That evening Joyce listened over the phone to Greg's news about Jennie, and although Joyce was skeptical, she agreed to meet with Jennie. Their meeting took place two days later on Thursday afternoon at Greg's townhouse. Jennie came prepared to move in.

To her own surprise, Joyce found Jennie refreshing. Joyce was also pleased with Jennie's qualifications and her interest in the boys. Hiring her was a green light as far as Joyce was concerned, and she told Greg so. So Jennie got the job and began moving in, with Joyce's help, as Greg prepared to fly to California. There wasn't time for Jennie to complete her move into the condo that afternoon, so Joyce agreed to come back the next morning to assist her.

The next morning, Greg was in a mingled state of relief and disbelief as he handed Jennie the keys to 486-B. He said goodbye to Jennie, Joyce, and the boys, and then dashed off to the airport, looking forward to his brother's rehearsal dinner that evening in Pasadena. As he settled into his airplane seat, he thought *how unlikely and amazing it is that this nanny challenge has worked out so well? It must be God behind all these miracles.*

Together, Jennie and Joyce got the boys off to school and together they finished moving Jennie's belongings into Greg's master bedroom, which would be Jennie's apartment because it had its own bath and patio. Joyce felt confident that Jennie would be a good caregiver for her sons.

Joyce was almost as amazed as Greg by this turn of events. Turning her thoughts to her own upcoming move with Larry to the Big Island of Hawaii, she looked forward to the rental house they had found with an ocean view in Hilo. Hilo was a quiet, family town, with far less people, away from the Honolulu buzz. Larry had secured a position building trails with the Forest Service and Joyce had a lead on an open dental hygiene position in town. She hoped this move to the Big Island of Hawaii might allow her to settle down for good. Behind her plans was the big idea of bringing the boys over from Oahu to live with her permanently in Hilo.

For Contemplation and Conversation

1. Have you ever experienced God's mysterious intervention? If so, how did that happen? Did it encourage your faith? If so, how?

2. Have you ever kept a journal about your spiritual journey and about crucial decisions you made by faith? If so, in what ways have you found journaling encouraging or helpful? Does journaling help you recognize how your faith has matured?

3. When you and/or your spouse are faced with a very difficult choice, what kind of guidance might you reasonably seek from God and from others?

4. When others seek advice from you about making difficult decisions, what kind of guidance do you normally offer them? What are some other ideas or thoughts you might suggest?

7   The Light Strikes

Greg's flight to California was smooth, but inside he was experiencing tremendous turbulence. He felt he had dodged a bullet with Joyce's threat for full custody. He also felt giddy at the appearance of Jennie at the last minute. Greg wanted to feel less turbulence—more relaxed and free as he anticipated a few days off with family at the wedding, and then skiing with his new stewardess friend.

Though feeling somewhat unsettled by Joyce's suggestion that she might take the boys to live with her in Hilo, Greg assured himself that this was not an issue at the moment. He would face that when and if she ever brought it up again.

Upon his arrival in California, Greg wasn't able to reach the stewardess, who lived in Santa Monica. She hadn't answered or returned his earlier calls from Hawaii. This was a little disconcerting, but skiing with her wasn't the main thing on his agenda, so he let it go for the moment and headed for Pasadena in a rental car.

His brother's rehearsal dinner that night and wedding the next day were enjoyable and went well. Greg was thankful he made it, but he wasn't able to share with anyone about the close call he'd experienced with Joyce or about hiring Jennie. As Greg looked ahead, he was becoming increasingly frustrated with his inability to connect with the stewardess. He only had a phone number, and she wasn't answering. If things had worked out so swiftly and smoothly with Jennie, why was this connection so hard?

Greg finally figured out by Sunday afternoon that the stewardess probably never really intended to join him skiing. She likely was doing her best to avoid him. A little disgruntled, Greg decided to abandon his Tahoe plans and called Joyce's brother Dean and his wife to see if he might visit them Monday evening to say hello. Having not seen Greg for two years, Dean and Carol were quick to extend a dinner invitation. When he arrived at their home in Whittier, Carol answered the back door with a bright welcome, "Dean's putting on a clean shirt. He'll be here in a minute," she said, motioning him to have a seat at the kitchen table. Greg sensed immediately that there was something very different about their home—something good.

Not knowing how to put it into words, he blurted out, "Something sure is different here!"

She replied, "Oh, good, I'm glad you noticed."

When Dean joined them they chatted briefly for a few minutes and then Carol said, "Let me apologize in advance. We're not going to be doing any drinking or drugs like we used to. We've changed."

Greg answered easily and quickly, "I don't care about that stuff. Whatever it is that's different is fine with me. You both seem really happy." In contrast, Greg was aware, achingly so, that he was not happy and he wasn't about to be happy any time soon. Furthermore, he had no idea how to get to the level of joy Dean and Carol were obviously experiencing. He thought *what a difference these past two years have made in my marriage—and in theirs! Two years ago, they were unhappy, as much at odds with each other as Joyce and I were. But now, there's love here, while Joyce and I are not speaking much at all to each other.*

He wondered, fleetingly, if he would ever have the opportunity to be married again and to share love with someone in the way that Dean and Carol apparently loved each other.

They said, "We'll tell you all about it after dinner."

As they sat in the living room later that evening, Dean said simply and directly, "We've become Christians." A brief silence hung in the air. The dishes had been cleared away from the dining table and a fire was crackling in the fireplace. Dean continued, "We always thought we were Christians, but we really weren't. Then a year ago, we went to church on Maundy Thursday and heard the Gospel for what seemed like the very first time. It was like the preacher was talking straight to each of us. So, we both received Jesus Christ that night. Jesus has given us the Holy Spirit, who has given us the power to make the changes you see in us. We couldn't have done that by ourselves. The Bible is actually *true*!"

Greg interjected, "Oh, I know the Bible's true. I just read it for the very first time about a month ago, and I saw that it's true."

"That's good," Dean said, "and Jesus is God. He's alive!"

"Jesus is God?" Greg said, his jaw dropping open a little.

"Yes," Dean said, "After He was crucified, God raised Him from the dead. He is alive. Father, Son, and Holy Spirit—the Trinity!"

Greg's mouth fell open. His face immediately brightened—it was as if he had been in a dark forest but now had walked out into a sunlit meadow. The black box had just been opened. "Oh wow! That makes sense."

Greg told Dean and Carol about some of the experiences he had been having over the last few months and that he had begun to realize, however vaguely, that God was somehow personally present and active in the universe. They smiled knowingly as Greg spoke, the light of the fire playing warmly across the room.

Nothing had prepared Greg for this kind of conversation, certainly not his attending church as a child. But here in a quiet living room among people he had counted as family, it was impossible to deny that a greater force was at work in his life and in theirs. Carol asked Greg, "Would you like to pray to receive Him?" Greg said, "Yes, I would like to do that."

Dean and Carol both said, "Let's pray," and they closed their eyes, bowed their heads just slightly and began speaking to God out loud, first Dean and then Carol—not to God far-off like in church, but as though God was right there in the room! Greg was intensely aware of his surroundings, and of what was happening—the fire in the stone fireplace, the mantle above it, Dean and Carol both speaking directly to God. When they finished, it was Greg's turn to talk with God.

The moment widened into a flat plane of time. Greg did not know what he would say to God, especially out loud. He felt very awkward, having never consciously spoken to God with any belief that God was personally listening to him, let alone invisibly present in the room with him! Even when he had led prayers in church as a youth, Greg had never prayed like Dean and Carol had just prayed. Until now, Greg thought that prayers were just words tossed into the air toward heaven, like a bottle tossed into the ocean with a message inside. Until now, a prayer was an expression of forlorn hope that might find its way to Something/Someone helpful out there. But to accept and believe that God—in the person of Jesus—was now present with him in this very room with the fireplace, mantel, Dean, Carol, and Greg—well—that was an entirely new possibility. Greg willingly took a deep breath and plunged in.

"Lord, I know You've been after me for a long time," he began, "and if You are who they say You are—and I don't think they're crazy—then I want to have what they have. I want You to come into my life. Will you please come into my life?" Then he fell silent, and the room was silent except for the gentle sound of the flames licking around the logs against the bricks in back of the fireplace.

Instead of feeling foolish or self-conscious, Greg found himself feeling relieved, even somewhat heartened. It became instantly clear to him that he was either certifiably loony, or that Jesus was actually now present in his life! Greg immediately saw himself like the man at the end of *Ecclesiastes*, living now in a way that would revolve around God. He would learn to fear God and keep His commandments. Greg had a strong feeling that his life was suddenly headed in a brand new direction. He had no sense of regret, doubt, dread, burden, or disappointment—rather, he felt freedom, relief, expectation, and delight.

Before Greg left their home that evening, Carol found a newsletter from their church and pressed it into his hand. She said it had a list of churches, including two on Oahu, similar to their church. "When you get back to Hawaii, seek to find a church to attend regularly—one that worships Jesus Christ and where the Bible is taught as God's Word. Any of the ones on this list should be okay." Greg thanked her and said he intended to follow up on her advice.

Greg completely forgot about Lake Tahoe. On the forty minute drive back to his parents' house, he wondered about what had happened. *Was this evening real?* At the same time, he felt a new peacefulness, deep-down, in trusting that his life was actually changed and that God would now be the main focus of his life.

His sister, Laurie, was there when he came in. She was staying at their parents' home temporarily to finish her paralegal studies before returning to Hawaii. Having become a believer in Jesus Christ the previous year, Laurie recognized the change in her brother's countenance the moment he walked through the door.

"Something's happened to you," she said with a quick smile. Greg told her he had just received the Lord Jesus as his Savior.

"I already knew it!" she said. "I could see it on your face!"

When Greg got back to Hawaii, he found that all was well with the boys and that Jennie had managed fine. He told all three of them, as best he could, how he became a Christian on the mainland. "Boys," he said, "we'll be going to church on Sundays from now on. I don't know where we'll go yet, but we'll find the right church for us." Jennie said she was already attending a local church, but asked if she might join them on occasion after they found a church. Greg was glad to agree.

The next Saturday Greg looked at the churches on the list Carol had given him. One, called North Shore Christian Fellowship, met at Waimea Falls Park in Sunset Beach. It was over an hour away on the far end of the island, but it sounded good—until he called and learned that they had only one service at 8:15 in the morning. That wouldn't work. The other church on the list didn't seem to have a regular meeting place, just a phone number.

Greg decided to look in the phone book for an alternative. He saw an attractive ad for a church in Waikiki and decided to try going there. On Sunday, he and the boys and Jennie went to the ten o'clock service. They were warmly greeted, and given leis. However, Greg felt something was amiss as the service progressed. The words sounded nice but there was nothing that touched his spirit the way he had been touched at Dean and Carol's house. As the service was coming to a close, it dawned on Greg, *He's not here!* Greg did a little investigating afterwards and was relieved to learn that the Waikiki church was not a traditional Christian fellowship. Rather, they believed *Jesus* was a divine teacher we all might come to resemble, not the third Person of the Trinity whom Greg had received as his Savior.

Greg concluded that his newfound desire for God was not going to be satisfied in Waikiki, so the next week he determined to make the long trek to the North Shore Christian

140

Fellowship even though the service was so early. The following Sunday morning, Greg roused his sleepy boys enough to get them into the car, having packed a breakfast of toast and peanut butter for them to eat on the way. At seven o'clock they pulled out of their driveway and began the drive across the full breadth of the island of Oahu—from the southeast corner to the northwest corner—to the North Shore Christian Fellowship. When he arrived, Greg found the church very simply set up in an open air tent across the lawn at Waimea Falls Park. Seventy-five or more adults were standing at picnic tables, singing—many of them in swimsuits and flip-flops.

A man younger than Greg greeted him on his way in from the parking area, "We have Sunday school classes for the kids, if you'd like, right over there." He pointed to an area where fifteen to twenty children were seated in small groups on a covered porch. The boys' faces brightened when they saw children their own ages. Greg nodded and said, "Thank you."

He found the first group of two and three-year olds sitting on a quilt, being led by an easy-going and warm-hearted couple about Greg's age. They gladly welcomed Todd into their group. Then Greg walked a little further with Geoff to two picnic tables where a half dozen four and five-year-olds were meeting. The couple teaching this group welcomed Geoff and released Greg to attend the adult service. Greg headed over by himself, across the lawn, toward the luau tent.

As he came near, Greg heard them singing. A young couple was leading with an acoustic guitar. They were singing to the Lord. The voices flowed freely in a simple melody offset with beautiful harmonies. Greg slipped into an open space behind a table at the back of the tent. There were no hymnals, just songbooks with words and guitar chords. Greg's heart unfurled, *they are singing to Him. He's here! I'm not the only one who is crazy!* Greg had a deep knowing that

God was here with him and all these people as they sang, praising Him, despite their lack of church attire—or lack of any special building. Beyond the edge of the tent, a peacock meandered through plantings of Ti leaves and flowering ginger. Greg sighed and smiled to himself in relief. Up to now, although he was certain he had begun a fledgling pursuit of God, there remained a tinge of doubt about whether he had lost his mind. That fear now vanished.

The congregation was a lively mix of young people, mostly surfers and young families with children. Greg soon learned that the early service time had been set to accommodate the congregation's large surfing community. Many came prepared to head for the beach immediately after the service.

The pastor preached a sermon from the Book of Joshua about the story of Ai and the tragedy of Achan. Greg had never heard of Achan or Ai, and he hadn't thought to bring his little blue Bible. Pastor Bill, as he was known, was teaching that Ai and Achan not only were real, but that the story was helpful for instructing his listeners how to live faithfully today. Bill was about Greg's age and height, bearded, a little stockier than Greg, but obviously fit.

For the first time in his life, Greg was witnessing a nurturing pastor of strong character who believed the Bible and everything he was teaching from it. Bill spoke in a down-to-earth manner, yet with a deep conviction that Greg had never encountered before. He preached the Bible as *truth*, not as an ancient tale.

They repeated the journey the next week. Pastor Bill continued to preach and teach through the book of Joshua. Greg couldn't help but be amazed at his own conversion and his desire to follow God. Greg quickly bought a new Bible so he could follow Bill's sermons. The Sunday trek to the North Shore became a weekly pilgrimage for him and the boys. Greg was also grateful that the boys seemed to enjoy their Sunday School classes. Each week on their return trip home, they stopped in Haleiwa for shave-ice at Matsumoto's, a happy habit!

When Greg mentioned all of this to Joyce, she seemed skeptical about his story and doubted that his spiritual conversion was genuine. In recent dealings with her, Greg had begun questioning her beliefs and suggesting possible church attendance. To Joyce, his words and behavior seemed like the same old Greg in a new wrapper—*with God now supposedly on his side!*

At the same time, Joyce was getting settled in Hilo. She and Larry had moved into a small rental house that had stood empty for many months. It had a small back yard for the boys and it was in good condition. Joyce had secured the dental hygiene position for which she had hoped. The dental office was very close to her home and just perfect for her practice. She was thrilled to have the three-day-a-week job.

After she and Larry were settled, Joyce's thoughts turned toward the boys over on Oahu in the Hawaii Kai townhouse with Greg. She compared her new living situation to Greg's. *It would be much better for the boys and for me if they lived here*, she thought. According to their divorce decree, Joyce still had legal custody of the boys. She talked the situation over with Larry, to see if he was open to the idea of Geoff and Todd living with them in Hilo most of the time. He was agreeable, saying it would be fine with him if the boys were with her, so Joyce began to plan for the boys to come live with them.

Joyce rightly suspected that Greg would probably disapprove and block this step, so she decided to pack the boys' things and take them to Hilo permanently without saying anything to him about it. She knew this would be similar to Greg's previous hijacking the boys from her place in California, except this time, she would be legally in the right. Joyce had already scheduled a weekend in April with Greg for the boys to visit her in Hilo. They agreed she would pick them up at his place on Friday morning, fly with them to Hilo and then bring them back the following Sunday evening.

When the Friday morning arrived, Greg received a concerned call at the office from Jennie. She reported that Joyce had arrived to pack the boys' stuff for the weekend—but it looked to Jennie as if Joyce was packing far more than they would need for one weekend. Jennie said it appeared that Joyce was packing everything! Jennie thought Greg should come home right away. Greg immediately left the office and drove straight home, but by the time he arrived, Joyce and the boys had already left for the airport. Frantically, he raced to the airport to catch them, but their flight was departing just as he arrived.

Filled with panic and anger, Greg drove back to his office. It didn't cross his mind to call Pastor Bill for advice or prayer. But he did decide to ask one of the other lawyers what to do. Locating one of the partners who handled some divorces, Greg explained what had happened. The partner advised Greg to avoid taking any legal action as the courts would probably side with Joyce, but rather, to go to Hilo as soon as possible to try to bring the boys back before more time passed. That advice appealed to Greg, even though he didn't see how he could pull off such a scheme. He was willing, however, to give it a try.

Early the next morning, Greg flew to Hilo, praying silently that God might help him convince Joyce to return the boys rather than keep them with her. It still hadn't occurred to him to call for prayer from anyone, or to seek Pastor Bill's advice. He had booked a room at the Hilo Hilton for the night and a return flight on Sunday that he hoped would include Geoff and Todd.

When Joyce received Greg's call from the Hilton announcing his visit to the Big Island, Joyce was very suspicious. He asked if he could come see the house and talk with her about the boys. She thought, *Hmmm, Greg has suddenly flown all the way to Hilo to see my new place? And to talk with me about our sons?* Larry was away on a work assignment, so at least he and Greg would not have to deal with each other. Reluctantly, Joyce agreed to let Greg come over for a visit that afternoon.

Their house was on the north end of town at the edge of cane fields. When Greg arrived, Joyce let him in, showed him the open backyard, and then the inside of the house. The house was quiet and bright, and its open windows allowed the trade winds to swirl in off the Pacific.

While the boys played outside, Greg asked and Joyce acknowledged that it was her plan for the boys to stay with her in Hilo rather than to return them to Honolulu. Greg began explaining his concerns, letting Joyce know about the many ways the boys' needs were being well met in Honolulu. But Joyce resisted, reminding him that she had legal custody and that she knew very well the needs of the boys and what was good for them. Finally, she asked him straight out, "Look, what are you going to do if I don't agree that you can take the boys back to Honolulu?"

Greg stumbled to find the right words, and finally said, "Well, I think I just have to take them back with me, even if you don't agree. I think that's what I have to do." Joyce reached for the piece of paper next to her by the phone and prepared to call the number on it—the Hilo Police Department.

"You know I have custody," she said. "I'm not agreeing for you to take the boys. If you try to do that, I will call the police and have them come and stop you." Her voice was cold, stern, measured, and full of passion. She stared at Greg. He looked back at her pleadingly, perhaps expecting God's hand to somehow intervene in a direct way. He blurted out, "You can do that if you want, but it's not right. The best thing for the boys is to come back to Honolulu with me.

So I'm going to go to pack a few of their things that they won't need here." When Greg stood up and moved toward the boy's bedroom, Joyce picked up the phone and called the police.

Within fifteen minutes, a police officer arrived at the front door. When Joyce asked Greg to come meet the police officer, the officer asked Greg for identification. Then, with Joyce looking on, he said, "So, Ms. Millikan told us that you are an attorney and that she has primary physical custody of the boys under your divorce decree. Do you understand and agree with that?" Deflated, Greg answered slowly, "Yes, she does. I do not disagree."

The officer then said sternly, but with a trace of compassion. "I can't allow you to take them, not without Ms. Millikan's approval. You must already know that, since you're a lawyer. If you want to change things, you'll have to go to court for that. Now sir, I think you need to leave the house unless Joyce has something more to say." Joyce shook her head, "No." Greg nodded and went out the door, drove his rental car back to the Hilo Hilton in despair and went straight to his fifth floor room. He slept fitfully that night.

Sometime before dawn, Greg had a vivid dream. He and hundreds of other people, maybe even thousands—all strangers to him—were walking down a long, wide ramp that led underground, out of the light and into darkness below. All the people were shuffling along mindlessly, without question or concern about whether they should be moving into the deepening darkness. There was no sign or promise of anything good in the darkness, only a deafening silence.

Suddenly Greg had a very strong conviction that he did *not* want to go into that darkness, so he stopped moving. He turned around and began to run back up the ramp toward the light. No one said anything to him—the others simply continued walking down the ramp. As he passed them he shouted, "Turn around! You don't have to go there! Get out of here, while you still can!" Greg continued to run, and at last, he emerged alone into the fullness of light, relieved but shaken and still quite terrified. Then he suddenly awoke—still feeling the fear and breathing hard. It was just after seven in the morning.

Getting out of bed, he went to the hotel window and pulled opened the curtain. A bright streak of light poured into the room. Looking westward, he saw the deep-green slope of Mauna Kea rising to its snow-capped crest in a clear blue sky. The contrast between the beauty through his window and the horror of his dream brought him fully awake. Instantly he felt the weight and anguish of his predicament, so he began to pray, asking God's mercy for his family as he continued to stare up at the mountain. Pleading to God, Greg sighed, speaking the only fitting words that came to his mind, "Lord, please reunite this family. If You will please reunite this family, we will certainly follow You and serve You all of our days."

Sharing that hope and concern with God, Greg somehow *knew* He had heard and would indeed hold *this family* in His hands, however things turned out today. Greg wondered, though, about his choice of words. *Who was this family? Did his family include Joyce? Why had he prayed "this family?"* He decided to leave the prayer as he had prayed it, trusting God to work out His best plan.

Before going to breakfast in the hotel, Greg called Joyce's number. There was no answer. He called again after breakfast. Again, no answer. He knew that if he drove to her house, none of them would be there. Instinctively he seemed to know that Joyce would not return to the house or answer her phone until after he had flown back to Honolulu. Checking out of the hotel and placing his bags into his rental car, Greg felt resigned to fly back without seeing the boys or speaking to Joyce again.

With several hours remaining until his flight, Greg decided to drive around to see the city. He drove up the quiet main street and recognized the address of his firm's Hilo office. Driving up and down various streets, aimlessly exploring, he drove by a large park with almost no one in it. There was only one car parked there in the small lot by the playground equipment. When he spotted it, he felt a rush and a sense of amazement. It was Joyce's VW Bus!

Greg slowed as he drew near the parking lot. Peering toward the play area, he could see Joyce and the boys playing together on the equipment—with lovely Mauna Kea in full view behind them. In stunned disbelief, he pulled over and parked his car. As he got out of his car, Joyce saw him. Astonished that Greg had somehow discovered them hiding out in this secluded location, Joyce walked over to him. "How did you find us here?" she demanded with an exasperated and suspicious tone, looking him squarely in the eyes.

Greg said, "I called and there was no answer. I knew you were gone and that I wouldn't be able find you. My flight doesn't leave until 2:30 this afternoon so I began driving around, just to see Hilo. I didn't have anything else to do. I came around that corner down there—it was a dead-end the other way, so I had to turn left. I drove down the street and there was your car! I had no idea you were here."

Joyce couldn't stand it—he had *accidentally* stumbled upon them? "Somehow I knew you'd find us!" she cried out with deep displeasure. Greg asked Joyce calmly if she had given any further thought about whether the boys should stay permanently with her. Looking at him for a long moment, she replied, "Let's ask the boys and see what they want to do."

She called for Geoff and Todd to come over to them and then in gentle, simple terms, she asked whether they would like to stay with her in Hilo or go back to Honolulu with their dad. Geoff, who was almost six years old, and Todd, who was not quite three, seemed to treat this as a natural sort of question to be asked in a city park on a Sunday morning. They took the question seriously. After a little thought

Geoff said he would like to return home with Dad. Todd, on the other hand, wanted to stay with Mom.

Joyce sighed deeply. Then she said, "Okay then." Geoff would return to Honolulu with Greg. It wasn't long before the four of them met back at Joyce's house and packed up Geoff's things, loaded everything into the rental car, and Greg and Geoff departed for the airport.

Over the next two weeks, Joyce realized that splitting the boys had been the wrong decision. Doing this was more painful and less practical for everyone. Larry's involvement with Todd would be slim at best. Despite her sorrow, Joyce made the difficult assessment that Todd would undoubtedly be better off living with his brother, Geoff, and Greg. So Joyce called Greg to make the arrangement, volunteering to bring Todd back to Oahu to live with him. Greg was extraordinarily glad, and readily agreed with her.

Joyce's Take

Once I dropped off Todd with Greg, I was suddenly miserable. Somehow this change seemed so final. When I made the move to Hilo, I was certain it would work out great to have the boys come live with me. After returning without Todd, I called to ask the airlines about our sons flying inter-island by themselves. The news was not good. Because of the boys' ages, I would have to purchase a round-trip plane ticket myself, each visit, to pick them up and return them to Honolulu. With my income I just couldn't afford doing that on a regular basis.

I had a wonderful job in Hilo—a very respectable, professional job where I was an essential part of a dental team. Evidently I was the only dental hygienist with the necessary periodontal skills on the island. My boss, the periodontist, was very busy serving many clients, so he very much needed and appreciated my availability to help.

Emotionally I tried to hold myself together, working my normal schedule. My external veneer, however, kept cracking, and I frequently found myself in the employee snack room sobbing over my situation. I was an emotional wreck.

Not long after that, I began making plans to move back to Honolulu. My boss was crestfallen and I felt terrible abandoning his busy practice. Larry was compassionate and seemed to understand. I felt quite uneasy, planning and making another move by myself.

This time I decided to look for a shared house rental *without* men on the premises. I had learned I was far too vulnerable for that kind of situation—so I found a nice condo to share with two other women in Hawaii Kai, near Greg and the boys. I wasn't sure exactly what I was hoping to achieve, but I did know I wanted to be near *my kids*, Geoff and Todd.

By the time Joyce returned to Honolulu, unknown to her, Greg had initiated a relationship with a woman named Adele. They had been dating casually for about two months. To Adele's surprise and delight, Greg said early on that as a Christian, he wanted to keep their relationship chaste. She had started attending church regularly with Greg and the boys. Adele was a local haole in her mid-twenties. Greg was thirty-one and enjoyed her company very much.

When Greg told Adele that Joyce was moving back from the Big Island to Honolulu, Adele very soon said to him, "I think it's wonderful that Joyce is coming back. The Lord has made it clear to me that you should remarry Joyce! That's certainly God's desire for you and it would also be best for your family. Of course, I like you, but just imagine how wonderful it would be long-term for you and Joyce to remarry and unite your family! It's best to stop our dating relationship—let's just be friends. I don't want to be in the way of your relationship with Joyce."

150

Greg was more than stunned. "You're not in the way!" he protested. "I don't have any idea about Joyce being interested in remarrying me, and I don't feel like remarrying her." Adele looked at him with a sympathetic but joyful smile—he could tell he wasn't going to get her to change her mind with his protests. Finally Greg said, "Okay. I don't agree with you, but if you believe that's what the Lord is doing, I'm in no position to change your mind." They continued to be friends, but nothing more.

Despite his unhappiness about Adele's decision, and doubtful about her advice, Greg did try to reestablish a friendlier relationship with Joyce. He invited her out to dinner one evening. To his surprise, she accepted.

Joyce surprised herself by finding and purchasing a new dress for the occasion. She asked herself *why am I buying a new dress to go out with Greg?* In hindsight, she realized she did think Greg was an extra-special guy, even though he had not treated her as well as she had hoped or wanted.

The two of them enjoyed their dinner meeting, but neither of them had the ability to talk about much other than their two boys and their schedules. Joyce had been burned before in asking Greg to reveal something meaningful about their being together, so she held herself back. After Greg dropped her off and said good night, Joyce reflected on the evening with mixed feelings of pleasure and disappointment. At the personal level, Greg seemed mostly interested in his new-found faith perspective on life. For Joyce, this seemed like a barrier to the two of them truly catching up with one another.

Greg also struggled, sensing their common failure and inability to discuss anything beyond everyday events and practicalities. Each in their own way was perplexed, wondering *why is our relationship so potentially promising and yet so incredibly difficult?* This mystery stood tall between them with no evident solution.

For Contemplation and Conversation

1. Have you ever *presumed* that you knew what was best for your family, without consulting God or others who knew Him? Did you consult with your spouse about your thoughts? What happened in your case?

2. How have you seen God demonstrate His care for the well being of your marriage or your family relationships?

3. In what ways have you served as an ally or an obstacle to God's efforts to restore and strengthen your family relationships?

4. If you have ever stood in the way of God's best for you in a relationship, what did you learn from this experience?

8 Single, Living in Faith, Stumbling in Romance

After their date, Greg abandoned any further efforts to pursue Joyce. He soldiered on as a single dad, grateful for Jennie's help as a housekeeper and nanny. As the weeks turned into months, another school year began. Geoff was now in the first grade and Todd remained in pre-school. Greg began to feel depressed with his overall life situation.

Greg did not doubt his faith in Christ or question his decision to follow Him. Geoff and Todd had each, by now, freely prayed to receive Jesus Christ in their young lives. They had come to believe in Him in powerful ways, and Greg felt assured that the two boys were adopting a way of life that would be a strong foundation for them, and also for future generations. Sometimes Greg would even admit jovially that he and his two sons were three disciples living together—his responsibility was to be "dad," while they got to be the kids—all of them on the same journey together following Jesus as their Lord. Greg had so much to learn, and the Bible had so much to say about how to love and discipline his sons in a healthy way. At times he felt like a true rookie. Once the boys even held him accountable when he failed to discipline *them*!

Greg's Take

I found it doubly difficult to learn to discipline the boys, because it took self-discipline on my part, which was quite inconvenient! One day I promised Geoff that I would take him to the park after work, and he said, "No you won't. You always say that and you never do it!" I was cut to the heart by his bluntness and accuracy. Things often seemed to get in the way of delivering on my promises to Geoff. I called Pastor Bill for advice, looking for a magic wand from God that would help me.

Instead of offering me a fast fix, Bill said, "Greg, God can't help you keep your word to Geoff. You have to keep it yourself." The ball was now obviously in my court.

I learned the same was true in regard to discipline for the boys. God wouldn't do it for me; I had to do it myself, and the Bible taught that this had to be done in love. Proverbs 13:24 says, "the one who loves their children is careful to discipline them."

From the Bible, I gathered that true discipline involves some surprising elements. It is always for *connection and engagement* with the child, never for disconnection, isolation or disengagement from them. True discipline is given in love, never in anger. If I felt angry, I had to wait and get over my anger before attempting any discipline. The purpose and effect of my parental discipline was to waken my son's awareness of what he had done and of its seriousness—like the prodigal son awakes when he comes to his senses at the pig trough (Luke 15:11-24). Discipline is never intended as punishment. Discipline is to be in private, just with the one son, so he is not shamed.

Once we were in private, we began with a discussion about what had happened. It is always the child's awareness that is at stake. Many times, our discussion would take us in a new direction because of his strong belief about what he did or failed to do. Once we were both on the same page of awareness, the disciplinary session would always conclude with forgiveness, prayer, hugs, and expressions of love for one another. Then the matter was finished forever—over and done with, washed away. The matter was never brought up again.

This was the path of discipline that I chose to adopt. It took time and regular prayer for me to establish this format, but I was determined to learn how to serve my children well and consistently in this respect.

After the breakup with Adele, Greg realized how tired he was of single parenthood. He understood the Bible to say he should remain single as long as Joyce was unmarried, and that it was a good thing for him to continue to wait for reconciliation with her (1 Corinthians, Chapter 7). Joyce, however, was not a professing Christian. Therefore, Greg didn't think it would be right for him to marry her even if she were interested—at least not at this time. Larry had by now moved back to Honolulu, and Greg wondered *why doesn't Larry marry Joyce? Or, Why doesn't Joyce trust the Lord and become a Christian?* If she did, Greg thought, then perhaps he might be willing and able to reconcile with her. But for now, there seemed no ready-made or quick solution to his problem.

The holidays came and went. The only bright spot for Greg was his sister Laurie's wedding just before Thanksgiving. Bill Lawson was a friend of his, a Christian lawyer he met playing on a lawyer's league volleyball team in Honolulu, and Greg had introduced them when Laurie returned to Hawaii from her paralegal studies at UCLA. Laurie and Bill would make their home in Honolulu, a dream come true for her, and a welcome family connection for Greg, Joyce, and their sons.

Greg muddled on with his daily grind, often with an unconsciously gloomy countenance and a sometimes sullen attitude. There seemed no light on the horizon for him with Joyce. After Larry's return to Oahu from Hilo, Joyce rented a house together with him in Manoa, not far from the University of Hawaii.

By May, Jennie had been working for Greg, caring for his home, and loving his boys for well over a year. She was well acquainted with Joyce and was also a good friend of Greg's sister, Laurie, and Laurie's husband Bill. Perhaps it was out of sympathy for Greg, or maybe with deeper feelings that had arisen in her, but one day Jennie ventured to suggest to Greg that perhaps he might consider the possibility of marriage with her as God's best choice of a partner for him. She assured him of her willingness to explore that possibility—even with some delight on her part.

Greg didn't have any romantic feelings toward Jennie. In fact, he hadn't thought of her as his type at all. She was good with the boys, but he didn't think she would necessarily be a better parent for the boys than Joyce. Even so, Jennie was a Christian. She was faithful and reliable in every way, and her influence on the boys was consistently good. So Greg began to consider Jennie's suggestion that she might be the woman God would have him to marry, even though he had no feelings for her. He didn't bring it up or discuss it with anyone else, but he prayed and thought about it.

After weeks of indecision, Greg finally concluded marrying Jennie must be God's will, and that his lack of feelings for her was just a test of his faith. Feelings for Jennie, he thought, would surely come along if he married her.

One night in early July, Greg asked Jennie if they could talk after he put the boys to bed. He invited her to have a seat on the couch. His words started out in something of a jumble but it finally became clear to Jennie that Greg was asking her to marry him. Jennie's eyes grew wide and serious and then her face lit up with amazement and delight. "Yes!" she exclaimed. "Yes, Greg, I'll be the best wife to you and a wonderful mother to the boys!"

She stood up and Greg stood too. Jennie stepped over to him and threw herself into his arms with a big hug, which he returned, but with some reluctance, which he hoped Jennie did not notice. They did not kiss.

The news traveled fast. Joyce was not moved, but she was quite surprised by this announcement. So were many of Greg's friends. Greg's sister and Jennie arranged an engagement party at Laurie's in-laws' home in Kahala.

Others didn't quite know what to make of the new couple. At the celebration party, Jennie was enthusiastic and effusive, but Greg didn't seem to be totally with it. Neither did he know anything yet about their plans. Both Greg and Jennie evaded questions about the details of their forthcoming wedding.

Greg's ambivalent feelings had not abated since he had popped the question. He was looking for his feelings for Jennie miraculously to change at any moment; it just hadn't happened yet.

The week after the engagement party, Pastor Bill called Greg. Greg had not yet told him about the engagement, but he was glad to hear Bill's voice on the phone. Bill said he had heard about Greg and Jennie's engagement. "Yeah," Greg replied, "I finally realized that this had to be God's will for me and the boys. So I proposed to Jennie and she accepted." Bill asked Greg if they might meet to share lunch together the next day and talk it over. "Sure," Greg replied, "that would be great." Bill said he'd drive into town from the North Shore, suggesting that they brown-bag lunch on the grounds of Iolani Palace. On Greg's tight budget, that sounded good.

The next noon, Bill and Greg sat down together with their sack lunches on the grass under a monkeypod tree. After giving thanks, Bill was about to take a bite of his sandwich when he paused. Carefully, he lifted up the top piece of bread to sneak a peek under the lettuce. He smiled, pulling out a small rubber alligator that had been tucked in between the lettuce and tuna. Then he laughed, "That Danita! She is always doing this kind of thing, just for fun. I have to be on my watch!" Bill dropped the rubber alligator into his lunch sack with a smile, and looked at Greg with a twinkle in his eye. Greg thought *how great to be married to someone who enjoys putting a toy alligator in your lunch!* How wonderful it would be to share that love with someone.

But then Pastor Bill grew very serious. "Do you love her?" he asked, referring to Jennie.

"No," Greg admitted candidly, but I'm sure I'm going to," telling his pastor how the Lord had spoken to Jennie about their relationship. Bill replied, "Look, Greg, when God wants people to marry, He speaks to both of them about it. I believe Jennie deserves to marry a man who truly loves her. If you don't love her, you're not being fair to her, and you're not giving her what she deserves." He explained that God loved Greg and his sons, and Jennie, and that He wanted the very best for each of them.

Then Pastor Bill asked, a little more quizzically, "Do you think God is finished with you and Joyce? Do you think God is done with your relationship with her?"

Looking at Bill, Greg thought for a moment and then replied simply, "No, I don't think so. I don't think He is."

"Well then," Bill said, "what do you think you should do?"

Greg replied, "I think I should break off the engagement with Jennie." The pastor replied, "That makes sense to me."

All at once Greg felt sheepish, embarrassed, humbled, sobered, and yet relieved. He also felt a glimmer of hope. God really *might* not be done with his relationship with Joyce. He spoke with Jennie that night, after the boys were asleep.

Jennie took the ending of their engagement hard. She immediately quit her position as nanny and moved out, finding an apartment in town while she looked for another position.

Joyce responded to the news of Greg's broken engagement with sympathy, but she certainly saw no link to herself.

She was supporting herself professionally as a dental hygienist in Honolulu, eager to marry—but with no real prospect of doing so unless Larry changed his mind about marriage. Her romantic life was no less messy than Greg's.

So Greg found himself alone, facing the labors of single parenthood unassisted again. He was relieved about the end of the engagement, but his countenance was so gloomy, one of his Christian lawyer friends offered, "Greg, maybe you need some pastoral counseling. I think it would really help with your depression. Try calling Pastor Harold at Kaimuki Christian Church, I think he could help."

On that suggestion, Greg called Pastor Harold, who was a friend of Pastor Bill's. Harold welcomed Greg to stop by his church office in Kaimuki. They decided to meet together one morning a week at Harold's office.

Over the next four months, Harold's listening ear and wise counsel brought fresh spiritual air into Greg's sails. In one of their first meetings, Greg told Harold how much he had enjoyed Joyce's company at a multi-family picnic with the boys at Bellows Beach back in June. Harold asked Greg if he could envision having a better relationship with Joyce, one where they each might maintain positive feelings *regardless of external events.* Greg said he thought so, and he hoped they would do so. The two of them prayed for that to come to pass. Harold also asked Greg to pray for Larry. That was harder for Greg, but he did.

Geoff, who was impacted by the emotional difficulties of both of his parents, began struggling in elementary school. Now in second grade, Geoff was not seeing eye-to-eye with his teacher. Unlike his kindergarten and first grade teachers, his second grade teacher gave Geoff no sympathy and cut him no slack. She preferred instead to shame him when he got out of line, which spurred Geoff on to act out negatively. Greg and Joyce each tried to work with his teacher, but to no avail. After a particularly demeaning conflict between the teacher and Geoff, Greg decided he would pull Geoff out of that school and find a Christian school in which to enroll him.

Kailua Christian Church and School (KCCS) in Kailua came well recommended from several friends, but it would take forty-minutes each way to drive there. When Greg called, he learned they had openings for both boys. That made it just barely feasible timewise, so he decided to risk it. His main hope was that the positive and encouraging environment of KCCS would make the extra drive time worthwhile.

Both Geoff and Todd immediately enjoyed the change. So Greg decided that somehow he would make it work. But Greg was weary and lonely, and he didn't mind telling God about it.

Just before midnight one evening in early April, Greg walked in from the porch with his last load of clean laundry to put away before going to bed. He glanced into the kitchen as he passed by, and immediately winced. He had forgotten about the dinner dishes! With a sigh, Greg put the clothes away and returned to the sink. He had learned to put everything in order before going to bed, so the house would be ready when he hit the ground running in the morning.

Standing there in front of the sink, tired, looking down at the dishes, Greg sighed to God, "Lord, when is this going to be over?" To himself, he thought *will I ever get married again?"*

He felt the Lord's gentle reply, "What if it's never over? What if you remain single and it's this way the rest of your life? Don't I give you enough energy each day to do all the things you need to do that day?"

Greg expected a little bonus time and energy *just for himself.* He thought about it briefly, and then admitted, "Yes, Lord, You do. I guess I can do it, one day at a time."

"Okay, then let's do the dishes," was the Lord's reply.

Somehow the dishes were a little less burdensome than they had been a few minutes before, but it was midnight before Greg got to bed.

In the following weeks, Greg's thoughts did turn to Joyce—to pray for her salvation—but his prayers were more self-interested than from a deep concern for her soul or her eternal destiny. Though Greg didn't want to admit it, his strongest motivation to pray for Joyce was for her to become a Christian so they could get back together and he could have some help with the laundry, dishes and marketing! It took a question from four-and-a-half-year-old Todd to break through and expose Greg's prayer motives.

The last Sunday in April, Greg and the boys were finishing dinner. Todd looked up at his father and said solemnly, "Dad, is Mom going to come to heaven with us or is she going to burn in the Lake of Fire?" Todd was just a preschooler, but he had been a disciple of Jesus for almost a year and he was evidently listening closely, and understanding his Sunday lessons at church!

Greg was taken aback by Todd's question. By the look on Todd's face, he could see Todd's question was sincere. Greg thought about it and replied, "Todd, I don't know. It says in the Bible, 'whosoever believes in Him shall not perish but have everlasting life.' I don't know whether Mom believes in Him or not."

Todd immediately responded with earnest passion, "I sure hope she believes! I don't want her to burn in the Lake of Fire. I want her to come to heaven with us!"

Greg was stopped in his tracks. All of his pretentious prayer motives regarding Joyce fell away in the light of Todd's pure desire for the well-being of his own mother's soul. Immediately Greg said, "Let's pray for Mom." They stopped eating and prayed for Joyce right then—asking God that she might come to believe in and receive Jesus.

Meanwhile, unusual things were happening in Joyce's life. Speaking with love, Jennie had previously shared a Bible verse with her: "Do you not know that the unrighteous will not inherit the kingdom of God? Do not be deceived. Neither fornicators, nor idolaters, nor adulterers . . . " Joyce had not known about this Bible verse! At the time Jennie shared it, Joyce discounted its value, thinking *the Bible is an old book. It doesn't matter any longer what the Bible says.* But God's Word penetrated her heart, and since Larry had no desire to be married, Joyce had decided in February to move into her own apartment. She hoped he would miss her and propose marriage but that never happened. In fact Larry didn't even call her. Joyce was quickly and easily replaced, which was painful for her.

Joyce quickly began dating others, even lowering her moral standards in the process. She just didn't feel *complete* without a man. This was what her mother had imparted to her early on. Joyce started questioning her neediness and her desperate dating behavior.

Greg's sister, Laurie, had been consistently kind to Joyce, listening patiently as Joyce told her how hard it was to be alone—and to date again. Laurie always assured her of God's care and interest to provide a future and a hope for her (Jeremiah 29:11). Laurie would remind Joyce, "The Word of God is true—you can count on the Lord to be with you and to guide you."

Joyce's Take

I grew up attending church, yet I never had any feeling of a relationship with God. After my conversations with Laurie I began to feel loved and cherished by God for the first time. Soon I wanted to honor Him and to live alone until the right man, God's man for me, proposed marriage. I decided to stop chasing men, trying to get them to love me and need me. I examined my desperate dating behavior and I was ashamed of myself. I wasn't honoring or keeping the simple standards I was taught as a child. I had always

known that sharing myself sexually was to be saved for
marriage, not used as a tool to manipulate others.

Joyce found her childhood Bible stored in a box in the
garage. She pulled it out and placed it alongside her cookbooks, up high in the kitchen. After a phone conversation
with her brother, Dean, she recalled him saying it would be
good for her to start reading her Bible in the Book of John.
Dean also said that after he asked Jesus to come into his
heart that God's Spirit helped him understand what the Bible was saying. This was interesting to Joyce, but she wasn't
quite ready for that. Secretly she thought, *I don't want to ask
Jesus into my heart, because then God will want me to remarry
Greg. Everybody would probably think remarriage would be so
nice for our family, but I just can't imagine it!* With those
thoughts in mind, Joyce broke down and cried. She was all
alone in her apartment. She was thirty-one years old.

Joyce decided she would go to a church service nearby
to see if God would show her the right man to date. Joyce
was surprised to meet a very nice, single young man named
Carl who met almost all of her criteria. It wasn't long before
the two of them talked, set a date, and shared an evening
together. Joyce was so impressed with him and their evening together she invited Carl to stay the night with her. He
was so handsome and winsome—for her, the invitation felt
very natural! When morning came, Carl arose, got dressed,
and said he had to leave. Surprised by his sudden departure,
Joyce walked him to the door. Carl turned to her and said,
"This relationship is moving far too fast for me. I'm going
to take some time out and think about things. I may or may
not decide to call you back in a couple weeks." And off Carl
went.

Joyce took his pronouncement hard, especially since she
had already been convicted about her behavior. She felt embarrassed and troubled. That evening, feeling very low, Joyce

fell face-down on the carpet and cried out to God, "Father God, I am so messed up and desperate to find a man to love me. Jesus, will you please come into my life and help me live honorably? The only thing I ask is that *you won't make me remarry Greg.* Thank you God..."

When Joyce arose from her prayer, her face was wet with tears. Looking over to her bedside table she saw her childhood Bible lying there, right next to her bed! She couldn't recall placing it there, so she wondered how her Bible had moved from the kitchen shelf to her bedside table. She was thankful about it though, figuring that God must have moved it there for her to start reading!

That very evening—Friday, May 1—Joyce started reading the Gospel of John. To her amazement, she was able to understand what the Bible was saying! It was such good news for her—it felt like eating very nourishing bread. Joyce had never read the Bible on her own past the two Bible passages she memorized as a child: John 3:16 and Psalm 100. Before that, Joyce thought that *regular people* weren't able to understand what the Bible said.

The evening Joyce prayed to God and asked Jesus into her life was *only five days* after Greg and the boys had prayed for her. This fact was not lost on Greg and their sons.

Joyce soon realized it would be unwise for her to continue associating with her current group of friends in Honolulu. She wanted to dive into a faith community where she could learn about God and allow Him to help her live wisely and more peacefully. She called her older sister, Martha, who lived on Kauai with her husband Marv and two daughters in Princeville. Martha and Marv were Christians, so Joyce was hopeful they would be able to help her. When Martha answered the phone, Joyce announced, "Hi Martha, you may be surprised, but I received the Lord Jesus last week. I wonder, would you and Marv help me locate a safe place for me to live near you?" Martha was instantly excited to hear

Joyce's news, as she and Marv had been praying for Joyce! Martha asked Marv if they might allow Joyce to stay in their guest bedroom—and Marv heartily agreed.

The following week Joyce finally told Greg about her conversion and plans to move in with Martha and Marv. He felt a sudden surge of hope. Greg suggested they get together for a bag lunch to talk about it, and they did.

Over lunch, Greg hinted at the possibility of renewing their relationship. Joyce replied with a paraphrase of 1 Corinthians 5:17: "If anyone is in Christ, they are a new creation; the old things have passed away..." She said, "Greg, *everything* is new for me now, I have a *new life!*" Then she let him know that from her perspective he was one of the *old things* from her previous life that had now passed away. She went on to express her genuine hope that Greg might find someone else to love and marry.

Joyce wanted to establish this new footing for her relationship with Greg because it would be good for their boys. Joyce firmly believed God would safeguard her new husband, a man of God—and someone *other than* Greg. When they finished lunch, the two of them bowed their heads and prayed together for one another's respective futures. Joyce prayed specifically for Greg and his future wife. Greg silently wondered if Joyce's prayers might actually apply to the two of them one day. Leaving the lunch meeting they wished each other well, but Greg was as baffled as ever. Joyce moved to Kauai in early June.

The first Sunday after Joyce moved in with her sister's family, she joined them for church at a very small chapel in Hanalei—thirty or forty were gathered there to worship God and to learn from the Bible teaching. Two thirty-something men played guitars and led worship. Many there held their hands up to God while they sang to Him. Joyce was astounded. *This is really special*, she thought, *all these people are singing right to God!* For Joyce, these people were truly worshipping God—something Joyce had never experienced before. This was nothing like the church of her childhood.

After the service, many stayed on for a casual volleyball game. Watching this group—some single, some married with kids—Joyce sensed all of them were authentic. This was no show. None of them were smoking, using drugs, or drinking alcohol! Seeing all of them in action together was a real eye-opener for Joyce, who thought *being with these people is almost like Heaven!* Joyce hoped she would someday be more like them. For her, the day marked a new beginning. She had encountered people who loved God, and were living very different lives than Joyce had ever imagined or known before.

She began to attend a mid-week Bible study, which she also had never done before. There in community with others she started learning for the first time how to live an authentic Christian life. About three months later, Joyce learned about baptism and that she could choose to be baptized now. Before then, she'd only known about baptism for babies. Joyce talked with one of the pastors and his wife about becoming baptized.

Joyce's Take

I learned that by being baptized and going under the water, I would be enacting the fact that my old life without Christ, and my sins with it, were now buried and dead. When I was raised from the water by my pastor, I would be enacting the newness of life I received from God by the power of the Holy Spirit due to Christ's resurrection!

Before he baptized me, Pastor Don asked me to read Romans 6:1-11. I'd never read about baptism in the Bible before that. The following Sunday, Pastor Don, his wife, and many from the church walked with me to the beach at Hanalei Bay, a short block away. There I was baptized in the midst of that incredible Hawaiian scene.

Immediately after moving into Martha and Marv's guest bedroom, Joyce began looking for a position as a dental hygienist. With more than ten years of experience and a warm professional rapport with people, she soon secured a job with an experienced dentist in Lihue, an hour down the road from Princeville. He was a practicing Christian, which pleased her.

As soon as she saved enough money to move into her own place, Joyce found a one-bedroom rental home in Kapaa, which cut her daily commute time to just twenty minutes. She also found and became active in a Bible-believing church in Kapaa.

Joyce continued hoping for a godly husband as she met a few single Christian men at the Kapaa church. When asked about her background, Joyce would openly acknowledge that she was divorced and had two young sons. It would naturally follow that her ex-husband was also a fairly new Christian. When the single Christian men heard about Joyce's background, one by one each of them would say, "Well, you and your ex ought to get back together!" Joyce would always disagree, using Scripture to support her point, saying, "See—here in 1 Corinthians 5:17? It says old things are gone and that all things are new for me! My ex-husband is one of the old things, right?" Not one of the single Christian men she hoped to date was completely convinced by her logic.

In the meantime, Greg was in a quandary, trying to figure out the best future for his family. Joyce was still personally appealing to him, and he enjoyed her company—even if he couldn't figure out how to relate with her very well. And Joyce's new faith in Christ had changed things. For Greg, it was now *permissible* for him to reconnect with Joyce, according to his theological understanding, and genuine love was a possibility. But he wondered *how would such a thing happen, and when? Should I try to reconnect with Joyce or should I move on with someone else? What is God's will?* Joyce wasn't offering any signs that she would even consider the possibility of a dating relationship with him.

167

People around Greg kept encouraging him to let Joyce know that he was interested in her. In August he attended a weekend marriage conference on Pastor Harold's recommendation. Between sessions, Greg asked the speakers, who were married, for their advice. Upon hearing about Greg's situation, the couple responded, "Joyce is not replaceable. She's the wife of your youth and the mother of your children! You need to reach out to her."

Pastor Bill had also advised Greg in a similar vein, "If you're interested in a loving marital relationship with Joyce, let her know where you stand. Give her plenty of time to think about it, and *then* if she's not interested, go on with your life and don't bother her or yourself about it any longer. If she doesn't want to be on board when your train leaves the station, so be it."

So Greg began to reach out to Joyce, even though he was on the island of Oahu and she was on the island of Kauai. His first approach was to send Joyce flowers at her Lihue dental office. When the flowers arrived, the dental assistants swooned over them, telling Joyce she should take Greg's rekindled interest in her seriously. After all, they said, "Your ex is amazing! What guy around here would send such lovely flowers to his girlfriend at work—let alone his former wife?" Joyce sloughed off their comments, thinking silently *you two just don't know him as well as I do!* Even so, Joyce found herself looking sideways at the lovely flowers throughout the day.

Next, Greg traveled to Kauai and took Joyce out to lunch. They shared a congenial time together, but Greg wasn't getting the positive response he hoped for.

Joyce didn't know that Greg's law firm wanted him to increase his hours in the coming year. He was hoping to find out before the end of October if he and Joyce could make a go of a new relationship. If not, he and the boys would have to sell their condo and move elsewhere. As usual, Greg kept this information to himself and didn't tell Joyce about it, but he did decide to launch out and implement his interpretation of Pastor Bill's advice.

When Joyce flew over to Oahu to visit the boys the first weekend in October, Greg sat with her watching them play soccer. At what he believed was the *right moment*, Greg took a breath and said, "You know, it's the beginning of October. If you would, I'd like you to seriously consider pursuing a relationship with me. How about letting me know by October 31 whether or not you are interested?"

Sensing a whole lot of tension and stress behind Greg's words, Joyce thought *what is Greg really wanting from me here—an immediate remarriage, or is it something else?* Completely uninformed about Greg's living or financial situation, Joyce was unmoved. Staring blankly back at Greg she said, "You can have your answer right now, because it will be the same answer in four weeks. I'm just not interested." Greg countered, "Wait, don't be so fast about it. Give it some time. I really want you to think about it!" Joyce gave him no assurance that she would do so.

At the end of October, Greg went to Kauai for a quick visit. During the visit, Joyce said nothing about his request. Just before he left for the airport, Greg asked her, "Well, what's your decision?"

Joyce replied, "Decision? About what?"

He said, "About our relationship, remember my offer?"

In a matter-of-fact tone, Joyce said, "Well, my answer is still no."

Feeling stunned, Greg looked back at her blankly, "Okay, well, thanks. I guess I'll see you later."

As he walked out to his plane, Greg remembered Pastor Bill's counsel that he needed to let Joyce decide, and then live with that result. Apparently his train was going to leave the station and she would not be on board.

When Greg boarded the plane for his flight to Honolulu and fastened his seatbelt, he silently cried out to God,

"Now what, Lord?" Instantly he felt the Lord speak in his heart, "Now you get to find out what it means to love Joyce unconditionally."

Greg's surprised response was *unconditionally? That means without any expectation of benefit in it for me?* In the confirming stillness, everything seemed to become very clear to Greg. Loving Joyce unconditionally was his responsibility, whether or not he ever became her husband. If he didn't love her unconditionally, why would marrying him be good for her? He thought *of course! It's my responsibility to love Joyce unconditionally because that is how Christ loves me. And right now loving Joyce unconditionally means loving her without regard to my future with her.* Greg doubted he knew how to do that, but he expected he would have to learn.

Joyce's Take

Christian single life away from my sister's family was challenging, but at thirty-two I did enjoy having my own place. The house was a newly constructed one-bedroom home with a loft for the boys. Being a social person, I wanted to invite others over. I considered asking a married couple over for dinner. However, I found myself too uncomfortable to socially navigate seating for three.

My church in Kapaa offered me ways to connect with others. I enjoyed activities where I could *get out of myself* and encourage others rather than to feel sorry for myself, or to perpetually seek someone to date. A musical play called *Colby the Computer* was to be presented at the church and an assistant director was needed, so I volunteered! Doing this gave me *deep joy* as a single person.

There also was an open competition game, sponsored by the high school group—something like TV's *Jeopardy!*, in which two teams were asked specific questions about the Book of Matthew. Anyone from the church could participate, so I jumped in. Each week, we all would study three chapters to prepare for the questions. I gobbled up this team sport, studying every detail of Matthew's gospel, in hopes our team might win that week's game. Gladly, I was learning God's truth along the way!

Greg had completed four years with his law firm in September. At his annual review meeting with his supervising partner in late September, Greg had received news that he wasn't prepared to hear—the news he was keeping from Joyce.

The partner had told Greg that the firm wanted him to become a partner at the end of his fifth year. They liked his work, and the clients liked him as well. However, the firm wasn't getting enough hours from Greg. The partner didn't spell out exactly what that meant, but Greg had thanked him anyway, saying he would consider it and get back to him after Greg assessed his situation. Greg already knew he had no more hours to give.

Greg had left the meeting both encouraged and dismayed. He was encouraged that the firm and his clients were pleased with his work. He was also certain the firm was making a good profit from the work he was doing. But he was dismayed because of the requirement of increased hours. Greg knew he didn't have two seconds remaining in any day to do more legal work. He could only give them more hours by subtracting them from the boys or from the Lord. This would mean compromising his role as a dad and as a follower of Christ. He wasn't about to make either of those compromises! Apart from attending church with his sons each Sunday morning and picnicking at the beach after church, Greg was pedal-to-the-metal the other six and a half days of the week. More time for his legal practice was not an option.

Greg had called his father for advice, figuring his dad would understand the situation as nobody else could. His dad gave him a very specific formula for making a decision.

He didn't suggest any compromise to meet the firm's re-
quirements. Instead, he told Greg, "You need to figure out
if you have enough time to earn a living as a lawyer. If not,
you'll have to find another line of work. It takes about 120
billable hours a month, in my opinion, for a lawyer to earn a
living. Keep a log of all your hours for the next two or three
months. See how many hours you actually bill for your work.
That way you'll learn if you're chalking up enough billable
hours to make it. If you have enough hours, you'll know
you have enough time to be a dad and a lawyer, though not
enough time for what this firm wants. If that's the case, you
can find a new firm or another place to practice with the
hours you do have."

His dad's words gave such sound and simple advice!
Greg felt immediate relief and assurance, like he had felt before after his conversation with his father thirteen years earlier about how to brief a case. Greg knew what he would do
now—and he knew that big changes lay ahead, both in his
work and in his family's housing.

Keeping very close tabs on his time, Greg quickly saw
that by his dad's standard he would be able to bill enough
time to be a self-sustaining lawyer. Greg would be able to
leave the firm and earn a living practicing law somewhere
else. But where?

Without the firm's regular salary, Greg wouldn't be able
to make his monthly payments on the townhouse. If, however, there was any chance that he and Joyce might get together and become one household, Greg thought keeping
the townhouse might be possible. So he had held off putting
it on the market until Joyce gave her answer at the end of
October. When Joyce turned him down he was genuinely
shocked. Greg thought *it would have been so easy, logical, and
natural—even right—for Joyce to say yes, as she had once before.*
But Joyce's refusal meant the door was now closed for Greg
to keep his townhouse.

Loving Joyce unconditionally wasn't the only thing on Greg's mind when he returned to Honolulu. The very next day he called his realtor and told him to go ahead and put 486-B on the market.

Within days the townhouse was placed in escrow as the result of a full-price offer that Greg accepted. At the request of the buyer, the sale was set to close the Monday after Thanksgiving.

Although Greg and the boys hadn't yet found a new place to live, Greg decided to take Geoff and Todd with him to Kauai to celebrate Thanksgiving with Martha, Marv, their two daughters and Joyce. *It is wonderful being in a family setting again with Joyce,* Greg thought.

When Greg explained his need to move out of the townhouse over the weekend, Marv was extremely generous. He volunteered to fly with Greg to Honolulu on Friday and help him move everything into storage over the weekend. A family in Greg's home Bible study allowed Greg and the boys to stay with them in their apartment at Pearl Harbor until Greg's housing decision could be made.

The same week Greg and the boys moved into their friends' apartment, he told the firm that although he had truly enjoyed practicing law with them, he couldn't offer them any more hours. Greg advised them he would be leaving the firm on January 31. This would allow the firm time to find his replacement. For his part, Greg would use those two months to assess his situation and decide where he might practice law and where his family would live.

This was not a clear or easy decision. Greg was known in Oahu, so he thought it would be logical to practice law in Honolulu and keep the boys in school at KCCS. As the weeks passed, Greg searched, but he wasn't able to find an appropriate place to rent. After discussion and prayer, Greg and the boys had decided to rent a place where their little dog, Sweetie Pie, would have a yard to play in and where no one would live above them. On this score, Greg was striking out.

In early January, Marv called Greg from Kauai with three bits of news. First, Marv knew a legal secretary at church who needed a job. She would probably be available to help Greg on a contract basis, as needed, if he decided to move to Kauai and set up a legal practice there.

Second, a family in their church was moving out of a two-bedroom rental home in Hanalei that would be available for lease through the end of June. Greg asked about a yard outside for Sweetie Pie, and Marv affirmed there was a yard. The single story house was located just two blocks from the Hanalei shopping center.

Third, Marv said there was a place available for Geoff in the local Christian school and that the local public elementary school would be very good for Todd in kindergarten. Both schools were within walking distance of the house. Astounded at the news, Greg thanked Marv for calling, saying he would get back to him as soon as possible.

Nothing else had opened up. Greg wondered if this was one of God's opportunities for Greg to learn what it meant to love Joyce unconditionally. After all, Geoff and Todd's cousins were there on Kauai, along with their aunt and uncle, and their mother. Greg made a few quick calls to see if his firm or other lawyers he knew might refer him work on Kauai if he set up a practice there. He received some mild assurances. Greg calculated he had just enough money to rent the house and a small office for his new sole law practice for five months through the end of June. Depending on how things turned out, he would decide at the end of June what to do next.

When Greg told his father his plans, his dad was supportive, but asked, "Where are you going to get business in Hanalei?" Greg said he was unsure, apart from any referrals he might receive. He would have to learn how to attract business. That seemed good enough for his dad.

Greg explained the situation to the boys. After prayer together, they all agreed that Greg should rent the Kauai house, set up his practice in Hanalei and see what would develop. Greg called the landlord to settle the lease. Their move to Kauai was planned for the weekend of January 30-31.

Greg gave away everything he wouldn't need in Kauai, including his fancy stereo set from law school and *his half* of the crystal glassware from his marriage with Joyce. It was a tightly trimmed set of belongings that arrived in Hanalei with Greg and the boys for his experiment in solo practice in a rural setting.

Within a week of their arrival in Hanalei, Greg had rented an empty office on Aku Road across the street from Ching Young Village. After buying a memory typewriter and some office equipment, connecting a phone, and opening a business checking account, Greg hung out his shingle. Painted on the office window was his sign: Gregory F. Millikan — Attorney at Law.

For Contemplation and Conversation

1. How has your faith helped to determine your course of action in challenging times? How has the faith of others helped you to determine your course of action?

2. How have you seen God at work in your recent circumstances?

3. Does knowing that God is active around you encourage your faith and decision-making? If so, in what way?

9   A Time for Every Purpose Under Heaven

The yard at Greg's new place in Hanalei had plenty of room for Sweetie Pie. An added bonus was finding several papaya trees on the property, loaded with fruit. The beach at Hanalei Bay was close enough for the boys to walk or ride their bikes there to play.

During their first two months living there, it rained over 100 inches. Except for the mold that grew inside Greg's shoes in his closet, the rain was more of a sensation than a problem. Heavy rains would cause the Hanalei River to rise and cover over the only road into Hanalei, which meant no school for the boys—to their delight. With not much legal work for Greg, he found plenty to do sorting the stuff from the boxes he and Marv had thrown into storage several months before.

As for his relationship with Joyce, Greg was working to learn how to move on with his life and still love Joyce unconditionally. The two of them were attending different churches. Joyce attended her new church in Kapaa, and Greg was attending the church Joyce had previously attended with Martha and her family in the Hanalei chapel.

Joyce was open to dating other Christian men, but Greg continued to believe that his future wife would be Joyce or nobody as long as she remained unmarried. In any event, Greg was busy enough parenting and establishing his new law practice. Life in Hanalei was challenging for Greg regardless of how things were going with Joyce.

Greg began attending a midweek evening Bible study led by Pastor George and his wife. Greg enjoyed Pastor George's friendship and counsel and the opportunity for the boys to play with other children each week. Plus, delicious homemade Filipino desserts were served to all each week.

When the rains subsided in April, Greg made a visit to Joyce's church while the boys went to their Hanalei church with their cousins. Not knowing what he would to say to Joyce, Greg decided not to call to let her know he'd be there. As a result, Greg learned very quickly that showing up unexpectedly at Joyce's church did not please her. She soundly reprimanded Greg, saying, "If you show up here at my church again, unannounced, I'm going to stand up in the service and call you out! You keep saying you trust God with your future. You keep telling me you think it is God's will for us to get back together, but you don't trust Him at all to do it! If it is His will for us to get back together, *He'll do it!* You talk a lot about God, but all I see is you, *you, you!*"

Greg knew Joyce would follow up on her threat. After apologizing and saying there would be no more unannounced visits, Greg drove back to Hanalei where he found the boys still playing with their cousins at the beach.

He went inside his house, knelt next to the couch and prayed, "Lord, I believed it was Your will that Joyce and I should be together. I sent her flowers. I took her to lunch. I've tried to love her unconditionally. I've moved to Kauai. I've prayed for her..." His voice trailed off.

Greg stopped talking and listened. He heard the Lord say, "You, you, you! Joyce is right. Don't you believe I'm able and willing to do what I purpose to do? Will you leave Joyce in My hands?" Stunned and chastened, Greg fell quiet. The Genesis account of God's creation of Adam and Eve came to his mind. Greg saw it afresh—Eve was not Adam's idea! *Adam was asleep* when God made Eve—she was God's idea. God created both of them. *It was up to Eve to decide whether or not she was interested in Adam.*

Greg finished his prayer, got up and called Pastor George for additional counsel. George reminded Greg, "Joyce knows where you stand; now you need to let things alone between you. Part of loving someone is to accept and value that person, even when there are disagreements. You must determine for yourself where God is leading *you*, and then allow Joyce to decide for herself where God is leading *her*." Greg acknowledged and thanked Pastor George for his wise counsel.

After he hung up, Greg wondered *how can I live this out?* He remembered Jesus' response to Peter's question in John 21:22: "What's that to you? You follow Me!" Greg decided he was called to follow the Lord, not to march around Joyce as if she were Jericho, waiting for her walls to fall. If Joyce wanted to join Greg in following the Lord, she would do that, if and when the right time came. So Greg turned his attention to following the Lord.

It was a good time for Greg to refocus, because he was facing a professional and financial challenge. It was becoming obvious that there was no need for a tax lawyer in Hanalei and maybe not in Kauai. Greg was stumped about the next step for his career prospects on Kauai.

In early June, Greg's parents came to visit him for a week. His father had recently completed three years of chemotherapy following surgery in 1979 for colon cancer. Their visit was enjoyable for all of them. Greg was glad to commiserate with his dad about the lack of legal business he had found on Kauai, but Greg noticed his father was acting uncharacteristically tired. Brad was only fifty-six years old, yet how weary he looked!

Within a few days of their return to California, Greg's mother called to say that his dad's cancer had come back. Brad had just received news from tests taken before the visit—evidently the cancer had migrated into his liver. The prognosis for Brad was not good. Stunned by this news, Greg called Joyce to tell her about it.

Joyce suggested that Greg fly over immediately to be with his father in California, and to see for himself what was happening. Greg welcomed her advice, thankful that she also offered to take care of the boys while he was gone.

On the flight, Greg remembered Old and New Testament passages about honoring one's father and mother. He wondered if following the Lord at this point might mean moving back to California to help in his dad's law practice. Greg's leases in Hanalei, both house and office, were set to expire at the end of June, with no possibility of extending the house lease, as the owners wanted to start living there.

Once in California, Greg quickly determined that his father's busy law practice would suffer without some immediate help. Brad's practice could not be carried on by his associates. Brad's tax and transactional work was outside of their expertise, but it fell squarely within Greg's areas of specialty. To Greg it seemed obvious he should leave Kauai at the end of June and join his father's practice in California. Such a move made sense to Greg, except for its impact on Joyce and the boys.

In the hospital, Greg explained his reasoning and waited to hear his father's response. Brad told Greg not to come to California for Brad's sake, but to come only if Greg was convinced that this was the Lord's direction for his life. Measuring his words carefully, Greg replied in a very serious tone that *he wanted* to come work in California because *he firmly believed* that God was leading him. On those terms, his father agreed.

Upon Greg's return to Kauai, he called Joyce to let her know about his plan to move to California at the end of the month. The two of them had previously agreed that neither of them would move away from Hawaii without mutual agreement. Although Joyce was sorry to hear about the declining health of Greg's father, she was upset by Greg's unilateral decision to move to California without talking with her first.

Joyce's Take

Greg's dad was a mountain of a man. At 6 foot 6 inches and 240 pounds, he made a big impression on me, both physically and intellectually. He had personal integrity. The prospect of losing Brad Millikan was a very tragic situation. He was very important to Greg and also to me. I felt great sorrow about this situation. At the same time, I really wanted our family to remain in Hawaii. As a result, this situation for me was doubly tragic. It seemed to compound the many family difficulties Greg and I were already working to navigate.

Gladly, Greg's attitude was now softer toward me. He didn't insist on taking our boys with him to California. I appreciated his respect on this point. My limited income as a dental hygienist, however, could only cover my own living expenses. Even beyond financial concerns, I knew myself well enough to know that I wasn't created to be a single parent, even if I could afford keeping the two boys myself. For me, raising children was a family matter. Parenting is a role founded *in marriage*—families are meant to stay together! My heart was still breaking over our divorce, and now here was another tragic problem to face.

While Greg wrapped things up in Hanalei, Joyce planned a summer vacation with the boys. She would take the month of July to stay with her brother, Dean, and his wife Carol at their mountain cabin in California, where Geoff and Todd could play freely with their other cousins.

Greg left Kauai and flew back to California on the 30th of June. When he saw his father, Greg knew immediately that his dad would not be returning to his law practice. The cancer was not responding to further chemotherapy.

Greg would take the California Bar examination the last week of July, so he had only three weeks to prepare. During that time, he and his dad talked regularly about what needed attention at Brad's office. Steadily weakening, Brad entered the hospital the day before Greg's three-day Bar exam began.

When Greg completed the exam three days later, he drove directly to his father's hospital room. He wasn't prepared for the shock. His dad was *much* worse than he had been on Monday. The chemo drip Brad was receiving, with a heavy dose of morphine to cover painful side effects, left him incoherent and unable to speak audibly. The doctor couldn't assure the family how long Brad might last. Greg and his mother wanted to communicate with Brad, so they told the doctor to turn off the chemotherapy.

The next morning when Greg arrived, Brad was lucid again and in his right mind. He urged Greg to call the office and request that Brad's junior partner, Jim, come right over to meet them at the hospital. "Tomorrow will be too late," Brad said.

When Jim arrived, he and Greg discussed the practice briefly with Brad. They agreed that Jim and Greg together would carry on the practice. The three of them shared Communion and then Jim left. Greg and his mother, Barbara, stayed the rest of the day with Brad at the hospital. By eleven o'clock that night, Barbara was exhausted and went home to rest. Greg leaned back in the chair next to the bed, held his father's hand, and waited.

Just after four o'clock in the morning, Greg was startled awake when a nurse ran in, "Your father!" she blurted. Greg looked at his dad, who seemed to be sleeping. Then a last breath escaped Brad's lips and he lay motionless and quiet. Stunned, Greg thought for an instant to pray for his father's revival, but then he looked at his father's emaciated body and instead prayed silently, *Okay Lord, he's with you.* After a few minutes, Greg got up and called his mother with the news.

A memorial service for Brad was planned for the following week in the Church of the Recessional at Forest Lawn. As soon as Joyce heard the news, she arranged to bring both boys with her to Glendale to attend the service. To Greg's surprise, Joyce and the boys filed into the service and sat right next to him in the family section. Joyce's main concern was for Greg's loss of his father. It was a completely natural gesture for Joyce to escort their sons to sit alongside their father. Soon after they all sat down with Greg, however, Joyce reflected on the importance of the three of them sitting with Greg in the Millikan family section.

Afterward, Joyce returned to the mountains with the boys. She had thought through and decided two things about what she needed to do. She would not attempt to raise their sons by herself as a single parent; rather, she would ask Greg if the boys could live with him at his mother's house when they returned from the mountains. Joyce also decided that she ought to remain near the boys in California, so she would seek employment in California and not return to Hawaii unless absolutely necessary.

Joyce phoned Martha and Marv about her hope to stay in California and not return to Hawaii. Martha cheerily replied that she and Marv would pack up all Joyce's things and ship them to California along with Joyce's VW Bus. Joyce was astounded by their generosity. Although Joyce had known that Martha and Marv had been praying for God to guide her and Greg back together, Joyce was incredulous. She thought *Martha and Marv must be angels! Wow, now I'm free to call my boss and ask for permission to leave my job and remain in California.*

The next amazing turn was that Joyce's boss in Lihue readily agreed to let Joyce off her job without notice. Joyce could barely believe everything that was taking place. When Dean and Carol heard all the news, they warmly invited Joyce to move into their Visalia home with them after she delivered the boys to Greg. Before long, the boys were safely delivered and Joyce was back in Visalia waiting for the shipment of her things to arrive from Hawaii.

Everyone involved in Joyce's life seemed to want her reunited with Greg. Joyce, however, remained firmly disinterested. As she waited for her belongings, she began to think about moving back to Santa Cruz as a place for her to settle and start a new life. Joyce was hoping she might be able to get her previous dental hygiene job back. For her, Visalia was both unfamiliar and unappealing. She also had no job connections there.

Greg had not yet connected with Joyce at any emotional level. Greg was not able to offer her anything openly about himself. He was still a closed book when it came to his innermost thoughts and feelings. This disconnect between them was the main factor that kept Joyce disinterested.

Greg's Take

When my friend Pastor Harold first proposed that I needed to pray for God's best for Joyce and for her boyfriend Larry, I had a difficult time with that prayer. But I had an *even harder time* forgiving Joyce. I just couldn't get past some of the things I had against her!

That changed after I heard a message about the importance of forgiving others. I learned that when we don't forgive someone, we keep that person locked in a prison cell in our heart, with a little blackboard on the door listing the things they have done against us. The speaker said, "To forgive is to unlock and open the door of the cell and say to the person inside, 'I'm not holding these things against you any longer. You are free to leave.'" This was a picture of forgiveness I had never imagined before.

I knew I needed to forgive Joyce. I had her locked in a prison cell in my heart, but I couldn't get past the stuff I had on the blackboard—rejection, abandonment, other men. I couldn't bring myself to unlock the door and release her. I also knew that if I couldn't get beyond the stuff on the blackboard, I wouldn't be able to get back together with Joyce.

I was completely stuck until I brought my difficulty to the Lord early one morning. As I imagined the blackboard on Joyce's cell, Jesus asked me, "Aren't you depending on My blood to cover all the things on *your* blackboard?"

"Yes, I am," I replied. Then He asked, "If My blood is good enough to cover your sins, why isn't it good enough to cover Joyce's sins?"

At that instant I saw that I hadn't allowed Christ's blood the same currency for Joyce's sin as for my own. And in that moment, I accepted it and saw the things on Joyce's blackboard blotted out under Christ's blood. *And I was freed!* Immediately and easily I was able to unlock that cell door, to open it and say to Joyce in my own heart, "I forgive you. I don't hold these things against you any longer, you are free!" Opening up to Joyce with that freedom took me much longer.

"I Miss Mom"

One night in early September both boys were already in bed when Greg came in to share prayers with them. The evening air was pleasant. Cricket songs echoed in the gathering darkness outside and the faint fragrance of sycamore leaves drifted through the open window. The multiplied stresses of the previous months and years were somehow submerged in this moment of peace. There was work ahead for him; plenty of challenges, but here in the house where Greg had grown up, with his newly widowed mother and her first two grandsons, his life suddenly felt acceptable and tenable.

After their prayers were finished, Geoff spoke into the stillness, "Dad, I miss Mom." Greg looked out the window, paused and then heard himself say, "I miss her too, Geoff." This was the first time Greg had voiced such feelings to Geoff, or anyone—even himself. He kissed Geoff and then Todd. Then, before he walked out the door, he blessed both of them aloud, as he did each night, "The Lord is loving you!"

Greg walked quietly down the hall and sat down at a table in the family room where he could write a letter. He wrote to Joyce, describing the quiet evening, how things were settled and seemingly at peace. He continued, saying how he had looked forward to sharing each of their son's weddings with her, becoming grandparents together, and that he had just realized tonight that he missed her and the dreams they had shared about that future.

In the letter, Greg didn't ask anything of Joyce or propose anything to her. He said he just wanted to let her know what he was thinking and feeling. All Greg wanted to convey to Joyce was the meaning of the moment he'd shared with the boys. When he finished writing the letter, he put it in an envelope and addressed it to Joyce at Dean's house in Visalia. He sealed the envelope, stamped it, and put it on the counter for the next day's mail. A few minutes later, the kitchen phone rang.

When Greg picked up the phone, he was startled to hear Joyce's voice. He had to shake himself to pay attention to what she was saying. She was calling to plan her next visit with the boys. They talked together about it briefly and set a time for her to come visit. Still flooded with the freshness of what he had just experienced, Greg interjected, "You know, it's amazing. I just wrote you a letter! I was going to mail it in the morning. Do you want me to mail it, or would you prefer for me to read it to you now over the phone?"

Joyce thought *why not, let's just get this letter over with!* She said, "Sure, that's okay, go ahead and read it to me." Greg reached over, reopened the letter, and began to read it aloud to her. When he began to read the part about seeing the boys get married and becoming grandparents together, Joyce began to breathe deeply; her emotion was rising. Bursting out, she interrupted him, "You can't say things like that to me any longer!"

"What?" Greg said, not understanding.

Beginning to weep audibly, totally confounded by Greg's words, Joyce stammered, "It's been four years. It has been too long. It's not fair!" And she abruptly hung up. There Greg was, dumbfounded, holding the dead phone, wondering what *this* could possibly mean!

Joyce's Take

Greg was normally so analytical, structural, official—these words of his were conveying something entirely new. In this conversation, Greg was suddenly sincere and expressing himself to me so meaningfully!

When he told me all the shared dreams we had talked about earlier in our marriage: being grandparents someday, loving our grandchildren, when he reminded me of those things, I was caught off guard. I felt upset, embarrassed, confused . . . and I cried. I hadn't imagined Greg would ever make me cry again, but he had touched something very deep inside me.

Looking back now, I can see how each of our sons was a kind of bookend, influencing each of us, even unconsciously, to do the right thing. Todd was four and a half when he asked Greg about God's love for my soul and whether I would join them in Heaven. Greg responded to lead all three of them to pray for me. God heard them and answered their prayers! Later Geoff freely confessed to Greg that he missed me, which helped Greg to reconnect meaningfully with me. In these specific ways, each of our sons helped both Greg and me to reconnect.

After the phone call with Greg, Joyce felt confused and sick. She had to lie down on the couch to allow her mind to stop spinning. When she finally was able to get up from the couch, she went out to the garage to assess all the boxes of her stuff that had recently arrived from Hawaii. Exhausted by the sight, she just couldn't imagine loading everything into her VW bus another time. She stood there, scratching her head, not knowing what to do...

She finally gathered herself and said out loud, "I'm so tired of moving! I've moved ten times in the last four years. I just don't have what it takes to move again. *I've had it* with moving and with this crazy, unsettled kind of life."

Joyce returned to the couch, fell back to relax, and prayed, asking God for His perspective on her present predicament. At this moment she had no idea or plan except to return to Santa Cruz and take up where she had left off. And then a strange thought came. *Maybe I should talk seriously with Greg about some way that we could safely explore getting back together.*

She had hated Greg's constant pursuit, making it impossible for her to move forward in any direction that didn't have him in the midst of everything. Everyone she knew who was a Christian kept saying, "You and Greg are both Christians. You should get back together." Something in him had clearly changed, the letter he read to her proved it. How could they possibly *talk* about all of this?

Joyce decided to risk calling Greg to ask if he'd be willing to meet to talk together some time during her next visit. He was surprised, but said cautiously that he was willing to do that. They decided to meet for a picnic lunch with the boys at Descanso Gardens. They would begin their conversation there.

The boys played in the woods nearby as Joyce and Greg took up their conversation in the picnic area near the gates of the Gardens. Greg stated plainly that he was indeed willing to begin a process—perhaps like a courtship—but as they continued to talk, Joyce began to sense the difficulty of the path they were discussing. The more they spoke, the more formidable the subject became for her. Near the end of their lunch, Joyce looked at Greg with sincerity. After weighing the pros and cons, she said, the process they were discussing wasn't going to work for her. She had reached a conclusion. She would move to Santa Cruz and make a clean start.

But this wasn't the old Greg or the old Joyce sitting together in the warm September sunlight. Greg looked back at her reassuringly and responded, "Well, if you do that, I'm just going to put on my driving shoes and come up to visit you!"

Completely flustered by his comment, Joyce laughed it off, saying "Oh, for heaven's sake Greg, don't do that!" But she thought to herself *oh no—here he goes again! If I move to Santa Cruz and put down new roots, Greg will just show up and ruin everything!*

The picnic was packed up and they called the boys. It was time to leave. The four of them parted with an air of uncertain amicability. Greg asked Joyce to give him a call to let him know her plans. She said she would.

Once again, Joyce stood before the wall of boxes in her brother's garage. All of them had been carefully labeled by Marv and Martha. Slowly looking them over, wondering which boxes would go with her in the VW Bus and which ones would be picked up later, Joyce felt a deep fatigue come over her. She sighed. She didn't want to be single and she didn't have to be—she could marry Greg. She didn't want to marry Greg. She didn't have to marry him. She could remain single, but she didn't want that. She thought *if I move to Santa Cruz, it would just become another time around the same mountain. I don't want that either!*

In the morning when it came time for Joyce to load up her VW van and take off, she realized she just couldn't do it. Finally she decided: She would not return to Santa Cruz, but she didn't know a better option. Joyce decided to call Greg at the office to let him know she had changed her mind. Greg picked up the phone after his receptionist said the caller was Joyce Millikan. He looked at the clock on his desk—it was not quite 9:30.

"Where are you?" he asked Joyce.

"In Visalia," she answered.

"Oh, okay. When are you leaving for Santa Cruz?" he asked, thinking maybe she had learned her new phone number and was calling to give it to him.

"I'm not going to Santa Cruz," she said.

"You're not?"

"No," she answered, "I'm coming down to La Cañada instead. I'll be there at my parents' house." She waited.

The silence between them was vibrating, full of energy. Greg felt like an astronaut strapped in his space capsule at *T minus ten seconds and counting*. For Greg, the whole room started shaking. He looked over at the wall panels in his office to see if they were vibrating. They were still.

"Can I come over and see you this evening?" he asked, breaking into the fertile, quaking silence.

"Yes," Joyce replied.

"About 7:30?"

"That sounds fine," she answered.

"Okay, I'll see you then," Greg answered back, "Good bye, have a good drive down."

"Okay, bye, see you then," Joyce responded and then hung up. Greg's calendar said, "Thursday, October 9." At that moment, he felt older than his thirty-four years.

Joyce's Take

I knew theoretically that it would be a good idea to remarry Greg, but at the same time I did not have the same loving feelings I once had for him.

I was surprised to find an old photo of Greg standing with two-year-old Todd after a shower, both of them with towels around their waists, each with their clean hair tousled. They were holding hands—Todd looked so small. So precious! My mind flooded with warm memories. The photo made it easy for me to remember family life with Greg. I found myself thinking *Greg is really a lovable guy. We've been blessed with two wonderful sons. I very much enjoyed living with him.*

Studying that one photo brought back the kind of feelings I needed, feelings of hope and a future. Perhaps I would have enough hope to outweigh the risks of remarrying Greg again—but not without some respectable fears!

Joyce's mother didn't know how to behave after hearing that Greg was coming over to talk with Joyce. She didn't know whether to serve them cookies and tea, or just be absent. As it turned out, she served, and then she went into the bedroom to watch television with her husband.

Joyce and Greg settled onto the couch together in the living room. After some small talk, Greg told her about his plans to fly to Washington, D.C. on October 17, a week from Sunday. At the invitation of his sister Laurie and her husband Bill, he would be joining a group of Hawaii lawyers there just for fun. The trip would include a ceremony at the United States Supreme Court where the Hawaii lawyers would all appear and be admitted to practice in the Supreme Court by motion of a Supreme Court bar member from Hawaii.

In the back of Greg's mind the countdown continued. Engines were rumbling and roaring to life. The time had come for them to get married. He looked into Joyce's eyes and asked, "How would you like to come with me to Washington, D.C. a week from Sunday?" He saw her break into a modest, but bright smile.

Joyce responded quickly with warmth, saying, "I'd like that very much. The trip sounds like a wonderful opportunity!"

Then Greg added just as quickly, "As a honeymoon." Greg waited.

As Greg's last words sunk in, Joyce's face transitioned from a bright smile into a still, thoughtful look. For Greg, the moment seemed to stretch on endlessly. Then a little Mona Lisa smile came to Joyce's face, and looking into Greg's eyes, she said softly, "Okay." For Greg, that moment felt like lift-off—the real journey was now inevitably underway.

The scheduled trip to Washington, D.C. was just ten days away, which meant their wedding would have to be on Saturday evening, October 16. They would fly into Washington, D.C. the following morning.

For the first time in four and a half years, the two of them agreed. Joyce would find a dress and ask Greg's Aunt Julia to help her with flowers. Greg would call the church, arrange the ceremony, find appropriate rings, and get a new marriage license.

The next day Greg found matching wedding rings at a nearby Christian store. The rings had a cross, a dove, fruited vines, and conjoined circles, indicating the couple's unity with the Father's purpose in the Lord Jesus and His Holy Spirit. When Greg showed the rings to Joyce, she was pleased and excited.

The Methodist Church that Greg's family had helped start was available that Saturday night, and also for a rehearsal on Friday evening. Greg worked alongside the pastor to educate Geoff, now nine, and Todd, now six, on how to offer the Communion elements to people gathered for the ceremony.

Joyce found a simple cream-colored knee-length dress, which seemed just right for the occasion. Greg and Joyce planned a dinner reception for everyone at Beckham Grill in Pasadena. Greg made the arrangements. Greg's sister, Laurie, surprised them both by bringing hand-made maile wedding leis from a friend in Hawaii for each of them to wear during the ceremony. Even with the short notice, about seventy family and friends indicated they were able to join them at the wedding.

At the Friday evening rehearsal, Joyce welled up with tears when she practiced the "til death do us part" line. The force of those words affected her far differently this time than they did at their first wedding. She was much more in touch now with what those words *really meant*. This time there would be no turning back for either of them—no pretenses about making things work out *happily ever after.* These words were the *real deal*—their simple and naked vows of faith between them, before and with God.

On Saturday evening, just after six o'clock, the music played softly. Joyce and Greg entered the church together, each of them with a long maile lei draped around their neck. Geoff and Todd came in with them to the front of the church. Greg spoke first, and then Joyce, welcoming their assembled friends and family, explaining that in honor of the Lord who had renewed their lives, Communion would be served first to all. After that, the ceremony would proceed.

The four of them served the elements and the pastor led everyone to partake together. He thanked God for the reunion of Greg and Joyce's lives, and honored the Lord for reconciling people and restoring their lives when He is given the opportunity. Then, with the boys at their sides, Greg and Joyce were married, repeating the vows the minister gave to them. At the pronouncement of their becoming husband and wife, Greg and Joyce kissed one another and everyone cheered! *This was a day to remember.*

The dinner reception was thoroughly enjoyed by everyone. It seemed they all knew they were celebrating a mystery, because no one present had any knowledge of *how* this reunion had come to pass. Greg and Joyce barely understood it.

By 9:30, it was time for Greg and Joyce to leave. They would spend their first night together at the Hilton, then fly to D.C. in the morning.

They both looked for Geoff and Todd to say goodbye. Greg's mother would take the boys home with her afterwards. Each of them hugged Geoff who was thoroughly enjoying talking with family and friends at the party. They found Todd curled up asleep on a plush chair at the side of the room. Smiling at one another, they didn't wake him. Todd was in good hands. Instead, they grasped each other's hand, turned to the door, acknowledged a few well-wishers, and quietly walked out together into the cool October evening. Greg was thirty-four, Joyce was thirty-three.

Greg's Take

Our second wedding was one of the most authentic experiences of my entire life. It was the beginning of a dream *actually coming true*—because the Lord of All was the author of it all. God had prepared me, and He had prepared Joyce. He was the composer who had drawn each of us to that moment. God had drawn each of us to Himself, and then to each other, and then to the altar of the church, not as an end, but as a new beginning.

Today, I tell people, "Joyce and I have been married for forty-four years, with four and a half years off for bad behavior!" That's the way it feels to me. On the day of our second wedding ceremony, I knew we would have a lot to overcome. But I also had an *unshakeable peace* in the certainty that God was going to continue to help us every step of the way.

For Contemplation and Conversation

1. Are you able to stand back from the events of your life and see how God has been, and is involved in your life and your spouse's life—without your direct knowledge? How does this awareness help you appreciate the goodness of God and His purposes for *your life* and marriage?

2. What difference does it make for a person to say "yes" to God and "no" to himself or herself? Have you ever *known what God wanted* for you in contrast to what you wanted for yourself? What was that like?

10 Building a Marriage and Family on the Run

Joyce's and Greg's exit from the wedding dinner was peaceful and unscripted. Their first steps alone together in the clear night air were refreshing, especially after the frenzied week before the wedding. Inwardly, there were awkward steps, too. Greg and Joyce were on their way to Greg's promised D.C. honeymoon, but as well-acquainted strangers. The real work for each of them was now at hand—learning how to walk a lifetime together.

In D.C., Joyce was thrilled to find that Greg had upgraded their room to a honeymoon suite in the Mayflower Hotel, not far from the White House. The room was simply stunning, with warm wood furniture and soft yellow satin sheets on the four-poster bed. Joyce felt very special, and glad to share the beautiful suite with Greg, despite the uneasiness she felt about going to sleep together on the lovely satin sheets. Neither of them knew how to talk intimately with one another. They had no script.

After the formal ceremony at the Supreme Court, Greg and Joyce enjoyed cracking crab with Bill and Laurie on the Maryland shore. The Lincoln Memorial was an especially moving and memorable highlight. Greg wanted to shop for a new watch for Joyce, as her previous one had fallen off her wrist on Kauai when she had plunged feet-first into a lovely hidden pool earlier that year. After searching, Greg bought her a watch she liked, perhaps as an unconscious symbol of starting a new time together.

When their short honeymoon week was over, Joyce and Greg returned to his childhood home to begin their life together as a reunited family. Living with Greg's mother brought another new challenge. It had been just ten weeks since Brad's death. During those ten weeks, Greg had been heavily occupied trying to get a grip on the law firm. Joyce was trying to figure out how to manage the household together with Greg's mother, while Greg focused on the office.

The firm had three fulltime attorneys, besides Greg, plus a paralegal, four legal secretaries, a receptionist, two file clerks, and a part-time maintenance man. The firm occupied the second floor of a three-story office building. They had an in-house computerized accounting system and four top-end word processors and printers, all only partially paid for.

All of this was now Jim and Greg's responsibility, who hoped the firm's inflows of cash would match the outflows with Brad gone. Each day Greg sorted through his father's law work, moved the active cases forward, and reassured his father's former clients that all was well. As it turned out, during the twelve months after Brad's death, the outflows exceeded the inflows by about $110,000, which Jim and Greg covered by borrowing from Brad's personal receivables. That amount would eventually have to be collected from their future work and paid out to Greg's mother. Letting extra employees go and terminating unprofitable casework was both painful and necessary, and not very rewarding.

Joyce was also assessing their housing situation with Barbara. As sympathetic as Joyce felt for her mother-in-law, it soon became apparent that Barbara's generosity and their shared living arrangement would have to be temporary. Barbara was in her mid-fifties and well able to care for herself and her own home; so with Greg's consent, Joyce began a search for a rental house.

Within a month, Joyce found a large three-bedroom house on Oakwood Avenue, just ten blocks from Barbara's place. With Greg's approval, Joyce signed a three-year lease.

Right after Thanksgiving they moved and settled in with all their combined items. The house was ample for them, and in a very good location. Joyce's mother kindly gave them some needed furniture as a second wedding gift.

Now for the first time, Joyce and Greg were able to consider their sons' school situation as a couple in their own home. It was no longer necessary to drive them to the private school near Greg's Pasadena office. There was a good public elementary school near their home, one that all the neighborhood children attended. Joyce and Greg soon decided that it would be best for Geoff and Todd to transfer to the closer school. In January, they enrolled the boys at Paradise Canyon Elementary School, Geoff in fourth grade and Todd in first grade.

Along with Greg and Joyce, both boys were making major adjustments: another new school, another new house, another new church, and now living together with *both* of their parents! In the span of one year, Geoff and Todd had moved from Oahu to Kauai, from Kauai to the mountains, from the mountains to their grandmother's house and finally to Oakwood Avenue in La Cañada. These were turbulent times for them.

Within six months, Joyce and Greg learned about a new church start-up in their area which reminded Greg of North Shore Christian Fellowship, so they began to attend. Quite soon thereafter, too soon from Joyce's perspective, Greg unilaterally volunteered to lead an adult home-Bible-study group that would meet mid-week in their home. Joyce was surprised that even though they were now married, Greg still wouldn't listen or talk with her *before* taking on leadership roles. If Greg heard her words, it seemed he would reflexively defend himself rather than give credence to what she was saying. And if Joyce persisted, she found that Greg would go silent and withdraw. Even as a new creation in Christ, Greg had communication patterns that seemed to Joyce like the Greg of old.

Joyce's Take

It seemed everywhere Greg went, whether to church or social occasions, he was constantly asked to lead in various capacities. As a family we served together at the new church start-up by setting up chairs. We enjoyed that because we did it together. Greg and I had not yet developed a shared vision or purpose for our marriage, and as a result, we didn't know how or when to say, "No, thank you" to requests for our time, especially Greg's time. After all, we had just remarried!

We still didn't know how to talk together meaningfully as a couple. The four of us as a family needed to connect with one another to have a well-ordered home; to enjoy family fun, schoolwork, occasional hospitality and Greg's daily work. With too many outside commitments, Greg and I weren't making progress toward that long-range goal. We needed wise counsel, but we didn't know where to find it! I also needed to learn how to turn down requests from others graciously. My tendency was to follow my previous pattern of yielding to what others wanted. This was my way of feeling needed and important, but that habit never brought good to our family or to me.

Most people assumed that Greg and Joyce's miraculous reconciliation meant everything was now *just fine* for them. There were no older couples available in the start-up church to be marriage mentors for them. Their pastor was newly married himself. Each week his wife sat silently in the back row with her arms folded. Everyone knew she was far from happy about her husband's job.

Greg and Joyce sought mentoring from other sources, but they struck out. No one seemed available to give them the help they wanted and needed.

The voice that spoke most directly into their situation was the new *Focus on the Family* radio broadcast by Dr.

200

James Dobson. In terms of practical biblical advice, this daily broadcast was most helpful for them, providing each of them with good spiritual insights into family life, marriage and parenting.

One of those broadcasts in early 1984 presented the perspective of home school pioneers Raymond and Dorothy Moore. Their message was that parents could educate their children as well as or better than traditional schools by homeschooling them, particularly boys. Joyce wanted to learn more and said she might like to start homeschooling Geoff and Todd the following school year. To her surprise, Greg was very supportive and in agreement. Geoff was doing well academically in fifth grade, but he was not thrilled with the social scene there.

The Moores hosted a homeschool conference a few weeks later in Pasadena. After hearing their presentations and reading the available literature, Joyce and Greg became convinced that homeschooling the boys would be a very good and viable option for them, if it could be arranged. Not only would it benefit the boys educationally, it would allow them to bond with Joyce in ways that would help all three of them overcome the separation they had endured during the four-and-a-half years between the divorce and the remarriage.

Greg was concerned about the legalities. Homeschooling was possible under California law if the local district adopted an independent study program, but their district would have to want the program. The superintendent of their district, a longtime friend of Greg's dad, welcomed Greg and Joyce into his office to talk about the idea. Although he seemed skeptical about how their boys' socialization needs would be met, he said he would be glad to support their request, adding that he was confident that Greg and Joyce would do what was best for their sons.

The independent study program was approved at the School Board's August meeting, and Joyce and Greg signed an educational agreement with the district concerning their sons' studies. In September, Geoff began the sixth grade and Todd started third grade at the Oakwood House with Joyce as their teacher and Greg as their principal. They were the only homeschooling students in the district's program that year. Homeschooling became the family's new core activity. Joyce schooled both boys through the eighth grade, Geoff for three years and Todd for six years until he started high school in September of 1990.

Bonding and Connecting as a Family

One evening the following spring, in their first year of homeschooling, Greg was reading aloud to the boys from C. S. Lewis' *Chronicles of Narnia*. Greg had first started reading the series to the boys when they were in Honolulu in 486-B, but life had placed the series on hold. The series was highly enjoyable for them all, including Joyce! Reading them aloud provided Greg a rare opportunity to express his creative side. He gave each Narnia character a unique voice as he read, which delighted the boys.

This particular evening, Greg and the boys were nestled inside a new family-backpacking tent Greg had set up in the living room. He had set it up there to glue the seams for rain protection. Now the tent was suddenly an enjoyable place for reading aloud before bed. Joyce was proud of Greg's desire and his ability to read to the family each evening in a way that engaged the boys' imaginations and made their family times so very special. As she listened to Greg's reading from the kitchen, she thought *there the three of them are—Greg reading aloud in a different voice for each character—and our boys are spellbound and laughing!* This was such a sweet and meaningful family memory. But Joyce also felt a pang. She couldn't help but wonder *where do I fit in this family picture?* Although she didn't talk much about them, Joyce was occasionally plagued by self-doubts.

During their four-year separation, Joyce's visits with the boys were usually in a mode of having fun together, whereas Greg had been the family provider for their food, shelter, homework help, church attendance, and discipline. Now the four of them needed to *become a family*—a father, mother, and two sons.

Joyce's Take

I was a new follower of Christ, trying to understand what it meant for Greg to be the spiritual leader of our relationship and our family. Greg seemed to think a Christian wife should be seen, but not heard. I felt labeled with roles that didn't fit me, labels I didn't want!

I wondered who I was and who I *could be* for our family. As it was, my role was limited to planning the menu, marketing, decorating, loading the dishwasher, and teaching the boys their lessons. I wanted to be an *actual partner* with Greg—a partner with Greg in life and partners together as parents. I didn't know how to talk with Greg about this, mostly because I was fairly certain that Greg would not be able or willing to be an *equal partner* with me. I was feeling sidelined in many respects, and uncomfortable... but at the same time, I knew there was no walking away.

The tent in the living room was being prepared for their first big family adventure—a backpack trip in the Sierra Nevada Mountains. It had been two-and-a-half years since their remarriage. Although Joyce had been backpacking before, she agreed to this kind of vacation only if Greg and the boys would plan the menu and cook the meals—otherwise it wouldn't be a vacation for her. To her pleasant surprise, Greg was very supportive and readily agreed to handle the menu and meal prep. Joyce was thrilled, and she agreed to wash all the dishes.

Greg took full charge of planning and executing the six-day backpack trip. It was to be a two-day hike out of Mineral King Valley, going over Franklin Pass at 11,800 feet on the second day—then two nights at Little Claire Lake. They would then retrace their steps for two days and return to Mineral King.

Greg's backpacking book said they would all be just fine carrying packs, as long as each person's load was limited to twenty-five percent of his or her body weight. They each packed their own clothing and equipment from the list that Greg put together. Without checking with Greg, Joyce decided to add in extra clothing, assuming she would want a clean shirt for each day.

When all of the clothing, food, snacks, and cooking equipment were packed, it was time for Greg to check the weight that each family member would carry. When Greg weighed the packs, he had to remove a lot of food and cooking equipment from Joyce and the boys' packs to meet their weight limits.

Maybe some of their clothing is extra, Greg thought, but he wanted this first trip to be a success. He thought *what if Joyce or the boys really need the extra clothing?* Silently, Greg decided to carry the extra twenty-one pounds in his own pack, giving him sixty-eight pounds to carry instead of his limit of forty-seven pounds. He didn't say anything about this to Joyce or the boys, as he was confident he wouldn't have any real problems with it. After all, he was a former pro athlete, body surfer, and now a healthy thirty-six-year-old *man*. Greg felt slightly heroic as he carefully stuffed all the remaining items into his own pack.

Their backpack trip was memorable—fishing in crystal clear alpine lakes, marvelous mountain vistas, tranquil campsites, and trails laden with wildflowers. These lovely sights contrasted with Greg's near-total collapse upon their arrival to set up camp at Little Claire Lake.

Achy, feverish, and completely spent, Greg lay down on his sleeping bag in the tent while the boys began fishing in the lake. Joyce pulled out the first aid kit and took his temperature. It was 102.8 degrees! She gave him some aspirin, then gave him some food and kissed him goodnight, hoping and praying for his healing.

Joyce wondered *what bug does he have? How sick is he? What would I do if he doesn't get better? We're miles from habitation, with no way of contacting anyone!* Their only option would be to hike out for help. As Joyce and the boys went to bed, they prayed together for Greg's recovery. Mercifully, Greg slept calmly throughout the night.

When Greg woke the next morning, there was no sign of any continuing illness. Joyce and the boys were so pleased! Joyce asked Greg what he thought this sickness might have been. After a moment, Greg sheepishly confessed how he had violated the weight limit, guessing he must have just overdone it. "Dad!" the boys and Joyce protested. After receiving a scolding from each of them for his foolishness, Greg gave in. A new pledge was made by all of them: "None of us will *ever* carry more than twenty-five percent of our body weight in our backpacks!"

Little Claire Lake was the first of many adventurous trips their family took together over the next seven years, summer and winter—until Geoff graduated from high school. Both boys swam regularly with a YMCA Swim Team, and Joyce and Greg enjoyed planning regular one-on-one, parent-son weekend outings with each son. Their family also participated in mission trips to the Navajo Reservation sponsored by their church. These adventures built strong bonds between them and provided new friendships that helped heal the wounds and communication gaps the four of them had endured from their years of separation. Alongside the lesson that had been learned, their first family backpack to Little Claire Lake was filled with great memories.

Home and Office Collide

On the business front, three years after Brad's death things were still difficult. Greg and Jim had stopped the financial hemorrhaging at the firm, and were just beginning to make ends meet—but it was an ongoing battle for them. The building had been sold, and the firm's two-year lease had only one more year to run. Greg and Jim and their wives were seriously considering taking their law practice out of the Los Angeles area. If there were ever a prime time to make such a move, this would be it.

Joyce was excited about the idea of moving the practice and their home to a quieter place with a small-town lifestyle. She was hoping such a move might give her and Greg time and space to smooth out some bothersome wrinkles that kept haunting their relationship.

Unfortunately, Greg and Jim finally decided they weren't able to take on the risks of moving the practice out of Pasadena. They assessed their odds of surviving a move as a two-man team at about fifty-fifty. They reasoned that if they stayed in Pasadena, they at least could work with existing clients who paid their bills. There were no clients available yet in any of the new locations they had discussed, and Greg's mother still needed to be paid off. The two of them agreed to stay in Pasadena and make a go of their practice there. Even more unfortunately, their wives were not part of their final discussions. Greg did not review the facts with Joyce before he and Jim made their decision.

When Greg announced the final decision to Joyce in early December, she was stunned as well as terribly disappointed. After all, with no knowledge about the financial considerations Joyce couldn't understand why she and Greg had looked for office space in Atascadero and even looked at homes and property for sale. *What was wrong with Greg? How could he have made such a decision with Jim and not talked with her about it? What was the reasoning for turning away from this opportunity? What were the risks?*

Greg had no capacity to endure Joyce's challenging questions, or her verbal assaults that felt to him like mischaracterizations. Feeling frustrated, Greg refused to talk any further with her about it. He told her that their decision had been made and there was nothing more to consider.

In the wake of this shutdown, Joyce tried to nurse her wounded heart back to life. She simply had no skills on how to communicate through Greg's stonewalling. She wondered *how can my conversations with Greg become more mutual, effective, and complete?*

About the same time, their start-up church entered a deep crisis. The stress of pastoral church ministry turned out to be too great for the pastor and his wife. They were bailing out of the ministry, and likely breaking up as a couple. Greg was asked to serve on the church board to help the church through the transition. As was his pattern, Greg accepted the request before discussing it with Joyce or considering with her the broader ramifications.

Building a New Home

Since it appeared to Joyce their family would be stuck in the L.A. area for the foreseeable future, she began cautiously looking with Greg to purchase a home, as the lease on the Oakwood Avenue house was expiring soon. Greg had some money coming due from the purchaser of 486-B which they could use for a down payment. Joyce wanted a place with access to trails, and possibly space for a horse or two. She thought that might help cover for the loss of the rural lifestyle she had envisioned for them.

One Saturday morning, on his way to a church board meeting, Greg noticed some open space, and a few small horse paddocks here and there among the homes in the low rolling hills between Burbank and the San Gabriel Mountains. His interest was piqued. After the meeting, Greg drove around, wondering what the area was called. When he got home, he told Joyce about his find and they called their realtor. "It's called Shadow Hills," she said. "There are some nice horse properties out there for far less than where you've been living for the past three years. Sure, I can help you look for a place there."

Greg and Joyce began looking in Shadow Hills and found a place with some acreage that ran through a secluded valley surrounded by grassy hills. There was space there for keeping two horses. Having grown up riding horses, Joyce found the area very appealing. The property was near the wide-open Hansen Dam recreation area, a terrific location for horseback riding, and mountain biking for the boys. After arranging to continue homeschooling with their previous district, they decided to make an offer on the property, and it was accepted. The small, outdated house there would be torn down and replaced. Greg and Joyce planned to work with an architect to design and build an appropriate home for their family. They would borrow the necessary funds through a mortgage on the property.

Over the next six months plans were drawn with an architect and necessary contractors were found. Greg and Joyce located a used sixty-foot house trailer, with a pop-out living room, and moved it onto the property to live in while the existing house was demolished and their new house was constructed. At the right time, they would watch a bulldozer completely demolish and haul away the existing house, including its foundation. This would be a real adventure— sharing family life together *in a trailer*!

As Joyce and Greg's housing plans were gradually coming together, their little start-up church was *not* recovering. From Shadow Hills, it was now a fifteen-mile drive to the church, and Joyce could see that her family was starving for spiritual care. Greg was slow to accept this. Finally Greg promised Joyce that as soon as a new pastor was hired, he would step down from the board and they could find a different church.

A new pastor was hired just as the framing began to rise on the concrete foundation of Greg and Joyce's new house, releasing them to find a new church. The church they chose to attend delighted ten year old Todd who said he enjoyed his Sunday class and the other kids who went there. Greg and Joyce remarked to each other about the evident love, character, and warmth of the pastor and his wife, who were in their early sixties. This change was a relief for Joyce who was thrilled to be attending a church that offered true pastoral care, the first such church since her remarriage to Greg.

Their trailer-house adventure in Shadow Hills became more stressful than Greg or Joyce originally anticipated. The demolition of the existing home could not begin until *after* they obtained a City permit to live in the trailer during construction. They had to appear before the City Planning Commission in Los Angeles to request a special waiver before the permit was finally granted. Meanwhile, Joyce had found two riding horses that were now penned in the pipe-stalls that came with the property. To make way for the dump trucks, the horses and their stalls had to be moved to within a few feet of Joyce and Greg's bedroom in the trailer. This experience gave both of them a whole new appreciation of the sounds and smells of horse life.

When demolition finally got underway, the family escaped the noise and dust for a few days by taking a late spring ski trip to Mammoth Mountain. As they began the drive home from the cozy ski condo with its well-equipped kitchen and quiet vistas, Joyce burst into tears. Before anyone had time to ask her why, Joyce volunteered, "And now we go back to the trailer!" Life in a cramped, leaky trailer while building their dream house was clearly an adventure, but *only to a point.*

While Greg kept business moving at the office, the responsibility for the construction of the new house fell on Joyce's shoulders. Todd was with her, homeschooling in the trailer and watching the way his mother functioned as the general contractor. He enjoyed observing the builders, bricklayers, and plumbers assemble the house. He was also a good sport after accidently breaking his nose during a practice-run with the plumber's pipe-cutting tool. Joyce saved her necessary downtown excursions for building permits until the afternoons, when Todd and Geoff were at swimming practice with their YMCA swim team.

When the new house was finally completed a year later, the family's activities expanded further. By now Geoff was so good with plants that Greg and Joyce decided to help him install a greenhouse. A distant uncle had given Geoff dozens of beautiful orchid plants, and Geoff was excited to continue growing and cultivating them.

Their summer backpacking trips continued in the High Sierras, some of them off-trail. Greg taught both the boys how to read topo maps, after which Geoff and Todd enjoyed planning and navigating short excursions to and through high places. Both of them grew to appreciate their Mom's sense of humor and willing ability to follow their lead and do some hand-over-hand rock climbing!

One of their most memorable trips was Geoff's idea to climb Mount Whitney. It was an eleven-day trek from the Cottonwood Lake trailhead. Each night before going to sleep, Greg would pull out their current book (*The Dry Divide* by Ralph Moody) and read a chapter or two aloud by the light of his headlamp. On day eight, fresh fish was planned as the only entree on the dinner menu. That meant catch fish or eat tomorrow's trail snacks for supper! The four of them fished all the way around Middle Crabtree Lake, two miles in circumference. It was already three o'clock and nothing had been caught. Dinner was looking slim.

Something finally hit Joyce's spinner just before four o'clock. "It's a big one!" she cried out. A moment later, she pulled hard on her rod and flipped a sixteen-inch Golden Trout over her head and out onto the rocky shore. A moment later Greg landed a twenty-incher. Geoff and Todd were delighted, pulling in several more. They could hardly believe what was happening. These fish were the largest trout any of them had ever seen—and all them had been caught in the *last half hour* of their fishing day. The catch supplied them an abundance of food for their final ascent to the top of Mount Whitney, where they would spend the night for Todd's eleventh birthday.

These family adventures—and planning them—helped build strength, flexibility, and connectedness into their relationships with one another. These relational qualities would prove invaluable when Greg and Joyce addressed some of the deeper relational issues that had remained hidden below the surface all along.

Digging into Reality

These were issues that would not go away unless and until they were intentionally addressed. Greg would often find himself on his knees in prayer after a failed conversation with Joyce, asking God what to do. For Greg, the best guidance he knew was found in the Bible in Ephesians 5. His responsibility was to love Joyce, not to judge her or rule over her; however, these verses did not help Greg to learn how to *communicate better* with Joyce.

Greg's Take

In my childhood, my parents never called a plumber or an electrician. If something wasn't working, Dad fixed it. My dad did *all our repairs*! I emerged from my childhood with a deep and abiding desire to *try* to fix things.

In many ways, that was my approach to my relationship with Joyce. I *wanted* to find the broken part and fix it, but I couldn't discern what I needed to repair to make the problem go away. Most of all, I just wanted things to work!

Even though I knew that *loving* Joyce was the way to go, I would *still* approach our problems with a desire to find and fix the broken parts. And one of the *things* I knew needed fixing was our communication. I didn't understand that my approach itself needed fixing, or how much change that would require of me.

Much of the communication between Greg and Joyce was marked by overtones of stress. Just simple communication about mundane questions, or everyday mood swings, were enough to set off a conflict, which sometimes was loud and turbulent.

One day Todd—who was a skilled observer of his parents—bluntly advised them, "Hey, Mom and Dad, stop arguing! You are *saying exactly the same thing*, in different ways!" Before this, Greg and Joyce had been oblivious to the fact that they might be saying the same thing differently. They had only been aware of their differences. This long-standing issue of their failed communication was a minefield that definitely needed clearing.

Joyce took the initiative, asking Greg for a special birthday present. She invited him to come with her to a professional counselor to learn how to communicate better as a couple. When Greg unexpectedly and without any hesitation said yes, Joyce smiled and immediately set up their first counseling appointment. Their first meeting with the counselor opened their eyes. Greg was forty-one and Joyce was forty. Although it had been *twenty years* since they were first married—finally, they were obtaining help in learning how *to listen* and *really hear* one another.

Learning to Communicate

After getting acquainted with them and their background, the counselor asked Greg to say something objective but personal to Joyce, but to say only one sentence. Then she asked Joyce to repeat back to Greg what he had said to her. After hearing Joyce's answer, the counselor turned to Greg.

"Did she get it?" the counselor asked him.

"No," Greg answered, a little bit surprised and embarrassed.

"I didn't think so either. Okay, try it again. Say it again to Joyce."

Greg said it again. Joyce repeated what she heard. Same result. This was repeated five times before Joyce was able to repeat back exactly what Greg had said to her.

In another exercise, the counselor asked Greg and Joyce very objective questions concerning their relationship and their marriage. They each gave their answers. The counselor asked Joyce, "Do you think Greg understood my question and answered it appropriately?"

Joyce replied, "I don't think so."

Greg realized that he was so absorbed in his own perspective that he could not be objective about his relationship with Joyce. This was an eye-opener for him—one he was glad to be learning, even at this late date! This process of discovery also revealed that Greg found it difficult to acknowledge his lack of consistent emotional connection with

Joyce and his tendency to retreat or withdraw from her when their conversations became over-heated.

The counselor helped them by using simple metaphors, such as "Greg has his garage door closed," to describe when Greg had stopped listening in order to protect himself. Joyce understood what that meant. Greg also understood it. What the counselor advised, however, was that Joyce refrain from *pounding* on Greg's garage door. The counselor let Joyce know there was no way for her to *require* Greg to open up. Joyce would therefore need to *give up trying* to do so.

Furthermore, Joyce believed that by *telling* Greg outright what she wanted or needed, she was being self-centered—extracting romance from Greg, rather than allowing him to offer love to her *without her asking for it*. As it was, when Greg failed to read Joyce's romantic mind, she would let him know that by getting in his face. Greg would then retreat and slam down his garage door!

The counselor advised Joyce that she must learn to tell Greg what she wanted from him, without feeling apologetic for her own needs. The counselor asked, "How can Greg know what you want if you don't tell him?"

Joyce's Take

I was embarrassed it took me *five times* to repeat back exactly what Greg had said to me! I was so stuck in my own assumptions. I *thought* I knew what he was saying without listening closely enough to *hear the words* accurately. I suddenly recognized I had a huge problem with listening.

In my family growing up, everyone voiced their feelings and opinions, whether invited to do so or not. No one paid much attention to the content. All of us wanted to be heard, but no one was listening. The words we spoke were not very important. What carried the day in my family was the *emotional content*, not what was actually said! Not so with Greg's family.

At times, the volatile atmosphere in my family seemed to be tinged with violence, both in tone and behavior. Discipline was direct and confrontation was to be *expected* as a regular part of daily life. I didn't know anything about diplomacy until Greg taught me the concept. In my family, there was no diplomatic behavior—we were all in each other's face with our viewpoints and demands. Nothing much was subtle.

As an adult, I had difficulty refraining from speaking before I could think through the words. One weekend Greg asked me, "What are you trying to *accomplish* with the words you're speaking to me? What do you want your words to do?" This was the very first time I knew that when a person says something they want to *accomplish something*. I had never imagined linking my words to some kind of goal—ideally, to make things *better*. Realizing and accepting that my childhood family's communication was so dysfunctional was difficult.

There I was, already in my forties with two sons, realizing that I didn't know how to communicate purposefully, authentically and meaningfully! Beyond that, it had also become clear that I was married to a sincerely well-intentioned man who had a very different communication style than mine. I had so much to learn!

A Key Parenting Lesson

A year later, Greg and Joyce passed their first major test of their improved ability to communicate with one another. Geoff was a high school senior, pushing curfew boundaries set by his parents, and causing conflict between them. Greg and Joyce had differing, strongly-held views about the best way to discipline Geoff. Unable to reach a decision, they started to argue—Joyce pushing and Greg withdrawing— over what to do to enforce their curfew limit with Geoff.

215

Greg's Take

Our counselor had easily exposed my propensity to make pronouncements to Joyce without accommodating Joyce's viewpoint or consulting with her in advance. This was startling for me to learn—that I would do better to consult with Joyce before I announced my plans for us. I never intended to hurt Joyce or to overstep my bounds with her. I just didn't know there were boundaries! It had never occurred to me that my caring, husbandly role meant I was to be inclusive! I thought my leadership role was to make pronouncements and announcements! There was a lot more to communication in marriage than I had ever anticipated. I had no idea that effective communication was supposed to be relational. I didn't know myself as a relational sort of guy—I knew myself as a fix-it guy!

On top of that, in my childhood home everything was placid and ideal on the surface. So when Joyce would get in my face about things, I didn't know how to respond. I would become overwhelmed and retreat into my garage and pull down the door!

It was a breakthrough moment for Joyce when she recognized what she was doing and quit pushing on Greg. Instead, she said, "Let's talk to Pastor Stiles to see what he says. I'd be willing to follow his advice." Greg thought this was a good idea.

When they met with their pastor, Joyce complained to him, saying she wanted Greg to be stronger—to stand up to Geoff with clear enough boundaries and consequences so that Geoff would come home on time. Greg wouldn't bend toward this idea, as he was very uncomfortable operating in a tough-guy mode, especially now with Geoff as a senior in high school.

Their pastor offered a completely different type of advice: "The most important value for Geoff in this situation is that *the two of you agree.* That's what's important. There is no perfect curfew time and no right discipline for Geoff breaking your curfew. Whatever curfew and consequence the two of you agree on is good enough! Every child instinctively knows *all I have to do is get my parents to disagree with each other, and one of them will come over to my side. This way, I'll probably get my own way!* Agreement between the two of you is the very best plan of all. Do this, and your whole family will succeed."

The advice their pastor offered was a unique concept to Joyce who had hoped for some power to be exercised. Greg had previously understood that all parental decisions had to be black or white, right or wrong. *What?* Greg thought *there's no right answer to this problem?* Neither Joyce nor Greg had imagined that a *unified parental agreement* would be enough—even exactly what was needed. Whatever the two of them mutually decided together would always be the best answer.

After some prayer, brainstorming, and a talk with Joyce's parents, Greg and Joyce presented Geoff a firm curfew time and a consequence if he violated it. If Geoff chose to come home late, he would need to move out—to Joyce's parents' guesthouse.

And that's what happened—Geoff stayed out too late, moved to his grandparents' guesthouse, and returned home within a week. He wasn't defiant. Rather, he was matter-of-fact in his decision to live at home with his family and not with his grandparents—home was *better!* From then on, Geoff kept to his curfew.

This episode gave Greg and Joyce a new perspective. Asking their son to move out would previously have been considered a parental failure. Now they learned that agreeing on a mutually *acceptable* boundary for their son, and *keeping their agreement* about the results, had ultimately worked, even though Geoff's obedience had not followed a straight line. Greg and Joyce had seen Scripture in action: "Let the wise listen and add to their learning, and let the discerning get guidance" (Proverbs 1:5). In this parental crisis, their pastor's guidance led them into a new realm of mutuality and freedom that would change their lives in coming years.

Finding Alone Time Together

Like many couples with children, Joyce and Greg felt challenged in their desire to find time alone together, especially after Greg began his longer commute from Shadow Hills to Pasadena. Joyce was clear with Greg about her relational needs. She wanted just twenty minutes alone with Greg each day for the two of them to catch up and be adults together. For Greg, this didn't seem possible! His life was so tightly scheduled there simply wasn't a twenty-minute slot before things got rolling in the morning or after the boys went to bed in the evening—but with faith and patience, the two of them came up with three solutions:

- First, Greg resigned from several non-profit boards and Bar committees on which he had been serving.
- Second, Greg went to work earlier once a week so he could share a late breakfast with Joyce at a nice Pasadena hotel after Geoff and Todd were at school. They both looked forward to these private breakfasts together.
- Third, and this item was the most difficult—and rewarding—for them. Each quarter Greg and Joyce scheduled a Friday and Saturday night away together. Both sets of grandparents agreed to trade off keeping the boys for them, on alternating quarters.

Each quarter Joyce was challenged to keep to their plan. She *enjoyed* her daily routine with their sons. But after six months, and the first two weekends Greg and Joyce took away, they both realized how *incredibly important* those two nights away were for their marriage. These weekend times alone were exactly what the two of them had needed for a very long time. As challenging as they were to orchestrate, these dates were an investment that enriched their vision and planning. The practice paid them immediate relational dividends as a couple.

For Contemplation and Conversation

1. What are some of the main challenges you face in trying to find time alone with your spouse? What are your main stumbling blocks?

2. What ideas or other resources might your friends or study group offer so that you and your spouse can get away and reconnect?

3. Greg had some ongoing difficulties talking with Joyce about his work. What communication difficulties typically surface when you and your spouse discuss your work, or the boundary between home and work? What are some new or creative ways that could be used to address this important topic?

4. What unique problems do *parents* face in communicating? What have you learned that helps the two of you make time to talk or reassess your priorities?

5. After a time of separation—even if traveling apart for only a short time—what helps you and your spouse bond back together? What is it that ties you together when you're apart?

11   A Family Takes Wing

The summer Geoff graduated from high school, all four Millikans biked together along California's Mendocino coast where the scenery was especially lovely—with stands of tall redwoods, shady glens, and winding inland valleys. The excursion offered all of them time to relax and enjoy the northern coast of California to the fullest. The only problem they faced was the occasional danger of heavily loaded logging trucks roaring past. They made a mental note for the future to avoid bike touring on any road used by logging trucks.

Geoff departed in mid-September for Pahi, New Zealand, where he joined others in the Youth With a Mission Discipleship Training School (DTS). He was scheduled to be gone until the following March, and to be away from easy communication most of that time. His group's outreach would be in remote areas of the South Pacific and Australia.

With Geoff gone, their home felt strangely empty to Joyce. As Christmas approached, Joyce wasn't able to bring herself to decorate the house, and she wondered why. Then she realized her reluctance was an unconscious expression of her sorrow over Geoff's departure and absence. Even so, with Todd still living at home, life was good. Todd was a self-starter who enjoyed school, athletics, church activities, and people in general. As a sophomore in high school, he was growing tall and strong—and developing his own talents.

In March when Geoff completed his DTS and flew back from New Zealand, his parents and Todd met him in Honolulu where they enjoyed reuniting for several days together in a modest B&B tucked away on the windward side of Oahu. Greg and Joyce immediately noticed how Geoff had matured. He had gathered assurance, balance and perspective on his life objectives. Even though Geoff had been the youngest member of his DTS team, the team had selected him to serve as their team's finance manager during their multi-month, international outreach.

When the family returned home and settled in, Geoff was on his own schedule. He worked part-time at a sporting goods store and took on a full class load at a local junior college—aiming to transfer to Cal Poly San Luis Obispo. Both Greg and Joyce celebrated Geoff's mature outlook on life, but several weeks later, Greg was taken aback when Geoff approached him to ask him a question about their house.

"Dad, who owns this house?" Geoff inquired.

Greg looked at him, puzzled for a moment, "What do you mean?"

"Right," Geoff replied, "I know you and Mom own this house. But what I mean is, who *owns* this house, you or the bank? If the Lord asked you to leave here and go on a mission somewhere else, could you follow His direction? Or would you have to stay and keep working to make the monthly payments to the bank?"

When Greg understood Geoff's question, he felt a little sheepish. "Well, in that sense, the bank owns it. You're right. I couldn't just up and leave at this point for any length of time. We don't have enough savings to make the payments unless I'm working."

Geoff nodded his appreciation for this answer and didn't press the matter any further. A seed, however, was planted in Greg's mind. He and Joyce had never considered such a question when they bought the property and built the new house. Greg wondered *how could we consider following a new direction of the Lord, when we are so heavily encumbered with a large house, two cars, two horses, a horse trailer, financial demands at the office, plus a sizable mortgage?*

During Geoff's absence, Greg and Joyce had accepted a request by their church to advise and oversee its college-career ministry. With Geoff now college-age and Todd soon-to-be, they thought this ministry would be a good fit. It was their first official church responsibility in six years since Greg had resigned from the board of their former church. Their current church had a strong commitment to mission work—more than fifty percent of the church's annual budget. The church also emphasized the importance of sending its young people into Christian service. That aspect of the college-career ministry excited Joyce and Greg. They were in ministry together *and* in agreement about it this time!

Leading the college-career group was a new and satisfying challenge for Joyce and Greg. They had never done anything like this before, and yet they were enthusiastic about the opportunity to become acquainted with and positively influence several dozen young adults for the Lord. The group was hungry for whatever time and content Joyce and Greg could give them, and they were both on the lookout for suitable ideas and content. Greg heard from a friend about a highly regarded course, called "Perspectives on the World Christian Movement." His friend said it would revolutionize their understanding of Christian mission.

When Greg looked into the course, it sounded very good indeed—an eighteen-week, college-level course presented by the U.S. Center for World Mission based in Pasadena. The next session would be taught at Lake Avenue Church in Pasadena, beginning in January. If Perspectives measured up to its billing, there would be plenty for Joyce and Greg to share with their college-career group.

When January arrived, Joyce and Greg both enrolled in the course. Week by week, their eyes were opened to a missional perspective on the Scriptures and on God's actions in the world, past and present. Both of them were moved by what they were learning and they sensed that their lives would somehow be changed as a result. Joyce wondered how God might be leading her personally through the course content.

In the fourth week of the course, Joyce received shocking news of Martha's sudden death. Martha had taken her own life. She and Marv had divorced several years previously. After that, Martha's behavior had become increasingly erratic. Although Joyce had tried to maintain contact with Martha, that had become very difficult. Now Martha was irretrievably and terribly gone! Her suicide left Joyce confused and disoriented. Lacking anyone close who could understand how she felt, Joyce unconsciously suppressed her natural need to grieve, and just plowed ahead with life and the Perspectives course.

The course was guiding Greg and Joyce to see the importance of an *intentional lifestyle*. Using the metaphor of a luxury ocean liner, they were told about the RMS Queen Mary, which carried 1,750 passengers with 1,250 crewmembers during peacetime, but had transported 15,000 soldiers and 500 crewmembers during World War II. Class members were asked to consider the lifestyle each of them was pursuing, whether it was one of peacetime luxury or wartime efficiency? For Greg, this metaphor immediately brought up Geoff's question, "Who owns this house?"

Both Greg and Joyce soon became convinced that a more economical, and compact lifestyle would allow them more time, talent, and treasure to invest in God's mission. As the end of the Perspectives course neared, they put their heads together to consider how extra things that were devouring their resources might be peeled away. An idea soon surfaced. They wondered *what about living in the small office downstairs from Greg's Pasadena law offices? We could turn that into an apartment!* This change would eliminate Greg's forty-minute commute and let them test out a compact lifestyle. Geoff would soon leave for college in San Luis Obispo, and Todd was entering his senior year at high school. With their sons' assent, they decided to give it a try.

They set up the apartment, with plans to move there in late summer, unaware that their church's new youth pastor had already decided to take over leadership of the college-career group in June. When they heard that news, Joyce and Greg were seriously disappointed. After all, they had taken the Perspectives course in order to serve the college-career group! But because of the value they had gained from the Perspectives course, they went ahead with the move, being persuaded by faith that God had something good in it for them.

After leasing out their home in Shadow Hills, Joyce, Greg and Todd moved into the 380-square-foot apartment downstairs from Greg's office and Geoff headed for Cal Poly San Luis Obispo. The move challenged all of them. Geoff and Todd helped by moving nearly all the family furniture into storage. Observant Geoff quipped that this was probably one of the few times ever that parents had *left the nest* before their kids did! Although both Geoff and Todd were being uprooted, Greg and Joyce hoped that God's good purposes would somehow be fulfilled by what they were doing.

Todd set up his own space in the apartment and launched into his senior year in high school in his customary energetic, but low-key way—playing varsity water polo, earning good grades, heading up his high school's student Christian club, and singing in the school's madrigal choir. The change was not so easy or straightforward for Greg or Joyce, or for Geoff. Most of their things were necessarily in storage. The move had reduced their family living space by eighty percent.

Grief Counseling for Joyce

Their new proximity to Greg's office brought Joyce much closer to Greg's daily existence, yet she felt as distanced from his law practice as ever. In her work as a dental hygienist, Joyce was now driving more than forty minutes each way. She felt frustrated by that. Also she had not yet come to terms with Martha's death. Joyce was feeling increasingly frustrated about this and many other things, including her relationship with some of her family-of-origin. Joyce didn't know anyone that she could talk safely with about these things, but she listened regularly to a live Christian counseling program on the radio.

One day on the program, Joyce heard about something called a panic attack. The program's timing was providential, because she experienced such an attack less than two weeks later. She recognized the symptoms—heart racing, as in fear, but nothing nearby to cause that symptom. The apartment was quiet. She concluded God must have prepared her for this event.

Joyce immediately picked up the phone and called the Christian Counseling Center, saying she had just experienced a panic attack and she didn't like it. She asked about coming to the Center. The Center recommended that she take part in a ten-day residential program as soon as possible. A session was starting the next week, and there was an opening for her.

Psychological counseling was not yet part of Joyce or Greg's church world. Church people generally did not perceive themselves as candidates for counseling. Joyce had grown up in a family where such counseling was resisted owing to fears of social stigma.

When Joyce told Greg what had happened and shared the information she learned from the Counseling Center, Greg felt a little frightened, but he agreed without hesitation to support her going to the clinic. Their first counseling experience had been very helpful for the two of them. He hoped this experience would be equally good for Joyce. Greg told her that he and Todd would hold down the fort while she was away.

A few days later, Greg drove Joyce to the Christian Counseling Center. It was three weeks before Christmas. If asked, Greg was prepared to explain to their parents (and any others) that Joyce was attending an educational conference in Orange County.

Greg visited Joyce after five days, a little unsure what to expect since they had not talked. They went out to dinner and enjoyed catching up, and Joyce affirmed her progress so far. Both of them felt somewhat inhibited—after all, there were five more days to go. Their reunion was far happier when Greg picked Joyce up at the end of the ten-day program. She was relieved, having regained her footing. Joyce felt much better prepared for her next season of life.

Joyce's Take

During those ten days, I was learning *to be myself!* Prior to my counseling at the clinic, I thought the whole world was watching me, everyone seeking to expose my weaknesses, and then judge me for my faults and flaws. As a result of my fears, I had walked through life covered with emotional armor—as much as I could muster! I didn't want to be hurt, so I thought I had to be stronger than steel.

Yet, after the clinic, *I knew who I was* in Christ Jesus! I had begun to feel tender, vulnerable, and soft. I had gained understanding about the many painful things that had happened to me. I learned that going forward I *was capable* of surviving such things. Being emotionally hurt would not be fatal.

God took good care of me. To be free of my symptoms, I needed to unpack the anger I had harbored against my mother, Greg, and against Geoff. I didn't *want* to be angry with these people I loved, but the anger was there. I didn't tell anybody other than Greg and Todd where I was going or why. Both of them supported me in getting the help I needed.

Part of the therapy I received involved writing *unsent letters* to express myself to those who had hurt me, telling them as fully as possible what each of them had done—

and the impact of their behavior on my life—especially *what I had lost* and could never regain. None of my letters would be delivered or mailed. Writing the letters, I *owned up* to all that I'd lost—it involved a necessary process of grieving. Amazingly, when my sorrow was accessed and poured out, the grieving somehow freed me from the hurt and anger I had habitually pressed down inside. I had carried it secretly inside me for far too long—especially in relation to my mother.

Todd had applied to three colleges—one nearby, one in the Midwest, and the other on the East Coast. Greg and Joyce toured two of them with Todd in late March to help him decide. Although the choice was difficult, Todd ultimately chose to attend Wheaton College near Chicago.

After returning from their college tour, the three of them sought to find a church nearby their home in Pasadena. Lake Avenue Church (LAC) was just six blocks away from their apartment. It was such a big church Joyce wondered if they might get lost among so many people, but as they drove by the LAC marquee, there they saw the upcoming sermon title: "A Christian Approach to Sex." Todd exclaimed, "Let's go there, I'd enjoy hearing a message about sex from someone other than my parents!" So the three of them went to the LAC service and fully appreciated the message. Joyce and Greg continued attending LAC and became members the next fall after Todd left for Wheaton College.

As a result of the Perspectives course, both Joyce and Greg were interested in becoming better acquainted with internationals. They began participating with LAC's ministry to local international students, including some Mainland Chinese grad students studying at the California Institute of Technology in Pasadena. Upon meeting with a bright young Chinese couple and their little daughter over a period of several months, Joyce became frustrated with her inability to introduce the topic of faith in God. The couple had no knowledge of God whatsoever—and Joyce wondered *how can we convey the news of Jesus Christ across this cultural divide when I can barely talk about pie and ice cream?*

Joyce wanted to learn *how*. She quickly discovered that a Masters Degree in inter-cultural studies was offered at Fuller Seminary. Joyce hoped this degree would give her what she needed to bridge any cultural gap—and incredibly, Fuller's Pasadena campus was within *walking distance* of their apartment below Greg's office! When Joyce called the school, she learned it was still possible for her to apply for the fall quarter.

Joyce asked Greg what he thought about the idea. "Well, it'll be hard work. Are you ready and willing to work hard at it?" he asked.

Joyce pondered a moment, and then answered with firm assurance, "Yes!"

"Then I'm all for it," he exclaimed, "I say, go for it!"

Joyce applied and was accepted to begin graduate-level studies at Fuller Theological Seminary in September, the same month that Todd would start at Wheaton College. She was forty-five years old. The Shadow Hills house went up for sale that same month.

Parents Adjust to an Empty Nest

Two weeks before Todd's first semester at Wheaton, he made plans to join thirty of his freshman classmates for a faith-building wilderness excursion before starting classes. The Saturday morning arrived for Todd's flight to Chicago. Joyce drove Todd and his gear to meet a friend to rideshare to LAX. Greg said goodbye at the apartment, deciding to stay home to do some backlogged chores. Joyce was gone about forty minutes.

When she returned, Greg was eager to show her their reorganized living room. While she was away, he had disassembled and removed Todd's bed and headboard from behind the bookshelf at the far end of the living room.

Joyce stood there shocked—even dismayed at the sight.

"What have you done, Greg?" she exclaimed. Greg knew that something was surely amiss. A bit puzzled, he answered that he thought it would be wonderful to have their full size living room back into full use. Greg had expected that Joyce would be pleased with the change.

Slumping down into the nearest chair, Joyce dissolved into tears.

"I wasn't *ready yet* to have Todd's bedroom gone! I'd hoped to hang on to the memories of him living here with us for a little while . . . " and she cried some more. This scene from their first day of an emptied family nest became a lasting memory of the day their youngest son left home.

Within a week, Greg and Joyce were headed to Wheaton, Illinois, in Greg's Ford Taurus, which was mostly filled with Todd's clothing and study materials. Todd's accumulated sporting gear was carefully lashed onto a bike rack on the trunk. Joyce and Greg were looking forward to the long drive across the country to see the sights, and hopefully to sell the Taurus at Wheaton College. The trip was a good one, full of new memories for the two of them.

Joyce read her first Fuller Seminary reading assignment aloud to Greg as he drove: George Ladd's, *The Gospel of the Kingdom*. After driving to Denver, they decided to visit McCook, Nebraska, the setting of Ralph Moody's *Dry Divide* (the book they had read on the Whitney backpack trip). Greg and Joyce wanted to stay off the Interstate freeways, traveling instead along the two-lane U.S. Highway 34, through sorghum and corn fields, family farms, and small towns, to Lincoln, Nebraska, and then all the way to Wheaton. It was delightful for them to see the land and people at normal life-speed, rather than Interstate speed.

The Taurus was quickly sold to a College staff member while Greg and Joyce were hosted for two nights at a Wheaton professor's home a block from campus. The second evening, just before their flight back to LAX, Joyce and Greg were talking softly, settling down for the night, when Joyce began weeping.

She couldn't understand it—there were no words or concepts to explain her sorrow. There seemed to be no cause. Joyce was just sitting there on her bed, weeping. This only made sense when she talked with Greg about it the next morning.

"When I think of what we're doing—dropping our son Todd off at college and flying back to L.A. today, my sorrow makes sense. But I'm so happy that Todd selected Wheaton College, and that he's so happy here with his new friends—how can my grief make sense when I also feel so much joy?" Months later, Joyce finally concluded that her spontaneous grief was a kind of sorrow she had never experienced before. Her body must have been grieving the loss of her youngest child.

Once Joyce's classes at Fuller got underway, she found student life both challenging and invigorating. She dove headlong into her class work. Even more amazing was the discovery that her professors not only wanted to know what she thought, but they wanted her to share her thoughts with others in her classes as part of the educational process.

Joyce's Take

Prior to enrolling at Fuller, to my knowledge I had never been asked, "What do you think?" My opinion had not yet been sought by anyone. Suddenly, now my thoughts seemed important to my professors! Not only that, but I was expected to *write out* my opinions—not by hand, but in print. I was to put my opinions into a document created on a computer. Since I had not yet used a computer to write anything, I felt very uneasy.

Learning to Communicate about Sex

Now that their nest was empty, Greg decided to take a big risk. He asked Joyce if she would accompany him to some counseling for help to improve their sexual relationship. "After all," Greg said, "it has been twenty-six years since we were first married, and now twelve years since our *remarriage!*" Greg confessed he was still conflicted and uncertain about *how* to communicate with her on this topic—plus he felt quite certain he was not hearing her perspective. With Greg taking the lead, *wanting* to have a better sexual relationship with Joyce, Joyce was happy to oblige.

Greg sought counseling assistance from a Christian married couple who were sex therapists. He called Dr. Cliff and Joyce Penner, and they agreed to work with him and Joyce. Greg wanted to learn *how to fix* his sexual relationship with Joyce so that it would *work* better.

The Penners led both of them through individual sexual histories. This helped them clarify Greg's confused perspective on his sexual responsibility. Although he felt it was fine for Joyce to tell him she wanted to take a walk with him on the beach, *it made him uncomfortable* for her to tell him what she would enjoy with him sexually. Greg thought that would feel humiliating or demanding. Instead, Greg wanted Joyce's pleasure to be *his responsibility*. He saw himself as solely responsible for figuring out how to please Joyce sexually. Naturally, Joyce was surprised and perplexed that Greg, who acknowledged struggling consistently with the fear of failure, was somehow *opposed* to her input—as if he wanted unilaterally to decide what was best for her and for them to enjoy as a couple.

The counselors listened to Greg and understood, but they were also insistent that Greg start to inquire of Joyce about her preferences, and to listen and take her perspective seriously. After Greg began to understand this, the counselors discussed with him and Joyce what was actually pleasing to each of them, and prescribed various activities to help the two of them explore other pleasurable options on their own.

Greg and Joyce were asked to *talk with each other* about what kind of touching gave each of them pleasure. This discussion was aided by homework assignments—but each assignment required time as well as practice. Greg thought *these exercises take time, and they are so intimate!* He had no idea that real intimacy would require vulnerability of him as well as responsibility from him.

Both Greg and Joyce learned that relating sexually went far beyond the sex act itself. The truth of that became clear as they followed through on one of the first assignments. The assignment was to take turns gently massaging each other's bare feet.

Joyce's Take

The first time Greg took one of my bare feet tenderly into his hands and began softly to caress my foot, I slowly but surely dissolved into tears. What a surprise this experience was for *both of us!* I had never been touched like that by anyone before. Greg's touch was purely personal and loving. My feet had never been loved before and the experience was delightful. The memories of those first loving moments are still powerful. This was a major shift for me to begin telling Greg what I wanted to share with him in our sexual relationship.

What I am amazed about and grateful for is that even after all the years, being married twice and with grown children, we both were still *willing to learn how* to communicate our thoughts and feelings to one another, even when it was difficult to do so. I thank God there were people available to help us! If the two of us could learn how to communicate and love one another, then *there's hope that any couple* can learn and grow!

Greg's Take

I persisted for too long in my confusion about sex—twelve years after our remarriage—before finally seeking help. When I finally sought help, with Joyce's cooperation, I was surprised to find the major obstacle to our sexual satisfaction was my overworked sense of responsibility. In my self-sufficiency, I was keeping Joyce from telling me what would bring her pleasure! What a *relief* it was for me to enter into a new level of openness and intimacy with Joyce!

During Joyce's first year at Fuller, Greg also began to search for ways in which he might be able to use his legal expertise as an avenue for international mission work. Fuller's students and faculty were from all over the world, and Joyce seemed to be on track and relishing her studies. So in Greg's spare time, he began consulting on foreign tax code revision with an international non-profit organization. It was interesting work, but there was no sign as to where it might possibly lead.

As Joyce pursued her studies in the second year, Greg became concerned about her increasingly assertive theological and doctrinal views. She was sharing new perspectives, saying things he didn't want to hear. Greg was uncertain where her new outlook might lead them after her graduation, and that was adding a new kind of stress to their relationship. Happily, both Geoff and Todd were coming home to stay with them during their summer college breaks, beginning in June. This would provide an opportunity for the four of them to talk seriously about the future.

Sensing these might be difficult conversations, Joyce enlisted the help of a family counselor who specialized in family systems. It helped that he was already known and trusted by both Greg and Joyce. When Geoff and Todd arrived home, they were glad to join in the family conversations at their parents' request.

This third round of counseling focused on all four of them as a relational system, rather than on any of them individually. The counselor sought to help them uncover patterns of *family relating* that might be stuck or rigid. This was why Geoff and Todd were encouraged to take part. Both of them did so in a very helpful way.

With the family counseling underway, Joyce took a step she knew would precipitate a crisis for Greg. The two of them had found a little cottage that would be their empty nest home right next to a lovely Pasadena park. It would replace their apartment, which they had decided was too small. Escrow was set to close at the end of June. Although the family had only met twice with the counselor, on the day escrow closed Greg found a note from Joyce on the apartment table. The note said she had moved into a rented room by herself in a house shared by three other Fuller Seminary students. Greg was dumbfounded, completely astonished. Joyce hadn't left a phone number, but the note said she would see him at their next family counseling appointment.

Joyce's Take

At that point I saw my relationship with Greg as a rigid concrete bottle, but I wanted it to change and grow into something beautiful. I knew God had something good in mind for us. But the only way I could see moving ahead was to break the bottle. I didn't want the same *old relationship*. Feeling stuck, I didn't want to live that way any longer. I wanted both of us to grow and change. I couldn't seem to get that across to Greg, so I concluded it was up to me to take responsibility for it myself.

I was participating with a vibrant, faith-filled learning community at Fuller, where I was encouraged to explore fully what I thought and then write my thoughts in formal papers. When I would come home and share with Greg what I was learning, it felt terrible to hear him say, "Don't talk like that. You sound crazy." I wanted respect and understanding from him, not judgment.

It was very important to me that we *both* hear from God about *His purpose* for our marriage. I was no longer willing to have the future of our relationship determined by Greg *telling* me what God's purpose was for us as a couple. We would need to discover this individually, to talk and agree upon our thoughts, and then live out what we could decide about this together.

Greg's Take

I had no understanding that I was judging Joyce for the ideas she was expressing, although I can see how she may have felt that way. I was fearful about being judged by others as heretical or off-the-wall. At the same time, I probably felt threatened by the new ideas she was sharing—I wasn't yet sure I agreed with her on some issues. I wasn't sure why I felt threatened by them.

Greg came to the next counseling session tongue-tied, upset, and angry. He wasn't entirely calm, but he was controlled in his usual way. Somewhere down deep he was steaming, feeling hurt and sorry for himself, but he wasn't showing it. Joyce gave Greg a slip of paper with her address and a phone number, but she didn't give any explanation. The counselor heard about her move, but didn't choose to focus on that during the session. Instead, he continued from the work they had done previously. Greg did not understand what was going on.

Greg went ahead and moved into the little cottage by himself while Geoff and Todd stayed in the apartment. Greg found himself alone in the house—a phenomenon he had not experienced for more than a few days for nearly two decades. Greg had thought of marriage as a tandem bike he and Joyce rode together, him on the front and Joyce on the back. He thought, *occasionally we have friction over which route to take, or how fast to go, but we talk it through and generally work things out. But now Joyce has just jumped off the bike without talking with me about it—and I'm stuck here on the bike by myself!*

After Joyce moved out, she waited for Greg to call her and initiate a conversation with her. She expected that if *he wanted to know* what was going on, he would have to call her up and ask. If he loved her as he claimed, he would need to move toward her to learn her perspective. But Greg's logic assumed that *Joyce* was the one who had moved out—and therefore it was *her job* to move toward him and explain to him why she was angry! They were at a new impasse.

The impasse was explicitly raised by Todd at the next family counseling session. Todd asked Greg, "Aren't you upset that Mom has moved out?" Greg replied, "Of course I am!" A little perplexed, Todd responded, "Well, you don't seem very upset." All eyes in the room were on Greg. He realized that Todd was expecting him to show some kind of emotion—yelling, crying, questioning. . . *something.*

Greg exhaled, as if letting off steam. Then he spoke, "Look, I'm struggling to keep all the balls in the air. I have a law practice to conduct, a firm to manage; I have to keep billable hours invoiced, and money coming in, and to get moved into the new house. What good is accomplished by showing emotion over Joyce leaving? I don't have time or energy for that! I can't *figure out* what Joyce is thinking, feeling, or trying to do. If she's angry with me, then okay, but since I don't know what drove her to leave, I don't see how sharing my feelings will accomplish anything!"

Joyce then interjected, "If you want to find out what I'm thinking, why don't you call and ask me? You can find out by listening to me!"

Greg came right back, "You mean you're waiting for me to call you? You moved out, and you're not angry with me? You're just waiting, wanting *me* to call you, like for a date?"

Joyce answered, "I didn't say I'm not at all angry with you, but I *am* waiting for you to call me—if you're interested *in me* and not just in your own ideas of the way things ought to be! You can find out what I'm thinking and feeling by actually listening to me, with no conditions attached."

Greg licked his lips. In Shadow Hills they had learned that when a horse licks his lips, you have his full attention.

Joyce now had Greg's full attention.

Greg's Take

My family kept asking me to reveal my feelings, but I could hardly *figure out* which factors in my life had changed or why! Mostly I was feeling like an etch-a-sketch slate. I thought I had some details of my life in place and then suddenly, the sheet was lifted and it was all gone. I was back to square one. It was a healthy blow to my ego! I discovered that I could only know the truth of my situation through communication with Joyce. I needed to invite her to tell me what *she needed* or wanted, and then I needed to listen carefully to her responses!

Joyce's Take

Finally, at this time in my life, I was willing to *press through* some long-standing relational problems for the greater good of what might open up. In my struggle with Greg, I knew I would have to deal with pain, sorrow, and loss, to become the kind of person through whom God could do His work. I had come to believe that if I were willing to confront my problem with Greg by faith, while allowing God's love to work in me, then a way might open for *both of us* to emerge healthier and more faithful, even through our problematic situation.

At last they were unstuck! Greg called Joyce and they began to talk. He knew that he had to accommodate and learn to understand Joyce's concepts and preconceptions. Greg also had to accept that as her husband he had no *entitlements*. He would need to trust God to help him relate honestly and authentically with Joyce. There was no roadmap for precisely *how* Greg would be able to talk effectively with her. Their remaining family counseling sessions helped Greg and Joyce to reframe their habitual ways of relating with each son, in order to strengthen and equalize their family relationships.

In all, Greg and Joyce were apart for one hundred days that summer. In that span of time, Joyce was able to cover the conversational ground she needed with Greg in order to go ahead and move in with him—into their little 1907 bungalow cottage on Mar Vista Avenue, where they still live today.

During those one hundred days, Greg gained new awareness about the gulf between his office life and his home life with Joyce. He developed a new respect for Joyce's role in all areas of his life. Even before she moved into the cottage, Greg asked Joyce if she would come and pray over his office and especially over his desk. She gladly accepted and said she would.

For Joyce, Greg's invitation to come and pray over his desk and his legal work, and to pray for his relationships with office staff and his clients, was *a breath of fresh air.* Greg had never made such a request before. Up to that moment, Greg's law office had been foreign territory, even when they were living just a few feet away in the apartment downstairs. If Joyce entered the law office during business hours, she experienced an unspoken chill from the staff, as though she were a stranger who did not belong there. Feeling out of place, she might be asked to sit and wait for Greg to come out into the reception area. Suddenly, with Greg's request, Joyce became a spiritual partner of Greg's. Now she was welcome into his office anytime!

The next morning Joyce came to the office early with Greg to pray. She prayed aloud as she walked slowly through the entry, through the reception area, and into Greg's office. There she paused and prayed specifically over Greg's desk, the phone, his calendar, and all that would go on there. Suddenly whatever had been standing invisibly between them was now gone. The two of them agreed that this was a new day for their relationship, for their home and for Greg's work.

As Joyce prepared to move in, she looked forward to sharing the same house with Greg again, however, she had learned not to yield all of her private space to him. She sought to remember her own priorities. Joyce wanted to set apart a private place in the house where she would meet with God each day. She remained cautious about *becoming too close, too soon* with Greg.

Their first night together in the cottage, Joyce enjoyed a perfect night of sleep. When she awoke, she could see the first morning light through the curtains. There on the side table stood the beautiful flower arrangement Greg had given her as a homecoming gift. She sighed appreciatively. Greg was still asleep.

Curious to see what it looked like outside, Joyce pulled back one of the curtains for a peek. The view caught her completely by surprise, and Joyce was suddenly delighted with their new home. The park across the street was simply beautiful. There were tall liquid ambers lit up with hints of yellow, and deep green oaks standing in the corners. Other trees already displayed streaks of brightly colored leaves, and a long line of stately deodar cedars stood proudly along the eastern sidewalk border. As the early sunlight beamed through and over the trees, the grass looked radiantly alive. A few early-risers walked peacefully along a winding concrete path that circled throughout the park.

In that moment, Joyce relaxed, fully appreciating the view and the expanse of the park across the street. She instantly hoped it would always remain there in front of their little empty-nest house. It was such a gift, and her future with Greg and their family was wide open—filled with promise! Joyce fell back onto her pillow, feeling flooded with appreciation and joy. She was finally home.

For Contemplation and Conversation

1. Have you and your spouse ever participated in formal counseling sessions? If so, what are some of the most helpful things you learned that might help others?

2. Have you or your spouse ever taken time apart—time alone to reflect on your life priorities? If so, how did this experience help you and your relationship?

3. 1 Corinthians 7:10-11 says:
"To the married I give this command (not I, but the Lord): A wife must not separate from her husband. But if she does, she must remain unmarried or else be reconciled to her husband. And a husband must not divorce his wife."

a) What are your thoughts about marital separation? Can you imagine any improvement in a marital relationship from a time apart? What questions does this topic bring to your mind?

b) Do you or your spouse have an image or metaphor—like Greg's tandem bike—for your marriage? If so, is this an image you can discuss or share—and perhaps improve upon—with your spouse or others?

4. In what ways or under what conditions do you and your spouse find joy working together as a team?

Epilogue

Today, Greg knows that a Bible-based marriage is not a tandem bicycle. It is not *something* a couple can *possess*. Marriage is not a thing at all. Marriage is a r*elationship that is always in place*—a special kind of place that God gives to each couple. Marriage is a holy, personal place for both of them to live in and to share. This *marriage place* is always present with each spouse, wherever he or she is. It makes no difference that the two of them are separated by space. One of them can be in an office setting, and the other can be at the grocery store. Wherever one of them goes, their marriage *relationship* is also in *place*—there with all of its hospitality, promise and blessing for others. For example, when Joyce prayed in Greg's office at his invitation, they experienced *the power God had invested* in their *marriage covenant*. Together they each sensed His presence with them in the office. Prior to Joyce's time of prayer in the law office, she had experienced Greg's office as her enemy, something hateful that stood firmly against their marriage.

Joyce completed her Master's Degree at Fuller Seminary in 1997. In 1998, Joyce and Greg launched Working Faith, a ministry to workplace leaders. For six years through 2005, Greg laid aside his law practice to serve in that ministry with Joyce. In 1999, Joyce commenced Ph.D. studies through the School of Intercultural Studies at Fuller Seminary, to study how Christ's gospel advances through people in rela-

243

tional systems such as families, churches, and work groups. Joyce received the Ph.D. from Fuller in 2003.

Geoff graduated from Cal Poly San Luis Obispo in 1996. He immediately began plant science research and production with a company in Watsonville, California, but within two years he moved north toward the Silicon Valley and began work in Internet services. He met Cindy Brown at their church in Aptos, California, where they married in 1999. Geoff and Cindy are now parents of four boys: Jack, Gabriel, Tyler and Preston. They live near Thousand Oaks, California, where all six of them are active in their church community, alongside camping, skiing, backpacking, gardening, and bicycling together. Geoff continues his Internet services work, currently supporting businesses with online financial services.

Todd graduated from Wheaton College in 1997. Soon afterward, he migrated to Aptos, California to reconnect with his brother Geoff. Todd worked on various construction projects with a church friend, and then became an intern and staff member at their church, The Coastlands Church, in Aptos, California. Todd met Hilary Brown, a friend and former roommate of Geoff's wife, Cindy, at church. Todd and Hilary were married in 2000. They have four children: Asher, Ethan, Larissa, and Joseph, and live in Santa Cruz, California. In 2006, Todd and Hilary became the Senior Pastors of The Coastlands Church. Their family enjoys hiking in the Santa Cruz Mountains near their home, and—in good weather—they ride bicycles together on Santa Cruz bike paths. Todd stays in shape mountain-biking locally with friends in *all* kinds of weather.

In 2005, Greg resumed his practice of law after their ministry board concluded that Greg's greater call was to serve clients as a lawyer. Greg continues in sole practice today, admitted to practice in both California and Hawaii.

Since 2003, Joyce and Greg have often met with engaged and newly married couples who sought a mentoring relationship at Lake Avenue Church. Each of those couples brought them questions about marriage because they wanted to begin their family life together well. Greg and Joyce have felt honored to serve such couples.

In 2012, Joyce and Greg were surprised and delighted to meet Diane and Bill Shaw, who had previously developed a marriage-mentoring program through their church, Calvary Church of Santa Ana. Since 2002, Bill and Diane have grown and developed a team of mature Encourager Couples to help bring hope and healing to hundreds of couples who were experiencing defeat or failure in their marriage.

The Shaws have graciously trained, allowed and enabled the Millikans to glean from the Shaws' ten years of experience and to utilize their curriculum. Serving under Working Faith, the ministry the Millikans founded in 1999, Lake Avenue Church in Pasadena has launched a similar *Hope for Marriage* mentoring program. Greg and Joyce want to extend the same marriage-mentoring model to other interested churches. To learn more about Hope for Marriage, an overview is provided on Working Faith's purpose page at www.workingfaith.com.

In their free time and for exercise, Greg and Joyce ride together on a tandem recumbent bicycle. Today they have no trouble making plans or navigating their tandem bike around obstacles!

As grandparents of the eight youngest Millikans, Greg and Joyce celebrate the opportunity of participating in the future they once had lost. Daily they give thanks to God that they each decided to *receive their marriage* and family *anew* from God's own hand.

Afterword

Three Life Lessons from *Romance & Reality*

God's Word promises:

"Therefore Jesus said again, 'Very truly I tell you, I am the gate for the sheep [to enter into abundant life]; whoever enters through me will be saved. They will come in and go out, and find pasture. The thief comes only to steal and kill and destroy; *I have come that they may have life, and have it to the full.*'" John 10:7, 9,10. (Text in brackets and italics are ours).

With this passage of Scripture as a backdrop, we, Greg and Joyce, offer three life lessons as *take-aways* for you, the reader. These are offered as specific additions to your toolkit for maintaining a good connection with the Lord of your heart, home and marriage. These are not the only lessons, nor are they necessarily the best lessons you might have drawn from *Romance & Reality*, but the three lessons below have been key for us. These are offered to you with hope for your success.

Lesson #1. Don't do life alone.

Time and again, the faithful input we received from pastors, mentors, family members, friends, competent counselors, and God's Word changed everything for us. These inputs were available, *if and when* such assistance and support was humbly requested. Occasionally help came to us without our asking, through merciful and loving interventions that either one or both of us *really needed*.

In contrast, we found the do-it-yourself myth—like junk food—to feed pride, but pride will starve your soul and relationships, with terrible results. Pride *always* left us isolated. Gladly—the Lord Himself rescued us!

Escape any and all temptations to go it alone. Get together with others *who demonstrate care*. Ask them for support and guidance—everyone needs it. God is able to give you many blessings through your brothers and sisters of faith. Watch for good spiritual fruit growing visibly in others' lives (Galatians 5:22-23). When you see that kind of spiritual fruit, ask God for confirmation. If you sense a good fit, go ahead and ask for encouragement, support, or counsel. Accept no counterfeits or substitutes.

Joyce's Take

For example, when I asked a friend for advice about how I could relate differently with Greg, he suggested I ask Greg a question! This may sound like an easy thing to do, but for me it was easier to imagine than to accomplish. Finally, with practice, I became better at a*sking Greg questions* about his day, something like, "How is your project at work coming along?" Or, "What went well for you today at work?" Questions like this from me to Greg helped him to open up, and to assess how he was responding to his work and other things. Asking questions also helped me begin to enjoy Greg and to know him better!

Until I learned to ask questions, I would often blame Greg for his being disconnected and *remote*. What I hadn't known before then, was that Greg *needed* my questions to help him recognize and share his thoughts and feelings with me. As it turned out, we *both* were *helped* when I took my friend's wise advice. I finally started to care *actively* for Greg, with real interest. I became able, with practice, to ask Greg about his day, his priorities and his faith. This kind of activity is not gender-specific. Your relationship with your spouse *can improve* as you care actively, with real interest about his or her day, life, priorities, and preferences.

Lesson #2. It is never impossible for you to forgive.

Even so, be patient for reconciliation because that is a two-way street.

In his book, *Forgiving the Unforgiveable*, David Stoop says forgiveness is something we do inside, by ourselves, alone—the other person does not need to be involved in our individual forgiveness process (Stoop 2003, p.46).

We have learned that freedom from bondage to our own pain is gained when we forgive the other person according to God's gracious gift. *God's gift of forgiveness* is always fair and just because Jesus Christ gave His own life and blood to pay the cost required by God *for all human sins*, not just our own sins alone (1 John 2:2).

Stoop adds that reconciliation is different from forgiveness. That is because reconciliation involves both people. Reconciliation is an option on each side. It is a choice, not a requirement. (Stoop 2003:46-47).

Reconciliation is an option that is incredibly worth pursuing, because if that can happen, everything is forever changed for those who are touched by your lives (Romans 12:18-21). We have placed a current family photo below and also on the back cover of the book. It is a three-generation family picture that *would not have been possible* without faith in God, forgiveness, patience *and* reconciliation. This means unconditional forgiveness—forgiveness that is enacted individually, then communicated relationally, and finally accepted. These are what helped make our family picture possible. Without all of those who prayed and assisted us, plus the above-mentioned precious resources, our family would have been entirely different, and such a picture might not have been taken at all.

Lesson #3. Faith and patience inherit the promises (Hebrews 6:12)

Joyce's Take

One day at Fuller Seminary, in the midst of a conversation with me about her recent separation and contemplated divorce, a classmate asked me directly, "Does Greg love you *perfectly*?" I had to think carefully about her words. Perfection was a very high standard! Suddenly it seemed her choice of words felt like an attack on Greg—and I felt the need to defend Greg. Of course, I knew Greg didn't and couldn't love me *perfectly,* so I responded honestly by saying, "Greg loves me the best way he can."

Without fully knowing what she was doing, my class-mate had exposed my own blameworthiness. Until that conversation, I had regularly and secretly demanded that Greg love me the way *I* wanted him to love me, and to do that *perfectly!* Of course, perfection is humanly impossible. From that moment, I was humbled. I felt a new freedom to allow Greg to *be himself* and to begin letting go of my too-high, too-perfect expectations for Greg. I made an important decision right then to move ahead with Greg *as he was*, rather than who I was demanding and expecting him to be!

Greg's Take

As I began to walk with Christ, I knew my life was new, and that all things now revolved around God. I wasn't expecting an instant transformation—and that was a good thing, because I certainly wasn't disappointed! I am *still* learning what it means to be a good communicator. I am *still* learning what it means to value *all others* as *equal with me* before God. I am *still* learning to seek and receive help from others, including capable counselors when needed.

The learning process seems *slow* to me at times, yet I learn again each day what a tremendous ally I and we all have in the Lord. God is *for* me, *for* Joyce, and *for* our marriage—day by day, all the time. I am learning to trust Him more and more as the author and perfecter of my faith, and also the faith of *all those I love*. I would never tell *anyone* that marriage is easy, but marriage is God's good gift. Marriage is a far better gift than we can know or imagine. In marriage, we are able to grow closer to God. That is because marriage is a picture of Christ and the Church. God created marriage for our benefit!

If you have not yet discovered this reality for your life and your marriage, we both pray that today you will come to know God personally! He has a unique and wonderful place for both of you in your marriage. If we can encourage you in any way—either to receive the Lord Jesus Christ as Savior of your life and marriage—or to grow in your relationship with Him, we are eager to hear from you! Please contact us by email at: hopeformarriage@workingfaith.com.

Acknowledgements

Romance & Reality was a far bigger project than either of us imagined! After years of encouragement from friends, family members, and mentors who urged us, saying, "You should write a book," we want to thank all of you *first*, for your faithful prodding and encouragement!

Our names are on the front of this book, however, many faithful hands and hearts have made this book possible. Pastor Roger Bosch at Lake Avenue Church selected us as a couple who might share a brief account of marriage, divorce, reconciliation and remarriage with LAC's staff-writer, Karly Pierre. Karly turned our conversations into the *seed article* for this project. Before that article, all the previous requests from our friends, asking us to "write a book" fell on dry ground. Thank you Roger and Karly.

A big thank you to Jim and Debbie Hogan, our long-time friends, who took us past the tipping point. After reading the LAC article in the Summer 2010, *Seasons Magazine*, they challenged us to make our story into a book. The Hogans said they knew couples who *really needed* to read our story. It was their faithful appeal that motivated us to begin writing.

The writing process seemed interminable. After many months, Jan Dargatz helped us turn many pages of wandering, fractured prose into a finished product. Thank you, Jan!

Barbara Winter carefully reviewed and made corrections, twice, of the entire manuscript. Thank you Barb!

Others who generously read and gave their insights: Debbie Hogan; Cameron Lee; Sharon May; Geoff Millikan and Cindy Millikan; Todd Millikan and Hilary Millikan; Joyce Penner, and Greg Waybright—thank you!

Greg's attorney colleagues, Richard Chinen and Bob Sloat, and Joyce's Morning Break prayer team generously provided their enduring prayer support. Thank you, one and all, for your encouragement and patience during our absences while we worked on this project.

Our final words of appreciation go to our sons and daughters-in-law, Geoff, Cindy, Todd, and Hilary. Each of you encouraged us immeasurably to take the big steps and the baby steps needed to put our story into this book, in a way that will ring true across the generations. To each of you and to each of your children—thank you! Each one of you is a *life-giving reward* of faith to us—and *far above anything* we could ask or imagine!